MINNESOTA POLITICS AND GOVERNMENT

*Politics and Governments
of the American States*

General Editor

John Kincaid
Robert B. & Helen S. Meyner Center
for the Study of State and Local
Government, Lafayette College

Founding Editor

Daniel J. Elazar
Center for the Study of
Federalism, Temple University

Editorial Advisory Board

Thad L. Beyle
University of North Carolina
at Chapel Hill

Diane D. Blair
University of Arkansas

Ellis Katz
Temple University

Charles Press
Michigan State University

Stephen L. Schechter
Russell Sage College

Published by the University of
Nebraska Press in association
with the Center for the Study
of Federalism, Temple University,
and the Robert B. and Helen S. Meyner Center
for the Study of State and Local
Government, Lafayette College

DANIEL J. ELAZAR, VIRGINIA GRAY, AND WYMAN SPANO

Minnesota Politics & Government

UNIVERSITY OF NEBRASKA PRESS
LINCOLN AND LONDON

⊗

Library of Congress Cataloging-in-Publication Data
Elazar, Daniel Judah.
Minnesota politics and government / by Daniel J. Elazar, Virginia Gray, and Wyman Spano.
p.   cm.—(Politics and governments of the American states)
Includes bibliographical references and index.
ISBN 0-8032-1852-4 (cl.: alk. paper).—ISBN 0-8032-6714-2 (pbk.: alk. paper)
1. Minnesota—Politics and government.   I. Gray, Virginia, 1945–
II. Spano, Wyman, 1938–   III. Title.   IV. Series.
JK6116.E43   1999
320.4776—dc21
99-20478   CIP

FOR THE PEOPLE OF MINNESOTA

CONTENTS

ILLUSTRATIONS

MAP

JOHN KINCAID

Series Preface

The purpose of this series is to provide information and interesting books on the politics and governments of the fifty American states, books that are of value not only to the student of government but also to the general citizens who want greater insight into the past and present civic life of their own states and of other states in the federal union. The role of the states in governing America is among the least well known of all the 85,006 governments in the United States. The national media focus attention on the federal government in Washington DC, and local media focus attention on local government. Meanwhile, except when there is a scandal or a proposed tax increase, the workings of state government remain something of a mystery to many citizens—out of sight, out of mind.

In many respects, however, the states have been, and continue to be, the most important governments in the American political system. They are the main building blocks and chief organizing governments of the whole system. The states are the constituent governments of the federal union, and it is through the states that citizens gain representation in the national government. The national government is one of limited, delegated powers; all other powers are possessed by the states and their citizens. At the same time, the states are the empowering governments for the nation's 84,955 local governments—counties, municipalities, townships, school districts, and special districts. As such, states provide for one of the most essential and ancient elements of freedom and democracy, the right of local self-government.

Although, for many citizens, the most visible aspects of state government are state universities, some of which are the most prestigious in the world, and state highway patrol officers, with their radar guns and handy ticket books, state governments provide for nearly all domestic public services.

Whether elements of those services are enacted or partly funded by the federal government and actually carried out by local governments, it is state government that has the ultimate responsibility for ensuring that Americans are well served by all their governments. In so doing, all of the American states are more democratic, more prosperous, and better governed than most of the world's nation-states.

This is a particularly timely period in which to publish a series of books on the governments and politics of each of the fifty states. Once viewed as the "fallen arches" of the federal system, states today are increasingly seen as energetic, innovative, and fiscally responsible. Some states, of course, perform better than others, but that is to be expected in a federal system. Each state is unique in its own right. It is our hope that this series will shed light on the public life of each state and that, taken together, the books will contribute to a better, more informed understanding of the states themselves and of their often pivotal roles in the world's first and oldest continental-sized federal democracy.

DANIEL J. ELAZAR

Series Introduction

The American domain is given form and character as a federal union of fifty states whose institutions order the American landscape. The existence of these states made possible the emergence of a nation where liberty, not despotism, reigns, and self-government is the first principle of order. The great American republic was born in its states, as its very name signifies. America's first founding was repeated on thirteen separate occasions over 125 years, from Virginia in 1607 to Georgia in 1732. Each colony became a self-governing commonwealth. The American revolution and second founding were made by those commonwealths, now states, acting in congress, and the new nation's constitution was written together and adopted separately. As the American tide rolled westward from the Atlantic coast, it absorbed new territories by organizing thirty-seven more states over the next 169 years.

Most of the American states are larger and better developed than most of the world's nations. Territorially, Minnesota is one of the larger states with 84,402 square miles, but in terms of its population (1990: 4,375,099) and its gross state product, it ranks with the smaller nations of the world and is a small power in its own right. Minnesota is located near the geohistorical center of North America, which places it just north of the mainstream of the United States, crossed by the great waves of migration that spread settlements across the country in the nineteenth century from the middle states, the South, and New England, and reinforced by the great migration streams from Europe and by African Americans, Hispanics, and Asians in the nineteenth and twentieth centuries. Nevertheless, its location north of the mainstream meant that its southeast originally was settled as part of greater New England, and its central and northern areas, which mark the end of the eastern big woods and the eastern beginning of the western prairie plains, were heavily settled by Scandinavians with south Slavs in its mining areas. Its southern third attracted German settlers in large numbers. Among the three great spheres into which the United States is divided—the Greater Northeast, the Greater South, and the Greater West—most of the state is in the Greater West.

The American states exist because each is a unique civil society within a common American culture. First given political form, the states then acquired their other characteristics. Each has its own constitution and laws, its own political culture and history, and its own relationship to the federal union. It is in and through the states, no less than the nation, that the great themes of American life play themselves out. The advancing frontier and the continuing experience of Americans as a frontier people, the drama of American ethnic blending, the tragedy of slavery and racial discrimination, all have found expressions in the states.

Some states began as commonwealths devoted to establishing model societies based on a religiously informed vision (for example, Massachusetts, Connecticut, and Rhode Island). At the other end of the spectrum Hawaii is a transformed pagan monarchy. At least three were independent for a significant period of time (Hawaii, Texas, and Vermont). Others were created from nothing by hardly more than a stroke of the pen (for example, the Dakotas, Idaho, and Nevada). Several are permanently bilingual (California, Louisiana, and New Mexico). Each has its own landscape and geographic configuration, which time and history transform into a specific geohistorical location. In short, the diversity of the American people is expressed in no small measure through their states, the politics and government of each of which have their own fascination.

Minnesota Politics and Government is the eighteenth book in the series being produced by the Center for the Study of Federalism and the Robert B. and Helen S. Meyner Center for the Study of State and Local Government at Lafayette College and published by the University of Nebraska Press series The Politics and Governments of the American States. The aim of the series is to provide books on the politics and governments of the individual states that will appeal to three audiences: political scientists, their students, and the wider public. Each volume examines the specific character of one state, looking at the state as a polity—its political culture, traditions and practices, constituencies and interest groups, and constitutional and institutional frameworks.

Each book reviews the political development of the state to demonstrate how the state's political institutions and characteristics have evolved from the first settlement to today, presenting the state in the context of the nation and section of which it is a part and reviewing the roles and relations of the state vis-à-vis its sister states and the federal government. The state's constitutional history, its traditions of constitution making and constitutional change, is related to the workings of the state's political institutions and processes. State-local relations, local government, and community politics are examined. Finally, each volume reviews the state's policy concerns and their implementation from the budgetary process to particular substantive policies. Each book concludes by summarizing the principal themes and findings to draw conclusions about the current state of the state, its continuing traditions, and its emerging issues. Each volume also contains a bibliographic survey of the literature on the state and a guide to the use of that literature and state government documents in learning more about the state and its political system. Although the books in the series are not expected to be uniform, all focus on the common themes of federalism, constitutionalism, political culture, and the continuing American frontier, so as to provide a framework within which to consider the institutions, routines, and processes of state government and politics.

FEDERALISM

To many Americans, thoughts of federalism conjure up images of the rattle of drums and the fluttering of flags as blue and gray confront each other on a hundred battlefields of the Civil War, or of hundreds of thousands of Americans, black and white, singing "We Shall Overcome" as they confront the forces of segregation speaking in the name of law and order; or of slogans such as state's rights and secession. Federalism is all that—it is the First Minnesota Regiment gallantly charging the Confederates at Gettysburg to buy time for the Union army to consolidate its position, the Rainbow Division with units from all the then forty-eight states advancing against the Germans in the Argonne Forest, and the more recent weekend flights of the cargo planes of the Minnesota National Guard to Honduras to support the U.S. intervention there.[1]

Both the greatest conflicts of American history and the most prosaic day-to-day operations of American government are closely intertwined with American federalism. Federalism relates to the structure and process of government and the relationship that unites them. Throughout the years American federalism has been characterized by several basic tensions. One is between state sovereignty—the view that in a proper federal system, authority and power over most domestic affairs should be in the hands of the states—and national supremacy—the view that the federal government has a significant role to play in domestic matters affecting the national interest. The other tension is between dual federalism—the idea that a federal system works best when the federal government and the states function as separately as possible, each in its own sphere—and cooperative federalism—the view that federalism works best when the federal government and the states, while preserving their own institutions, cooperate closely to carry out joint or shared programs.[2]

Politically, Minnesota has long been one of the states most committed to the national agenda in any given period. Solidly pro-Union during the Civil War, Minnesota claims to have been the first state to offer troops for President Abraham Lincoln when the war broke out. Minnesota's deviations from national policy generally were anticipatory of the direction the country as a whole would later take. After the Civil War the state developed a progressive or liberal reputation on policy matters.

With regard to federal aid, Minnesota has been both a giver and a receiver throughout the years and has benefited politically and economically in other ways from its influence in Washington DC. Its location gave it major transportation advantages, both in the days of the railroads and in the airways of our time. The railroads brought federal grants-in-aid and contracts, and aviation has brought different forms of federal assistance. Still, Minnesota remains relatively less dependent on the federal government than many other states and more of a net contributor to the others.

CONSTITUTIONALISM

The American constitutional tradition grows out of the Whig understanding that civil societies are founded by political covenant, entered into by the first founders and reaffirmed by subsequent generations, through which the powers of government are delineated and limited and the rights of the constituting members are clearly proclaimed in such a way as to provide moral and practical restraints on governments. That constitutional tradition was modified by the Federalists, who accepted its fundamental principles but strengthened the institutional framework designed to provide energy in government while maintaining the checks and balances they saw as needed to preserve liberty and republican government. At the same time, they turned nonbinding declarations of rights into enforceable constitutional articles.[3]

American state constitutions reflect a melding of these two traditions.

Under the U.S. Constitution each state is free to adopt its own constitution, provided that it establishes a republican form of government. Some states have adopted highly succinct constitutions such as the Vermont Constitution of 1793 with 6,600 words, which is still in effect with only fifty-two amendments. Others are just the opposite, for example, Georgia's ninth constitution, adopted in 1976, which has 583,000 words.

State constitutions normally are far more comprehensive than the federal Constitution, which is one of limited, delegated powers. Because states are plenary governments, they automatically possess all powers not specifically denied them by the U.S. Constitution or their citizens. Consequently, a state constitution must be explicit about limiting and defining the scope of government powers, especially on behalf of individual liberty. So state constitutions normally include an explicit declaration of rights, almost invariably broader than the first ten amendments to the U.S. Constitution.

The detailed specificity of state constitutions affects the way they shape each state's government system and patterns of political behavior. Unlike the open-endedness and ambiguity of many portions of the U.S. Constitution, which allow for considerable interpretive development, state organs, including state supreme courts, generally hew closely to the letter of their constitutions because they must. This means that formal change of the constitutional document occurs more frequently through constitutional amendment, whether initiated by the legislature, special constitutional commissions, constitutional conventions, or direct action by the voters, or, in a number of states, the periodic writing of new constitutions. As a result, state constitutions have come to reflect quite explicitly the changing conceptions of government that have developed over the course of American history.

Overall, six state constitutional patterns have developed. One is the commonwealth pattern, forged in New England, which emphasizes Whig ideas of the constitution as a philosophic document designed first and foremost to set a direction for civil society and to express and institutionalize a theory of republican government. A second is the constitutional pattern of the commercial republic. The constitutions fitting this pattern reflect a series of compromises required by the conflict of many strong ethnic groups and commercial interests generated by the flow of heterogeneous streams of migrants into particular states and the early development of large commercial and industrial cities in those states.

The third can be described as the southern contractual pattern. Southern state constitutions are used as instruments to set explicit terms governing the relationship between polity and society, such as those that protected slavery and racial segregation or those that sought to diffuse the formal allocation of authority in order to accommodate the swings between oligarchy and factionalism characteristic of southern state politics. Of all the southern states, only Louisiana stands somewhat outside this pattern, because its legal system was founded on the French civil code. Its constitutions have been codes—long, highly explicit documents that form a fourth pattern in and of themselves.

A fifth pattern is that found frequently in the states of the far West. Here the state constitution is first and foremost a frame of government explicitly reflecting the republican and democratic principles dominant in the nation in the late nineteenth century but emphasizing the structure of state government and the distribution of powers within that structure in a direct, businesslike manner.

Finally, the two newest states, Alaska and Hawaii, adopted constitutions following the managerial pattern developed and promoted by twentieth-century constitutional reform movements in the United States. Those constitutions are characterized by conciseness, broad grants of power to the executive branch, and relatively few structural restrictions on the legislature. They emphasize natural resource conservation and social legislation.

Formally, Minnesota retains its original constitution of 1858, which combines the commonwealth and frame-of-government patterns. Minnesota's constitution was drafted in two separate conventions—one Democratic and one Republican—reflecting the nation's divisions on the eve of the Civil War. Two separate documents emerged; thus, the state's single constitution is embodied in both those documents. To compound matters, in 1971, in an effort to simplify the constitution without replacing it, the Minnesota Constitutional Commission reworded and restructured the document, reducing the number of articles it contained by a third. Their new, simplified document did not become the state's constitution for purposes of adjudication but is the version used in public discussions, giving Minnesota yet a third constitutional document for its single constitution.

THE CONTINUING AMERICAN FRONTIER

For Americans, the very word *frontier* conjures up the images of the rural-land frontier of yesteryear—of explorers and mountain men, of cowboys and Indians, of brave pioneers pushing their way west in the face of natural obstacles. Later, Americans' picture of the frontier was expanded to include the inventors, the railroad builders, and the captains of industry who created the urban-industrial frontier. Then television began to celebrate the entrepreneurial ventures of the automobile and oil industries and more recently the computer industry, portraying the magnates of those industries and their families in the same larger-than-life frame once depicted for the heroes of that first frontier.[4]

As is so often the case, the media responsible for determining and catering to popular taste tell us a great deal about ourselves. The United States was founded with a rural-land frontier that persisted until World War I, more or less, spreading farms, ranches, mines, and towns across the land. Early in the nineteenth century the rural-land frontier generated the urban frontier based on industrial development. The generation of new wealth through industrialization transformed cities from mere regional service centers into generators of wealth in their own right. The urban-industrial frontier persisted for more than one hundred years as a major force in American society and perhaps another sixty years as a major force in various parts of the country. The population movements and attendant growth on this frontier brought about the effective settlement of the United States in free-standing cities from coast to coast.

Between the world wars the urban-industrial frontier gave birth in turn to a third frontier, one based on the new technologies of electronic communication, the internal-combustion engine, the airplane, synthetics, and petrochemicals. These new technologies transformed every aspect of life and turned urbanization into metropolitanization. This third frontier generated a third settlement of the United States, this time in metropolitan regions from coast to coast, involving a mass migration of tens of millions of Americans in search of opportunity on the suburban frontier.

During the 1970s, despite the widespread "limits of growth" rhetoric, a fourth frontier stage was opened in the form of the rurban, or citybelt-cybernetic, frontier, generated by the metropolitan-technological frontier just as the latter had been generated by its predecessor. The rurban-cybernetic frontier first emerged in the Northeast, as did its predecessors. The Atlantic Coast metropolitan regions merged into one another to form a six-hundred-mile-long megalopolis—a matrix of urban and suburban settlements in which the older central cities yielded importance if not prominence to smaller ones. It was a sign of the times that the computer was conceived at MIT in Cambridge, first built at the University of Illinois in Urbana, and developed at IBM in White Plains, three medium-size cities that have become special centers in their own right. This in itself reflects the two primary characteristics of the new frontier. The loci of settlement are in medium-size and small cities and in the rural interstices of the megalopolis.

The spreading use of computer technology is the most direct manifestation of the cybernetic tools that make such citybelts possible. Both the revival of small cities and the shifting of population growth into rural areas are as much a product of long-distance direct dialing, the fax, and the internet as they are of the continued American longing for small-town or country living. The new urban-cybernetic frontier is finding its true form in the South and West, where these citybelt matrices are not being built on the collapse of earlier forms but are developing as an original form. The present sunbelt frontier—strung out along the Gulf Coast, the southwestern desert, and the fringes of the California mountains—is classically megalopolitan in its citybelt form. It is cybernetic in its content with its aerospace-related industries and sunbelt living made possible by air conditioning and telecommunications.

The continuing American frontier has all the characteristics of a chain reaction. In a land of great opportunity each frontier, once opened, has generated its successor and, in turn, has been replaced by it. Each frontier has created a new America with new opportunities, new patterns of settlement, new occupations, new challenges, and new problems. As a result, the central political problem of growth is not simply how to handle the physical changes brought by each frontier, real as they are. It is how to accommodate newness, population turnover, and transience as a way of life. That is the American frontier situation.

Minnesota has enjoyed a highly positive relationship with the continuing American frontier.[5] It is one of the few states that has moved smoothly from one frontier to the next without hiatus or pause. The initial American settlement of Minnesota came relatively late in the history of the land frontier, and its settlement period lasted long, well into the twentieth century, to overlap the next frontier stage with hardly a break in momentum. The history of its settlement parallels the history of American settlement on the West Coast, one of many indications of how isolated from the mainstream of American development Minnesota was during its formative years and, in some respects, continues to be.[6]

THE PERSISTENCE OF SECTIONALISM

Sectionalism—the expression of social, economic, and especially political differences along geographic lines—is part and parcel of American political life. The more or less permanent political ties that link groups of contiguous states together as sections reflect the ways in which local conditions and differences in political culture modify the impact of the frontier. This overall sectional pattern reflects the interaction of the three basic factors. The original sections were produced by the variations in the impact of the rural-land frontier on different geographic segments of the country. They, in turn, have been modified by the pressures generated by the various frontiers.

As a result, sectionalism is not the same as regionalism. The latter is essentially a phenomenon—often transient—that brings adjacent state, substate, or interstate areas together because of immediate and specific common interests. The sections are not homogeneous socioeconomic units sharing a common character across state lines but complex entities combining highly diverse states and communities with common political interests that generally complement one another socially and economically.[7]

Intrasectional conflicts often exist, but they do not detract from the long-term sectional community of interest. More important, certain sectional bonds give the states of each section a special relationship to national politics. This is particularly true in connection with those specific political issues that are of sectional importance, such as race in the South, the megalopolis in the Northeast, and agriculture and agribusiness in the West.

The nation's sectional alignments are rooted in the nation's three great historical, cultural, and economic spheres. The greater Northeast includes all those states north of the Ohio and Potomac rivers and east of Lake Michigan gathered in these sections: New England, Middle Atlantic, and the near West. The greater South includes the states below that line from the Atlantic to west Texas and Oklahoma. All the rest of the states comprise the greater West, both Northwest and far West.

From the New Deal years through the 1960s, Americans' understanding of sectionalism was submerged by their concern with urban-oriented socioeconomic categories, such as the struggle between labor and management or between the haves and have-nots in the big cities. Even the race issue, once the hallmark of the greater South, began to be perceived in nonsectional terms as a result of black immigration northward. This is not to say that sectionalism ceased to exist as a vital force, only that it was little noted in those years.

Beginning in the 1970s, however, there was a resurgence of sectional feeling as economic and social cleavages increasingly came to follow sectional lines. The sunbelt-frostbelt division is the prime example of this new sectionalism. "Sunbelt" became the new code word for the Lower South, Western South, and far West; "frostbelt," later replaced by "rustbelt," became the code word for the New England, Middle Atlantic, and Great Lakes states. Minnesota is part of the frostbelt but not the rustbelt, because its economy was never dominated by the urban-industrial frontier and it made the transition to the metropolitan-technological and rurban-cybernetic frontiers with relative ease. Its sectional position actually gave it additional strength on the rurban-cybernetic frontier. A reorganization of the nation's communications and banking systems strengthened the position of the Twin Cities west to the Rockies and south as far as New Mexico.

THE VITAL ROLE OF POLITICAL CULTURE

The United States as a whole shares a general political culture rooted in two contrasting conceptions of the American polity, which can be traced back to the earliest settlement of the country. In the first the polity is conceived as a marketplace in which the primary public relationships are products of bargaining among individuals and groups acting primarily out of self-interest. In the second the polity is conceived as a commonwealth in which the whole people have an undivided interest, and the citizens cooperate in an effort to create and maintain the best government in order to implement certain shared moral principles. The influence of these two conceptions can be felt throughout American political history, sometimes in conflict and sometimes complementing each other.[8]

This general political culture is a synthesis of three major political subcultures—individualistic, moralistic, and traditionalistic. Each of the three reflects its own particular synthesis of the marketplace and the commonwealth. All three are of nationwide proportions, having spread, in the course of time, from coast to coast. At the same time, each subculture is strongly tied to specific sections of the country, reflecting the streams and currents of migration that have carried people of different origins and backgrounds across the continent in more or less orderly patterns.

The *individualistic political culture* emphasizes the democratic order as a marketplace in which government is instituted for strictly utilitarian reasons, to handle those functions demanded by the people it is established to serve. Beyond the commitment to an open market, a government need not have any direct concern with questions of the good society, except insofar as it may be used to advance some common view formulated outside the political arena just as it serves other functions. Because the individualistic political culture emphasizes the centrality of private concerns, it places a premium on limiting community intervention—whether governmental or nongovernmental—into private activities to the minimum necessary to keep the marketplace in proper working order.

The character of political participation in the individualistic political culture reflects this. Politics is just another means by which individuals may improve themselves socially and economically; it is a business like any other, competing for talent and offering rewards to those who take it up as a career. Those individuals who choose political careers may rise by providing the government services demanded of them and, in return, may expect to be adequately compensated for their efforts. Interpretations of officeholders' obligations under this arrangement vary. Where the norms are high, such people are expected to provide high-quality public services in return for appropriate rewards. In other cases the primary responsibility of an officeholder is to serve him or herself and those who have provided direct support, favoring them even at the expense of the public.

Political life within the individualistic political culture is based on a system of mutual obligations rooted in personal relationships. Political parties serve as the major vehicles for maintaining the obligational network. Party regularity is the means for coordinating individual enterprise in the political arena and is the one way of preventing individualism in politics from running wild. Because the individualistic political culture eschews ideological concerns in its businesslike conception of politics, both politicians and citizens look on political activity as a specialized one, essentially the province of professionals, of minimum and passing concern to the public, and with no place for amateurs to play an active role. Furthermore, there is a strong tendency among the public to believe that politics is a dirty—if necessary—business, better left to those who are willing to soil themselves by engaging in it. In practice, then, where the individualistic political culture is dominant, there is likely to be an easy attitude toward the limits of the professionals' perquisites. Since a fair amount of corruption is expected in the normal course of things, there is relatively little popular excitement when any is found, unless it is of an extraordinary character. It is as if the public is willing to pay a surcharge for services rendered and rebels only when it feels the surcharge has become too heavy. (Of course, the judgments as to what is normal and what is extraordinary are themselves subjective and culturally conditioned.)

Public officials, committed to giving the public what it wants, normally initiate new programs only when they perceive an overwhelming public demand for them to act. The individualistic political culture is ambivalent about the place of bureaucracy in the political order. Bureaucratic methods of operation fly in the face of the favor system, yet organizational efficiency can be used by those seeking to master the market.

To the extent that the marketplace provides the model for public relationships in American civil society, all Americans share some of the attitudes that are of first importance in the individualistic political culture. At the same time, substantial segments of the American people operate politically within the framework of the two other political cultures.

The *moralistic political culture* emphasizes the commonwealth as the basis for democratic government. Politics is considered one of the great activities of humanity in its search for the good society—a struggle for power, it is true, but also an effort to exercise power for the betterment of the commonwealth. Consequently, both the general public and the politicians conceive of politics as a public activity centered on some notion of the public good and properly devoted to the advancement of the public interest.

There is a general commitment to using communal—preferably nongovernmental, but governmental if necessary—power to intervene in the sphere of private activities when it is considered necessary to do so for the public good or the well-being of the community. Accordingly, issues have an important place in the moralistic style of politics, functioning to set the tone for political concern. Government is considered a positive instrument with a responsibility to promote the general welfare, though definitions of what its positive role should be may vary considerably from era to era.

Politics is ideally a matter of concern for every citizen. Government service is public service, placing moral obligations on those who serve in government more demanding than those of the marketplace. Politics is not considered a legitimate realm for private enrichment. A politician is not expected to profit from political activity and, in fact, is held suspect if he or she does so.

The concept of serving the commonwealth is at the core of all political relationships, and politicians are expected to adhere to it even at the expense of individual loyalties and political friendships. Political parties are considered useful political devices but are not valued for their own sakes. Regular party ties can be abandoned with relative impunity for third parties, special local parties, nonpartisan systems, or the opposition party if such changes are believed helpful in gaining larger political goals.

In practice, where the moralistic political culture is dominant today, there is considerably more amateur participation in politics. There is also much less of what Americans consider corruption in government and less tolerance of those actions that are considered corrupt, so politics does not have the taint it so often bears in the individualistic environment.

By virtue of its fundamental outlook, the moralistic political culture creates a greater commitment to active government intervention in the economic and social life of the community. At the same time, its strong commitment to communitarianism tends to keep government intervention local wherever possible. Public officials themselves initiate new government activities in an effort to come to grips with problems as yet unperceived by a majority of the citizenry.

The moralistic political culture's major difficulty with bureaucracy lies in the potential conflict between communitarian principles and large-scale organization. Otherwise, the notion of a politically neutral administrative system is attractive. Where merit systems are instituted, they tend to be rigidly maintained.

The *traditionalistic political culture* is rooted in an ambivalent attitude toward the marketplace, coupled with a paternalistic and elitist conception of the commonwealth. It reflects an older attitude that accepts a substantially hierarchical society as part of the ordered nature of things, authorizing and expecting those at the top of the social structure to take a special and dominant role in government. The traditionalistic political culture accepts government as an actor with a positive role in the community, but it tries to limit that role to securing the continued maintenance of the existing social order. To do so, it functions to confine real political power to a relatively small and self-perpetuating group drawn from an established elite that often inherits its right to govern through family ties or social position. Those who do not have a definite role to play in politics are not expected to be even minimally active as citizens. In many cases they are not even expected to vote. Those active in politics are expected to benefit personally from their activity, although not necessarily by direct pecuniary gain.

Political parties are not important in traditionalistic political cultures because they encourage a degree of openness that goes against the grain of an elitist political order. Political competition is expressed through factions, an extension of the personal politics characteristic of the system. Hence, political systems within the culture tend to have loose one-party systems if they have political parties at all. Political leaders play conservative and custodial roles rather than initiatory roles unless pressed strongly from the outside.

Traditionalistic political cultures tend to be antibureaucratic. Bureaucracy by its very nature interferes with the fine web of social relationships that lies at the root of the political system. Where bureaucracy is introduced, it is generally confined to ministerial functions under the aegis of the established powerholders.

Although ethnically very diverse from the first, Minnesota, because of its geohistorical location, most easily attracted New Englanders and northern

Europeans since its earliest days. They gave the state a strongly moralistic political culture.[9] Minnesota looks very different from the inside, that is to say, to Minnesotans who live in the state, than it does from the outside in certain significant ways. In this respect, it is no different from any other place when seen through the different prisms of intimacy and distance. To its citizens and residents, Minnesota looks "pretty good," a state that has achieved a relatively decent way of life but is faced with serious problems that its people and governments have not been able to overcome, problems that are usually perceived as getting worse. Outsiders with similar values often cannot believe how good Minnesota appears to be and how laughable are their citizens' perceptions of its flaws when compared with other places. Both these perspectives are valuable. The constant desire of Minnesotans to improve, to be better than they or their civil society has been, is laudable, as are their achievements to date.

This book attempts to view the state through both prisms and to establish some perspective based on both. Indeed, one of the strongest confirmations of Minnesota's political culture also presents one of the greatest problems in writing about it. Because Minnesotans are moralistic, they rarely feel that they are doing well enough in their politics and government. They invariably feel that they could be doing better. At times Minnesotans even seem to try to highlight their minor problems to be in tune with the rest of the nation, where the same problems are major. This attitude is especially true among those recognized in their communities as leaders of local improvement and reform.

Normal human fragilities are often taken by many people in Minnesota to be reasons for feeling guilty—self-flagellation—and for issuing jeremiads, that is to say, commentaries on the weaknesses of their society. When Minnesota is viewed by outsiders, however, they often fail to understand that guilt because, for them, Minnesota looks so much better than what they see in the politics and government of their own states and localities. If this book impresses some Minnesotans as too good to be true, it is not meant to suggest that. Like every civil society, Minnesota certainly has its faults and weaknesses, only that, taken in the context of fallible humanity, Minnesota is in most respects a shining example.

That favorable assessment is a product of Minnesota's successful combination of a moralistic political culture with a strong entrepreneurial spirit, leading to commercial and technological innovations with a minimum of negative side effects. This is made possible in great part by the kinds of people who settled in Minnesota. Only recently has there been any substantial departure from earlier patterns in this regard, and the citizens of the state are working hard to assimilate newcomers, who must acquire the habits of the heart that have made Minnesota the place that it is. No doubt, in time, they will.

Minnesota, then, has been a successful polity, once we recognize human weaknesses and how hard it is to eliminate them. If, for some, this kind of flawed success is off-putting for many Minnesotans, it is usually viewed quite differently by the rest of the county.

Authors' Preface

What most Americans have traditionally known about Minnesota is that it is cold, liberal, and has 10,000 lakes. In fact, it is cold. Only Bismarck, North Dakota, is colder in January than Minneapolis/St. Paul and Duluth. But Minnesota's liberalism is overrated, and it has not 10,000 lakes but 15,291 lakes of ten-plus acres. On 4 November 1998 most Americans learned a new, and to them amazing, fact about Minnesota: its voters had elected former pro wrestler Jesse "The Body" Ventura to its highest office. In this book we put the "Jesse phenomenon" into a broader context; we explore myths and realities about Minnesota politics and develop explanations for how it differs from politics in the rest of the country.

This book is a collaborative effort of the three authors. Daniel J. Elazar, a native Minnesotan, is a longtime student of Minnesota political history, institutions, and political culture. Virginia Gray teaches state government and politics at the University of Minnesota and specializes in research on the politics of the fifty states. Wyman Spano is a political analyst and lobbyist deeply involved in the political life of Minnesota. This combination of talents and interests ensures a broad coverage of Minnesota's politics and government in light of the state's history and development. In terms of the writing, Elazar was responsible for chapters 1, 2, 3, and 9; Gray was responsible for chapters 4, 6, 10, 12, and 13; and Spano was responsible for chapters 5, 7, 8, and 11.

During the course of this project many individuals and institutions provided support, for which we are grateful. The University of Minnesota furnished able graduate assistants; Rowzat Shipchandler, Tom Rudolph, John Transue, Larry Grossback, Amy Gangl, and David Peterson skillfully constructed most of the graphs and tables. Assisting us in other phases of production were Paul Neal, John Wesley Leckrone, Mark Ami-El, Rachel Elrom, and Kim Robinson. Several knowledgeable Minnesotans read early versions of the book and furnished comments that greatly improved the final product. For this valuable service, we thank Sarah Janecek, John Brandl, Charles Backstrom, James Pederson, Marcia Keller Avner, and Ann Wynia. Two other colleagues—Don Ostrom and John Kincaid—served as reviewers for the Press and further refined our prose and sharpened our thinking. Phil Frickey, Sam Krislov, the Honorable A. M. "Sandy" Keith, and Ted Kolderie read and commented on individual chapters. The Minnesota Historical Society, the Campaign Finance and Public Disclosure Board, and the Legislative Reference Library provided mountains of information, and the Minnesota Poll furnished valuable survey data. All the governors serving between 1960 and 1998 graciously consented to lengthy interviews; more than twenty other Minnesotans were interviewed as well. Once again, Minnesota's political system proved to be open and accessible.

MINNESOTA POLITICS AND GOVERNMENT

CHAPTER I

Minnesota as a Polity

THE CHARACTER OF THE STATE

One of the most striking sights in Minnesota is the state capitol in St. Paul, designed by Minnesotan Cass Gilbert, one of the great architects of his time. When constructed in 1905, it stood alone on Capitol Hill, a visible sign of how small Minnesota government was in those days. Now it crowns a campus that stretches nearly a half mile long toward the Mississippi River and a quarter mile wide from the capitol itself on the north end to the massive Minnesota History Center, with other state departments in between.

The area below the crest of Capitol Hill was developed after World War II according to a master plan that demolished the slums around the area and transformed it into an architectural expression of the majesty and extent of contemporary state government. Today's capitol center embodies the character of Minnesota and its people—open and expansive, orderly and manicured—blending rural and urban styles. Some of the buildings are architecturally striking. Others were clearly built with tight budgets in mind.

The overall impact is pleasing but not opulent. The people of Minnesota clearly see the capitol complex as their property. Nearly every grade-school student in the state tours it. Dozens of yellow school buses are a daily sight during the school year, especially when the legislature is in session. The hill is used for the St. Paul Winter Carnival and, in the summer, for the annual "Taste of Minnesota" festival. Music, food, and fireworks entice more than one hundred thousand people to use the capitol grounds over the July 4th holiday.

The capitol is one of St. Paul's four focal points that give architectural expression to the character of Minnesota. Looking from its steps straight ahead, one sees the tall buildings of downtown St. Paul, representing Minnesota commerce, as well as the museums, auditoriums, and convention centers found in any modern capital city.

To the right of the capitol steps, one sees on an adjacent hill the Cathedral of the Diocese of St. Paul, a substantial structure built at approximately the same time as the capitol. More recently, the Minnesota Historical Society, using legislative appropriations and private gifts, constructed the Minnesota History Center on a slightly lower point between the capitol and the cathedral to add the dimension of historical preservation and interpretation to the skyline. The Minnesota Historical Society, the oldest public body in the state, was incorporated in 1849, the same year Minnesota became a territory. In 1995, remodeling and additions to the old historical society building just east of the capitol resulted in an ornate new judicial center.

The prominent position of the capitol also symbolizes the degree to which Minnesota exists because it is a civil society whose citizens are linked through its polity more than in any other single way.[1] This is true of every state in the Union, just as it is of the United States as a whole. As a nation of immigrant settlers, the commonwealths of the United States derived from the deliberate acts of founders who established political and social institutions designed to create and order political societies of newcomers.

Minnesota, like other states, exists because it is a political entity located on a particular territory, with its own government serving a specific population. Minnesota was given full form as a civil society when it was admitted to the Union as a state on 11 May 1858. Its constitution defines the state's boundaries. The internal divisions—the counties, townships, cities, villages, school districts, and special districts that give Minnesota its character—are the products of state government action in response to popular demand. The many different peoples that have come to Minnesota have formed their links with the land, the state, and one another through these political subdivisions. Even in this age when government is more intrusive in our lives, most people are unaware of the degree to which their lives are shaped by their political institutions and become aware of those institutions only when they fail to deliver promised or expected results.

Minnesotans have grown accustomed to being the envy of outside observers. In 1947 John Gunther, in his famous *Inside U.S.A.*, characterized the state as "spectacularly varied, proud, handsome, and progressive."[2] In 1973 a *Time* magazine cover story said, "If the American good life has anywhere survived in some intelligent equilibrium, it may be in Minnesota." In 1997 *The Economist* called Minnesota "surely America's promised land."[3] Of all the various laudatory writings about Minnesota, the most salient comes from Neal Peirce, the late-twentieth-century chronicler of the American states, who subtitled his chapter on Minnesota "The Successful Society":

> Its leaders . . . have played an increasingly prominent role in national life, far out of proportion to the state's modest two percent of the national population. Its political structure remains open, issue-oriented, responsible. Its state government has been a leader in services for people, even though citizens and corporations alike have had to pay a high tax bill for those services. Few states exceed Minnesota in the quality and extent of the education offered its citizens; none appears to provide health care of comparable quality. Economic growth has been strong and steady, encompassing the brainpower industries of the electronic era along with traditional farming, milling, and mining. And Minnesota maintains a clear focus of economic and cultural leadership in her Twin Cities, towns whose great industries have resisted the siren call of the national conglomerates.[4]

This book has as one of its themes an evaluation of the truth of these tributes. There have been dissenting voices. The February 1997 *Governing* magazine contained an article about Minnesota entitled "The Sick Legislature Syndrome."[5] In 1995 the *New York Times* called Minneapolis "Murderapolis."[6]

The elevation of former pro wrestler Jesse "The Body" Ventura to the governorship in 1998 provoked considerable amused commentary from the national media. The *New York Times*, in its front-page article on the governor-elect, featured a color picture of "The Body" stomping a wrestling opponent. *Time* magazine put Ventura on its cover (only in Minnesota) under the headline "Body Slam," and David Letterman offered his version of Ventura's top ten campaign slogans (for example, "A Man in Tights Has Nothing to Hide"). Once Ventura has been in office for a while, Minnesotans hope that more substantive evaluation will emerge.

Minnesota moves into the twenty-first century with a nationwide reputation as the exemplar of a state that has succeeded in providing a high "quality of life." Its people are, on one hand, proud and confident of their future, principally because of their polity and its political system, and, on the other, worried about a perceived deterioration in Minnesota's quality of life. Minnesota's situation as a well-respected yet perpetually concerned civil society was far from inevitable. It required a great deal of effort and the right combination of people and circumstances, brought together with the right timing.

GEOHISTORICAL LOCATION

Despite its continental centrality, geohistorically Minnesota is a relatively isolated part of the American Trans-Mississippi West. The advance of the land frontier in fits and starts made Minnesota, which was off the main routes of the westward movement, the farthest outpost of American penetration into the Northwest for many years and one of the last of the contiguous states to have an open-land frontier.

Five major regional physiographic patterns meet in the state, each of which has demanded its own forms of social organization and technology.[7] The Native Americans who inhabited the land that is now Minnesota before European settlement accommodated themselves to these regions. The tribes of the Dakota (Sioux) nation who originally lived in the Big Woods were forced westward by the Ojibwe (Chippewa) tribes moving into their territories from the east.[8] One consequence of the migration of the Dakotas westward was their transformation into Plains Indians, while the Ojibwes continued the lake-and-woods culture they brought with them. Today about fifty thousand American Indians live in Minnesota, approximately twelve thousand of whom reside on one of eleven Indian reservations located primarily in rural areas while more live in the Twin Cities.

The European Americans arriving in what is now Minnesota first encountered the lowland prairies drained by the Mississippi and Minnesota river systems. The new settlers applied essentially the same forms and techniques of organizing land settlement as had been used on the prairies to the near west. North of the prairies were found the so-called Big Woods, in part an extension of the forest-and-rock desert known as the Canadian or Laurentian Shield, the area of Minnesota first penetrated by Europeans, the French-Canadian voyageurs. In Minnesota this is the area of the state's "10,000 lakes." Settlement on the shield required adaptations not dissimilar from those required to settle the mountain deserts of the far West. On the northeast is Lake Superior, the largest, most rugged, and coldest of the Great Lakes, which are Minnesota's principal sea-lanes to the world. The western third of Minnesota, though initially thought to be simply a continuation of the humid prairie, was discovered by its settlers to be a transition zone between the humid grasslands and the high, dry plains. These conditions required modification of lowland prairie farming and settlement patterns to accommodate human needs in a climatically harsh, semiarid environment. All told, approximately two-thirds of Minnesota represents a difficult physical environment even by the standards of the greater West. This fact led, in turn, to the establishment of a marginal civilization, one prone to seek radical solu-

tions to its recurrent problems. The challenges of a harsh environment are reflected in the impact of the frontier on Minnesota.

THE CONTINUING FRONTIER IN MINNESOTA

The first Europeans to appear in present-day Minnesota were the French
voyageurs, who established fur-trading posts throughout the state. Minnesota's true rural-land frontier opened with the establishment of Fort Snelling
at the confluence of the Minnesota and Mississippi rivers in 1819 (now at a
point next to the Twin Cities Metropolitan Airport).

Minnesota's nineteenth century was dominated by the land frontier.[9] One
hundred years of intensive effort ended with permanent human occupation
and civil organization in every part of the state.[10] The advancing national line
of rural settlement reached Minnesota in the 1830s, and the state's land frontier continued until sometime between 1907, when the railroad reached
Rainy Lake, on the Canadian border, and 1919, when the collapse of the
World War I agricultural boom ended massive homesteading in the state. As
late as the 1950s there were still federal land auctions to sell off leftover parcels from the original public domain, and in the 1960s there were still original homesteaders living on the lands they homesteaded in the state's northern
third. That is one of the keys to understanding Minnesota. It is still, by world
standards, new. Many older adults have memories of pioneer grandparents.
Minnesota's territorial history reflects the conflicts between European claims
in the New World, which began even before the advancing frontier reached
its soil. Although Minnesota was technically a part of Virginia before ever
being seen by Europeans, Virginia's claim was never exercised in the field.
With the possible exception of the medieval Vikings, the French were the
first Europeans to set foot on Minnesota soil. Minnesota's entire territory
was claimed by France from 1671 to 1763. After the French lost the last
French and Indian War, their claims east of the Mississippi River were ceded
to Great Britain, which ceded them to the United States in 1783. What is today eastern Minnesota was nominally part of Quebec and under the jurisdiction of the Quebec Act.

In 1762 France's claims west of the Mississippi were ceded to Spain,
which held them until they were relinquished to France in 1803 so France
could sell the territory to the United States under the terms of the Louisiana
Purchase (1803). Following that act, western Minnesota continued to be an
unorganized part of Louisiana and then Missouri Territory. Northernmost
Minnesota remained under British control until the U.S.-British treaty of

1818, which established the border between the United States and British North America at a point from Lake of the Woods westward along the forty-ninth parallel. This gave Minnesota the point of land at the north end of Lake of the Woods, which makes it the northernmost state of the lower forty-eight. The Northwest Angle is directly accessible from the rest of the United States only by water.[11]

A year later, in 1819, the first official American settlement in Minnesota was established at Fort Snelling. The military commander there exercised jurisdiction over the white people in Minnesota. When Missouri was admitted to the Union in 1820 and the Iowa Territory was subsequently organized, it included the part of Minnesota west of the Mississippi. In 1836, after Michigan became a state and the territory of Wisconsin was organized, the latter was extended to include the entire area of what is today Minnesota.

As settlers arrived, the Wisconsin territorial government organized St. Croix County to provide law and order. The county became the first formal civil government in the state, made possible by the signing of the 1837 treaty with the Ojibwes and a second treaty with the Dakotas, which opened Minnesota's territory east of the Mississippi for permanent white settlement. Although, after 1836, settlements were established that eventually became Minneapolis, St. Paul, and Mendota, most of the region's settlers were located along the St. Croix River, where Stillwater was their center. Another group of settlers came down from the Red River Settlement in the Hudson's Bay Territory, now Winnipeg, Canada, to settle around Pembina (now North Dakota), nearly four hundred miles from the St. Croix River.

Wisconsin was admitted to the Union in 1848, leaving Minnesota once again outside any territorial government. On 26 August of that year the residents of the area met in convention at Stillwater and adopted measures calling for the establishment of a new territory to be named Minnesota. On 30 October the Stillwater convention elected Henry Hastings Sibley its territorial delegate to Congress. Thus, Minnesota was founded by the sovereign act of its own people at their initiative.

The urban-industrial frontier opened in Minnesota in the last generation of the nineteenth century, principally in the Twin Cities and Duluth areas, to process the raw materials of the land frontier—food, fiber, and ore. Milling, mining, and the lumber industry were developed between the 1870s and World War I, as the last areas of the state were being settled. Urbanization and industrialization continued through the interwar generation, slowed but not stopped by the Great Depression, perhaps because of Minnesota's location at the northwestern edge of the urban-industrial belt.

Although the urban-industrial frontier became increasingly important in the state, Minnesota remained on the northwestern fringes of that frontier throughout its heyday, maintaining close ties between the land and the urban-industrial base. After World War II (1945) companies such as Minnesota Mining and Manufacturing (now called 3M) and Honeywell, founded in the interwar period, expanded their industrial capacities to generate the new technology associated with yet a third frontier.

The metropolitan-technological frontier opened in Minnesota in the aftermath of World War II and clearly dominated the state for a generation. Its principal expressions were located in the seven counties of the Twin Cities metropolitan region, but manifestations were also found in the state's medium-size cities, with the exception of Duluth. By the 1960s half the state's population was gathered in the seven-county region, creating a unique combination of woods and waters, commerce and industry, and homes. These were centered on the nodes of state government in St. Paul, higher education on the two campuses of the University of Minnesota, and the commercial sites of downtown Minneapolis. That region became one of the innovators on the metropolitan frontier in several ways.

Rapid expansion of the new technologies, particularly in electronics and cybernetics, was reflected in the growth of metropolitan Minnesota. The Twin Cities changed from twin but separate urban centers into a metropolitan region as large as the state of Delaware, with a concomitant decline in the central city populations of Minneapolis and St. Paul and growth of the suburban population in a seven-county area.

By the mid-1970s the metropolitan frontier had closed nationwide. Though metropolitanization continued, it was no longer at the cutting edge of socioeconomic development. This was not entirely true in Minnesota, where the distance between the state's metropolitan areas and the rest of metropolitan America was such that the widening of the metropolitan circle was still a major growth factor. At the same time, the new rurban, or citybelt-cybernetic, frontier had begun to emerge.[12]

Minnesota was poised to cross over to the rurban-cybernetic frontier in the late 1970s without a break in its step. The state was home to some of the most innovative cybernetically oriented companies. Control Data Corporation, Honeywell, and 3M were the largest, but there were many other, smaller ones too.[13] As these companies surged forward into the new cybernetic age, settlement in the seven-county area and in southeastern Minnesota generally began breaking out of the confines of urban and suburban municipalities to acquire rurban characteristics.

By 1982 Southdale, the Twin City Metropolitan Region's biggest suburban shopping center and one of the nation's most notable, grossed more in retail sales than downtown Minneapolis. Downtown Minneapolis was only one of ten major regional shopping areas, and downtown St. Paul did not figure at all. Significantly third after Southdale and downtown Minneapolis was Ridgedale, located in suburban Minnetonka, west of Minneapolis. Three of the top ten shopping concentrations in 1982 did not even exist in 1977. Ten years later all this had radically changed with the opening of the Mall of America, the largest shopping center in the country. Once again, Minnesota rode the crest of the advancing frontier. This pattern is what accounts for the state's continued prosperity and generally even development.[14]

There are many indicators of this frontier dimension in Minnesota's civil society. Some are demographic, based on migration patterns. Minnesota originally attracted settlers from greater New England, the Scandinavian countries of northern Europe, and Canada. Then its cities attracted migrants from the rural areas of the interior Northwest, from Sioux Ste. Marie to the continental divide in Montana and from Saskatoon, Saskatchewan, to Sioux City, Iowa.

Since the days of the metropolitan frontier, the state has been on one of the migration tracks of high achievers from throughout the country. Extensive in-migration is reflected in the fact that the state's leading elected officials often have been in-migrants themselves, today as well as in the days of the land frontier. Arne Carlson, governor from 1991 to 1999, was born in New York City; U.S. senator Paul Wellstone was born in Washington DC; Minnesota's most famous postwar politician, Hubert Humphrey, was born in South Dakota; Congressman Martin Olav Sabo was born in North Dakota; and former U.S. senator Rudy Boschwitz was born in Germany. In 1995 only three of the six constitutionally elected officers, four of the seven supreme court justices, five of eight members of the U.S. House of Representatives, and one of the United States senators were born and raised in Minnesota.

State and local governments in Minnesota have had to respond to these frontier stages, from the establishment of the first counties in what was still Wisconsin Territory to the organization of the Twin Cities Metropolitan Council to serve the state's metropolitan heart. When Minnesota's territorial government was organized in 1849, scarcely a thousand whites lived in Minnesota. The establishment of a territorial government made possible and stimulated a sixfold growth within the year. Three federal treaties liquidating

Indian title to most of the territory, negotiated in 1851, opened the lands west of the Mississippi, so that when the census was taken in 1857 on the eve of statehood, the population already exceeded 150,000. The boundaries of many if not most of the state's governments are based on the federal land survey that covered virtually all the area west of the original thirteen states.[15] The many different peoples that have moved into Minnesota have developed their connections with the land, the state, and one another through these political subdivisions.

Minnesota emerged as a civil society in the decade immediately before the Civil War, the decade with the most ideologically intense cleavage in the history of American politics. Between 1849, when Minnesota Territory was created, and 1858, when the state entered the Union, the fixation of the country on the problems that led to the Civil War was reflected in Minnesota. The emerging civil society divided into the Republicans—mostly antislavery Yankees—and the Democrats—mostly Middle State and southern moderates who accepted Illinois Senator Stephen Douglas's position of "popular sovereignty." There were ethnic overtones as well. These differences became so intense that representatives of the two parties would not even sit together in a single constitutional convention. The state constitution was drafted separately, in two conventions, and the two documents were harmonized by a conference committee after a bitter struggle. Because neither group of partisans would sign the final document with the other group, Minnesota still has two official "original constitutions."[16]

Because the most important of these issues were highly moral in character, the objective political environment encouraged the development of a strongly issue-oriented politics from the first. This commitment to issues was reinforced in the post–Civil War generation by social and economic factors relating to the establishment and development of a marginal society on the Minnesota frontier. The commitment to issues was further intensified by a majority of Minnesota's first settlers, who stemmed from the moralistic political culture, mostly New Englanders or descendants of New Englanders from upstate New York, northern Illinois, and southeastern Wisconsin. They combined moral concern with a desire to become economically successful.[17]

These products of the Yankee stream settled in the southeastern part of the state, on the humid prairie, applying the technology developed by their compatriots for the Illinois prairies a decade earlier. Unlike the Yankee settlers of Illinois, however, they were virtually the first to occupy their future commonwealth, so they did not have to compromise their communitarian individualism with any "rugged" individualistic elements already entrenched in power. Nor did their environment encourage the latter type of individualism, because even on the prairies, cooperation was required for survival. Actually, in light of the migrations that were to follow, the first Yankee settlers came in time to be considered the symbols of extreme individualism in Minnesota.[18]

Minnesota's second wave of settlement came during and after the Civil War and was dominated by immigrants who came directly from Europe—from the Scandinavian countries, Germany, and Ireland. Most of them were farmers, but substantial numbers of Germans and Irish settled in the burgeoning urban communities along the state's navigable waterways. From the first, the role played by these immigrants had important consequences for Minnesota's political culture, for the most part reinforcing the original contributions of the Yankees.

Most of the Europeans who came to Minnesota shared a version of the communitarian ethic similar to that found among the descendants of the Puritans. This has been true even of the Catholics, predominantly Germans and Irish, who represented something of a self-selected population. Many of the latter were attracted by the great Catholic Americanist bishop John Ireland, for just those qualities, to establish farming colonies in Minnesota's hinterland. Perhaps even more important, the overwhelming majority of those European emigrants came directly to Minnesota, where they settled on virgin land. Thus, unlike their compatriots who settled in the cities or in rural areas already occupied by others and who had to adjust their ways to established patterns, they could retain many of the basic attitudes of the cultures they brought with them from the Old World, if not their overt manifestations. This, too, contributed to Minnesota's uniqueness in the national picture, to the state's ultimate desire for a degree of semi-isolation, and to the particular political culture dominant within its boundaries. As the nineteenth century drew to a close, they were joined by southern and eastern European farmers, brought in by the railroads, along whose rights-of-way they created replicas of Old World farm villages, each with its distinctive culture.

A third wave of settlement began in the state sometime after 1880. Like the first two, its representatives sought the still-plentiful vacant areas on the land frontier. Though this wave included many farmers (predominantly Scandinavians), the element that gave it a distinctive character was composed of miners, mostly southern and eastern European in origin, who settled the three iron ranges on the Laurentian Shield. Settlement of the iron ranges was already a response to the demands of the national corporate economy produced by the urban-industrial frontier. The settlers were employees of large companies from the first. Most of them settled in the northeastern part of the state, and Duluth's demographic base was strongly influenced by them.

The lumberjacks who entered the state in great numbers at the same time were brought by the large lumber companies then engaged in cutting the Big Woods. Even the farmers who pioneered this stage of the land frontier, though still in the entrepreneurial pattern, were frequently settled on the prairies by the great land-grant railroad companies of the Northwest, eager to populate their rights-of-way. Meanwhile, the cities had begun to attract members of all these groups, plus Jews from eastern Europe, to form urban working- and lower-middle-class populations. By the turn of the century Minnesota had one of the most ethnically diverse populations of any state; most of its residents had come directly from their countries of origin to their new places of settlement. Hence, their Americanization was entirely a product of their Minnesota experiences. The miners and those lumberjacks who stayed to settle in the state brought a kind of proletarian radicalism to add to an already radical (by American standards) tradition of politics in Minnesota.

After the turn of the century a fourth wave of settlement occupied Minnesota's far north. Because of the duration of Minnesota's land-frontier period, this fourth wave was dominated by the descendants of the Yankees of the southeastern counties who had actually been born and bred in the state. Their efforts to establish themselves permanently in the north country ran right into the post–World War I agricultural depression, which transformed them into seekers for social solutions for their problems along lines most appropriate to the twentieth century, but in a spirit of communalism and political responsibility akin to that of their parents.

The fifth wave of settlement to enter Minnesota, though not particularly radical, has served to reinforce the state's distinctive subculture. These migrants moved from the rural sections of Minnesota's great Upper Midwestern empire (the Dakotas, Montana, and parts of Wisconsin, Nebraska, Iowa, and the Upper Peninsula of Michigan contribute most of this fifth wave) to the state's metropolitan centers, particularly the Minneapolis–St. Paul metropolitan region, which embraces most of the section's recent frontiers. They have sought new social and economic opportunities similar to those sought by rural and small-town Americans across the country. In the process, they have helped establish one of the most demographically self-contained sections in the United States, with Minnesota at its heart.

Drawn from the same cultural streams, these new migrants reflect the same cultural background as the state's original settlers. Hence, they reinforce the political culture already rooted in the state. Minnesota's unique subculture is further protected by an extensive out-migration of population, which tends to leave the "hard core" Minnesotans in control of every facet of the state's life.

Coincident with the opening of the rurban frontier in the late 1970s, a sixth wave of migration into the state began, one that rested heavily on the arrival of increasing numbers of people of color. Minnesota's previously small African-American population began to grow significantly, primarily in Minneapolis. The end of the Vietnam War in 1975 brought immigrants from Southeast Asia in substantial numbers, including Cambodians, Laotians (especially the Hmong), and Vietnamese, who settled in the Twin Cities and also in southwestern Minnesota to take employment in available unskilled jobs. Along with them came other Asians and, later, Somalians. The number of Hispanic migrants increased, particularly in places such as Moorhead, Owatonna, and Willmar, in connection with the food-processing industry. The number of Native Americans in Minnesota more than doubled, partly by natural increase and partly by in-migration from Indian reservations to the west. To this point, the sixth wave has not significantly affected the state's political culture; indeed, these new migrants have, as yet, minimal participation in the political process. One of Minnesota's ongoing questions is whether the state will be able to acculturate this sixth wave. It is the first substantial immigration wave with origins clearly outside the dominant Minnesota political culture.

Despite this new migration, Minnesota has an extraordinarily small nonwhite population. According to the 1990 census, 93.7 percent of Minnesota's population was Caucasian, 2.2 percent black, 1.1 percent Native American, 1.8 percent Asian, and 1.2 percent Hispanic. The white population declined from 96.7 percent in 1980, while all the peoples of color increased their share by approximately 30 percent.

Out of these six waves of settlement have emerged Minnesota's dominant socioeconomic groups. Agriculture, the predominant industry for many years, has provided two very divergent elements: the more conservative farmers of the relatively prosperous southeastern and central counties and the populist types from the more marginal farm areas in the rest of the state. Both groups have been very active on the state political scene, even though their relative population strength has drastically declined in recent years. Minnesota has become statistically "urban," but owing to the large role agriculture still plays in supporting subsidiary businesses and industries, only since the opening of the metropolitan frontier has urban Minnesota developed a substantial economic base divorced from "agribusiness." Because of the forest-and-rock desert in which it is located, the state's northeastern hinterland did not develop from an agriculturally based economy, a fact that has heightened its differentiation from the rest of the state. Instead, a timber-based industry developed in the late nineteenth century and then settled into routinized patterns.

By and large, the dominant elements in the state's business community are descended from the early Yankee entrepreneurs. Since World War I they have been joined by entrepreneurs from the other streams who have developed enterprises of various sizes in a spirit similar to that of the Yankees. The largest enterprises have institutionalized this spirit even where they have passed out of the hands of their founding families. Consequently, the entrepreneurial tradition with close ties to the communitarian culture remains reasonably strong.

As late as the early 1980s Minnesota had business and industrial concerns that were more moderate in size and more likely to be locally controlled when compared with the rest of the county. In addition, Minnesota companies often were headed by longtime state residents, frequently the descendants of the Yankee entrepreneurs. The result was a tradition of active civic involvement by business leaders. Whether that tradition will continue is a subject of considerable debate. Most civic and political leaders with a national perspective tend to think that Minnesota still leads the way in terms of the civic/business nexus, but the level of interaction is lower than it was two decades ago. In the twentieth century some of the locally owned companies—General Mills, Pillsbury, Cargill, Dayton-Hudson, 3M, to name only a few—have grown into worldwide corporate giants, but the location of their headquarters continued to be in Minnesota. Today, however, Pillsbury is owned by Britain's Grand Met; Dayton-Hudson has many more sales outside Minnesota than in it; and 3M has major facilities all over the world. In recent years there has been a concern that even when major corporate businesses remain technically locally owned, they are managed by people who do not have earlier generations' commitment to the state. This change is showing up both in the level of corporate contributions and, even more important, in the amount of time corporate leaders devote to civic affairs.

The rapid rise of a locally created electronics industry is testimony to the survival of the entrepreneurial tradition as a major factor in the state's economy. The Twin Cities area is a major center of electronics production in the

United States, despite its handicaps of location and its lack of federal defense contracts. The bulk of the area's electronics industry was developed locally by individual Minnesotans who wished to establish themselves in their native state despite its economic and climatic disadvantages, rather than by large corporations or outsiders seeking a more favorable business climate. It is primarily a product of local resources, from the inventiveness at the University of Minnesota to the financial support by Twin Cities banks to the supply of skilled manpower in the tradition of Scandinavian craftsmanship and German precision.

Duluth was the one significant exception to this pattern. From the 1870s it had been an industrial colony of the lower Great Lakes cities, particularly Cleveland, and a business colony of the Twin Cities. One result is that Duluth's politics partly reflected the struggle between a labor force that remained tied to its locality and corporate stewards serving absentee owners while holding great political power locally. In the 1980s this began to turn around. Duluth's recent renaissance is a result of its becoming more like the rest of the state in the sources of its economic development.

In view of the state's history it is not surprising to find an important labor movement, composed to a very large extent of highly skilled workers. Organized labor historically has been strong in politics, local as well as national, and is exceptionally successful in its ability to gain community support for its demands. As in the rest of the United States, union strength in Minnesota declined in the 1980s, but relative to other states, organized labor continues to be a leader in terms of political clout. This is, in no small measure, because unions in Minnesota have been able to organize middle-class elements, such as teachers, retail clerks, and state and local government employees, in a basically middle-class population. This, in turn, has created a labor movement with some goals markedly different from those of the labor movements in other areas, one concerned with civic responsibility as well as "bread and butter" issues. The organization of government employees has also increased the level of labor activity in the political realm by creating a dual stake in politics for a large segment of the local labor movement.[19]

An industrial base that rests primarily on skilled labor drawn from much the same population base as the business and professional people has limited the development of divergences in outlook between the business-professional subcommunity and the labor subcommunity in Minnesota. In other states, where the two subcommunities have, to a great extent, been drawn from culturally different streams as well as from different ethnic groups, such divergences are common. In the latter the earlier-arriving native streams had supplied the bulk of the business and professional elements while the latecoming European elements were more or less automatically assigned to the working class on arrival and were forced to "work up" as individuals. Perhaps paradoxically, however, the similarity in cultural background between the two elements at one point stimulated class conflict in the state to an extent not experienced elsewhere.

Although the complex origins of class cleavage in politics are not easily unraveled and, in any case, Minnesotans reject them as violating their egalitarian sensibilities, two factors stand out. First, because the Old World–originated streams flowed directly from Europe into Minnesota at the outset of its settlement, some of the class consciousness more common to European politics went into the very formation of the state's political system. Furthermore, class differences could not be masked by ethnic or cultural ones. Rather, the similarity in cultural backgrounds between those who became the business and professional classes and those who entered the working class made the latter more conscious of class as a factor.[20]

Since obviously inferior status and economic conditions could not be explained away by pseudohistorical rationalizations about the "rights" of earlier groups or pseudoracial theories about a "superior northern and western European stock," resentment between the two elements grew as the labor subcommunity demanded a better place in the local sun. In time, this led to a sharp cleavage between the two subcommunities which, in the European manner, came to be expressed through politics. Given that the Democratic-Farmer-Labor party (DFL) won much of what the radicals demanded after World War II, including a dominant position politically, while business-labor cooperation on common projects brought both elements to a new level of mutual communication and understanding, that cleavage now has gone by the board.

MINNESOTA'S SECTIONAL LOCATION

These conflicts were both exacerbated and balanced by Minnesota's sectional location as part of the Interior Northwest. This section was first defined by the railroads of the rural-land frontier. It was reinforced by the institutional patterns that followed in their wake, whether we are speaking of the circulation of Twin Cities newspapers throughout the section or the location of medical facilities. Long before interstate banking became an accepted practice in the United States, the three former great banks of the Twin Cities—First National Bank of Minneapolis, Northwestern National Bank, and the First National Bank of St. Paul—developed bank holding companies through which they established what were, in effect, branches throughout Minnesota, the Dakotas, and Montana.[21]

Minnesota is one of the best examples in the United States of the interplay between statehood and sectionalism. As a state, it is located in the transitional zone between the greater Northeast and the greater West, pulled in both directions but more western than eastern in its social mores. The balance was tipped by Minnesota's sectional position as the heart of what is variously known as the Northwest or the Upper Midwest, a section best delineated by the boundaries of the Ninth Federal Reserve district, designed in 1913 with the section in mind. Headquartered in Minneapolis, the Ninth District includes the Upper Peninsula of Michigan, northern and northwestern Wisconsin, all of Minnesota and the Dakotas, and Montana. The Federal Reserve headquarters ensures that the Twin Cities will remain central to just about all the financial activity in the district.

In other matters, since the 1960s the Twin Cities' grip on its section has loosened as the colonial relationship between the cities and their hinterland has been replaced by one of greater interchange. Nevertheless, the sectional pattern still helps define the North Star State.

Minnesota remains unique. Of course, the state is being shaped by many of the same trends that have had substantial influence on the other states in recent decades. Although it remains a state with a substantial home-owned economic base, an increasing number of its corporations have been acquired by out-of-state owners, and others that remain home-owned have a progressively smaller share of their activities in the state, having become nationwide and worldwide in scope. Nonetheless, relative to other states, Minnesota appears to continue to have more ability to control its business destiny. The days are gone, however, when Phillip W. Pillsbury, chairman of the board of the Pillsbury Corporation during the 1970s, could tell his board of directors that the company would remain headquartered in Minneapolis instead of moving to a more central and less expensive location "because I live here."[22] A result of declining business control is a perceptible decline in business leadership's interest in civic affairs. John Fischer, in a 1969 article, said, "The archetypical man-who-has-made-it in, say, Miami may enjoy his leisure on a yacht, and in Hollywood among his collection of starlets—but if he lives in Minneapolis he would spend it in committee meetings."[23]

That may no longer be so true, but the state's largest city continues to exhibit remarkable civic interest. In 1997 *Business Week* proclaimed, "Minneapolis shows the way," and praised the city for its low unemployment, well-trained workforce, and climbing salaries. A major study of fifteen mid-size American cities published in 1996 by the *Pittsburgh Post-Gazette* rated Minneapolis/St. Paul best overall in fifteen measures of economic vitality and livability. One measure, United Way contributions, in which Minneapolis/St. Paul led all fifteen cities, spoke to business involvement, because United Way contributions are typically generated through businesses.[24]

Minnesotans can revel in their relatively healthy economy and civically committed business community, but there are troubling indications of new realities in the two major cities, particularly in the very rapid growth in the 1980s and early 1990s in the number of census tracts with high concentrations of poverty. In addition, Minneapolis and St. Paul schoolchildren are not achieving well in comparison with the balance of the state. And, for a brief period, Minneapolis had an extraordinarily high murder rate, though criminality of all types in Minnesota's major cities had returned, by 1997, to levels generally below those of comparably sized cities.

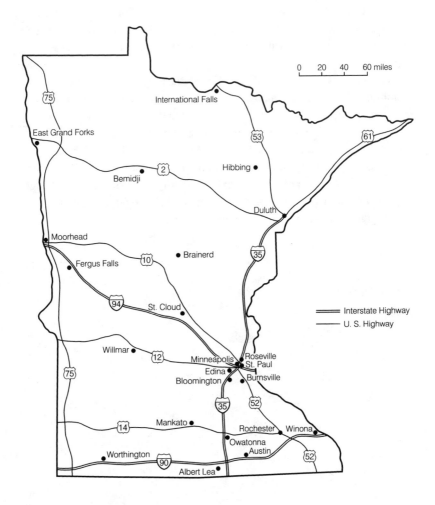

Major cities and highways of Minnesota

Source: Adapted from Facts On File, Inc. 1984.

CHAPTER 2

Epitome of the Moralistic Political Culture

Political cultural factors stand out as influential in shaping Minnesota's government. They do so (1) by molding the perceptions of the political community (citizens, politicians, and public officials) of the nature and purposes of politics and expectations from government and the political process; (2) by influencing the recruitment of specific kinds of people to become active in government and politics—as elected officials, civil servants, and political activists; and (3) by subtly directing the actual way in which the art of government is practiced by citizens, politicians, and public officials in the light of those perceptions. The cultural components of individual and group behavior also make themselves felt in the kinds of civic behavior dictated by conscience and internalized ethical standards in the forms of law-abidingness adhered to by citizens and officials and in the character of government actions.

MORALISTIC MINNESOTA

The introduction to this book describes the general concept of political culture and delineates the three subcultures extant in the American states: individualistic, traditionalistic, and moralistic. Minnesota is the archetypical example of a state informed and permeated by the moralistic political subculture: both the general public and the politicians conceive of politics as a public activity centered on some notion of the public good and properly devoted to the advancement of the public interest. The tone set by the state's political culture permeates Minnesota's civil society, its politics and government, giving Minnesota a "clean" image.

When Minnesota emerged as a civil society immediately before the Civil War, its founders confronted the most ideologically intense cleavage in the history of American politics—the struggle between antislavery Republicans, mostly Yankees, and popular sovereignty Democrats, mostly from the Middle States and the South. A highly moralistic, issue-oriented politics became vitally important in the state. This moralistic orientation and commitment to issues were bolstered by subsequent migrations. The Yankees and their descendants, who brought a moralistic political culture with them, were reinforced by settlers from the Scandinavian countries and, to a lesser extent, Germany.

The growth of home-owned industry and an influential, ideologically oriented labor movement intensified this issue orientation. Another feature of Minnesota's political life that may have contributed to the strong issue orientation is the periodic participation by academics in party and electoral politics and the drafting, by academic institutions, of former officeholders to participate in teaching. The very existence of these elements exemplifies the reality of Minnesota's special culture.

Academics were important in the founding period of the Democratic-Farmer-Labor party. That party rose to power after 1946 led by a collection of ex–college teachers who went on to success in politics, such as U.S. senators Hubert Humphrey and Eugene McCarthy, Minneapolis mayor Arthur Naftalin, and U.S. ambassador Max Kampelman.[1] Karl Rolvaag and Don Fraser grew up on college campuses as sons of faculty members. Other examples of professorial involvement in politics have been evident since then. A University of St. Thomas professor, Robert Brown, was chair of the Republican party and a state senator in the 1970s. U.S. senator Paul Wellstone taught at Carleton College before his election in 1990. The DFL U.S. Senate candidate in 1992, Ann Wynia, was also a college professor.

Academic institutions have also made use of former politicians. Former St. Paul mayor George Latimer teaches at the Hamline Law School. Former congressmen Vin Weber and Tim Penny facilitate a series of public policy dialogues under the auspices of the Humphrey Institute of Public Affairs at the University of Minnesota, whose dean, John Brandl, served in both houses of the Minnesota legislature. This cross-fertilization is a sign that the state's political order is attuned to issues that generate intellectual as well as moral excitement, and the state's political culture is so constituted as to make this relationship natural.

Today the DFL is a coalition of political activists, quite a few of whom are professional politicians in all but self-description, but others of whom are in politics avocationally as in the past. They are interested in the party as a vehicle for implementing progressive or liberal policies. A significant percentage of DFL activists are either teachers or members of public employee unions. At one time, the traditional labor movement (that is, Teamsters and building trades) provided the bulk of the metropolitan-area party workers because they had an economic as well as an ideological interest in politics. But the rise in the numbers and importance of public employees' and teachers' unions has resulted in their dominance of the labor movement and of labor's participation in the DFL.

For the Republican party, by the early 1960s young academics and intellectually attuned lawyers were rising from the grass roots to articulate new programs for a party in need of new blood. Perhaps reluctantly, the Republican leadership discovered how important this element was and began to accommodate it within the party framework.[2] Beginning in the 1970s, the Republican party has been increasingly dominated by persons whose political interests were based on their religious faith, usually Christian fundamentalist. Because of these activists, the Republican party today probably has more "amateurs" among its activists than the DFL.

All these elements, operating together in the state's political system, have generated a spirit of public concern with community problems that has led to popular recognition of Minnesota as one of the nation's most progressive states. The state's voting record indicates one way this progressivism has manifested itself.

Historically, Minnesota has tended to deviate from national voting patterns. Between the Civil War and the New Deal, Minnesotans tended to support third parties for state and federal office, except in the case of presidential elections, when they were virtually forced into the two-party mold. More recently, their consistent support for Democratic presidential candidates in the face of national Republican landslides has been conspicuous. For much of their history, Minnesotans maintained an atypical party system.

Minnesota became a state after the Republican ascendancy had already begun. The Democratic party, which had controlled the territorial government through presidential patronage, was almost immediately relegated to a residual role. Though Minnesota voters were even more committed to Republicanism in national elections than those of Wisconsin or Iowa, as Populist-Progressives, Minnesotans were the least faithful to the party's state candidates. Since Minnesota's second party was virtually nonexistent, these progressives rarely turned to the two-party system as an outlet, preferring to create their own third-party organizations from the first. Indeed, as the number of elections decided by plurality indicates, for most of the years between 1886 and 1944, Minnesota actually had a multiparty system, operating under a Republican umbrella only in national politics.[3]

The Populist-Progressive parties won elections only when they could unite among themselves or form a preelection coalition with a Democratic party that often polled a smaller vote than the largest "third" party. By 1928 this arrangement had so sapped traditional Republican loyalties that Minnesota voters began swinging Democratic nationally as well. However, only after the amalgamation of the Democratic and Farmer-Labor parties in 1944 made the successful progressive coalition permanent was the old allegiance to the GOP, which had been honored in the breach for two generations, replaced by a new Democratic allegiance.

With the DFL ascendancy, Minnesota often chose governors and presidents from different parties, a sure sign of an effort to separate state and national electoral politics. Even the state's formal arrangements were pointed toward that end, with two-year terms for state officers allowing for significant "off-year" state elections. The 1958 constitutional amendment increasing the state executive officers' terms of office to four years made this effort explicit by providing for their election in nonpresidential years.

For many years, political debate in Minnesota has been chiefly concerned with questions of how large a role government should have in society, not whether government should play a part in the first place. The state's pioneering role in railroad and utility regulation, conservation of natural resources, public ownership of public utilities, development of a progressive tax system, and creation of the cooperative movement is well known. Whether through governmental or public nongovernmental agencies, Minnesotans have an acknowledged record for communitarian activities.[4] Minnesota's widespread communitarian concern has not necessarily implied a simple bias toward government activity. On the metropolitan frontier, however, communitarian responsibility almost invariably came to mean a relatively high level of government participation on both the state and local planes.

Minnesota Progressives turned to nonpartisanship as well as to third partyism and, by World War I, had just about eliminated formal partisan competition for all except the highest political offices in Minnesota. Before partisan designations were reintroduced in state legislative elections in 1974, only 22 of 18,870 state and local elective offices were filled on a partisan basis. The state's constraints against partisan elections were applied to the localities as well.

Local nonpartisanship, however, did not signify an effort to escape participation in the state political system, as it did in many other states, but represented an effort by Progressives to capture their state whole. Party organization was accordingly identified as antiprogressive and, indeed, antidemocratic for many years. It was only in the 1920s that strong party organizations developed among the Progressives, and they were connected to the Farmer-Labor party, an outgrowth of progressive Republicanism. Though that party was later to run into trouble, in part because of its strong organization, it showed Progressives that political organization and progressivism were not incompatible. This, in turn, led to a renewed interest in strong political organization to promote progressive aims.

Politics in Minnesota consistently has been open to and dominated by activists interested in particular programs rather than people seeking careers in public office. This may be due to the persistence of issues as a central element in determining alignments in Minnesota politics, which in turn has meant the recruitment of new elements into the parties as issues change and the domination of the parties by issue-conscious people rather than by people interested in politics as a form of business. In this environment the number of people who earn their livelihood from politics is correspondingly reduced, particularly since the use of politics for economic advancement flies in the face of the accepted local morality. This, in turn, has a feedback effect.

Because there are few pecuniary benefits to be gained, professional politicians are few and far between, thus opening the ranks of political leadership to more amateurs. This is not to say that at times in the state's history party organizations have not followed their natural inclinations to become ingrown and exclusive groups of cronies interested in making a profit. Whenever they have moved in that direction in ways visible to the voters, however, party activists or the state's electorate have removed them from power. From the voters' perspective, the recent election of Jesse Ventura to the governorship is just another example of this.

Minnesota's twentieth-century political history is a case in point. The Farmer-Labor party was organized by a typically Minnesotan group of political amateurs in the 1920s. After the party gained power in the 1930s, it developed into just such an inner group, becoming well-nigh professional in its interests after a decade of officeholding. Typically, the newly developed professionals began to look on politics as their "business" and to indulge in the kind of monetarily self-rewarding activities quite common in Illinois and other states dominated by the individualistic political culture. Their actions were discovered, and a public scandal ensued, egged on, of course, by the opposition Republicans. The voters swept the Farmer-Labor party out of office with such force that it was crushed. Six years later, out of the depths of their hopelessness, the survivors were forced into an amalgamation with the Democratic party in order to revive the possibility that Farmer-Laborites would attain high public office again.

The minuscule Minnesota Democratic party with which they amalgamated had long been centered in (and almost confined to) St. Paul, where it was run by a group of professional politicians of the type that manned urban political organizations throughout the country. It was so thoroughly out of character with the rest of the state that it managed to win more than 12 percent of the statewide vote for governor only three times between 1918 and 1946. When Franklin D. Roosevelt was elected president, he preferred working with the Farmer-Laborites and did not even give the Democrats exclusive rights to federal patronage. Finally, they too were forced into this amalgamation, with FDR's active encouragement.

In the process of amalgamation the positions of both groups of professionals were destroyed, and a new group of DFL leaders, more in keeping with Minnesota's style, arose. They have been careful to maintain their "amateur" standing, if only because the party rank and file have challenged them whenever they have shown signs of becoming too "professional." For example, in the 1956 presidential primary the leaders of the DFL tried to deliver the state for Adlai Stevenson by virtually dictating to the rank-and-file DFLers that they vote for him in the name of party unity. The spontaneous reaction of the voters was to give Estes Kefauver the victory, a message pointed toward Hubert Humphrey. Humphrey got the message and, at the next DFL state convention, virtually apologized for overstepping himself. In 1960 there developed some feeling in DFL party ranks that their then national committeeman from Duluth was gaining unseemly material benefits for his law firm as a consequence of his official position in the party. He was accused of becoming "professional," was retired from his post, and never regained his influence in party affairs, though he did end up with an appointment to the federal bench.

Nearly thirty years later Republican U.S. senator David Durenberger, who had reached that office through active involvement in Twin Cities civic affairs and state constitutional revision, was found to have charged the U.S. government rent for his apartment in Minneapolis, using his senatorial office allowance and claiming it as his "local office." Not only was national media reaction against such "corruption" strong, but Minnesotans immediately rejected him as a viable senator. The argument within the state was whether Durenberger should resign or should be allowed to finish out his term before being replaced. From the moment of the disclosure he was finished as an effective force in Minnesota politics or in the U.S. Senate.

Democrats and Republicans have been equally subject to the effects of this aspect of Minnesota's political culture. The Republican party has traditionally been less organization-prone than the Democratic party throughout the country, perhaps because of the early influence of its founders. In Minnesota even Republican governors and senators have had a difficult time knitting the party together.

After replacing the Farmer-Labor party in the state capital in 1938 with the election of Harold Stassen to the governorship, the Republicans gave Minnesota a succession of organizationally independent governors. None was able to build personal power through the party apparatus, though some, particularly Stassen, tried hard to do so. These governors won elections not through the strength of the party organization but through their personal ability to attract voters. Their personal followings, no matter how loyal, could not be delivered to other candidates in other elections.

When the DFL did assemble an organization of devoted amateurs, the party acquired the extra momentum that took the statehouse and the state away from the Republicans. Since 1958, when Republicans copied the DFL party and instituted preprimary endorsements of candidates at all levels, the Minnesota Republican party has been trying with increasing success to build a winning organization within the confines of the Minnesota tradition.

The result has been a competitive two-party state politics since the mid-1970s, with Republicans succeeding more often in the U.S. Senate and gubernatorial elections and Democrats controlling the legislative branch. What is needed is for candidates to project the Minnesota image—straight and either nice or feisty—preferably with a strong populist streak and clearly amateur standing. What made for success in state politics often decreased chances for similar success in national politics, even though many Minnesotans have gained national recognition, perhaps because of political cultural differences between Minnesota and the nation.

The election of Jesse Ventura as governor in 1998 on the Reform party ticket marked a critical juncture in Minnesota party politics, returning the state at least temporarily to the multiparty system existing before 1944. Also, the Minnesota Taxpayers party attained enough votes in another statewide race to gain major-party status in 2002. Party competition in the new century thus will take on a new cast. Whether the new parties can shift from electoral success in one race to success in multiple offices over many years is an open question. But Ventura was the first Reform party candidate to attain statewide office anywhere in the country, and talk immediately turned to his prospects for making a presidential bid under the banner of Ross Perot's party, though Ventura himself discounted the idea.

CHANGING EXPRESSIONS OF A MORALISTIC CULTURE

Minnesota's political culture allows and even encourages local communities to extend their control over matters involving public morality. Municipally owned liquor stores and tight liquor regulation, limitations on Sunday sales, and similar forms of local law enforcement are features of the Minnesota scene. Horse racing, like gambling in any other form (except limited charitable gambling), was prohibited in the state until 1988. Since then casino gambling has been introduced, no doubt culturally legitimized by the fact that it is only on Indian reservations and is designed to benefit that group. In 1989, after state lotteries were well established in the rest of the country, Minnesotans adopted a lottery whose proceeds were to support environmental and other programs. Illicit activities are certainly carried on underground in Minnesota, as elsewhere, though their managers are considerably less influential politically than their counterparts in other states and are subject to continued harassment by law-enforcement agencies in most localities.

Since the 1960s there have been sharp changes in the expression of moralistic attitudes toward what were previously considered vices. For example, in the 1960s Minnesota became moralistically committed to the new individual freedoms. One result was that prostitution, which earlier had been repressed in the state, was allowed to become more open on the ground that there should be individual choice in the matter. A decade later, when crime began to rise in connection with prostitution, the state's major cities once again cracked down on it.

A significant aspect of state-local relations in Minnesota is the state's role in allowing local variations of the Minnesota political culture and style. This is particularly apparent in the case of Duluth, whose local political patterns differ markedly from those of the rest of the state.

The Yankee tradition in Minnesota has placed a high premium on local self-government. At the same time, other indigenous traditions that developed in response to sectional demands have encouraged statewide action in ways that in other states would be considered unseemly exercises of state control over local options. The result has been the development of strong positive state involvement in most Minnesota governmental activities, from education to municipal reorganization to law enforcement, but with the preservation of a high degree of local latitude within the framework of state standard setting or assistance. The state government, in essence, guarantees the right of its civil communities to develop acceptable local variants of the state political system in line with variations in local need while ensuring that no important civil community will develop a political system not in harmony with the state's political culture.

The state's requirements for nonpartisan local elections and its permissiveness in the realm of local control over issues of public morality furnish two divergent examples of this. Another is provided in the peculiarly limited form of "home rule" authorized under the state constitution. Although cities, townships, and, since 1958, even counties are granted the right to draft their own charters and theoretically to assume all permitted municipal powers, the legislature has either limited the effects of the constitutional provision or, in the case of counties, simply refused to pass the necessary implementing legislation in all but one instance. Thus, the legislators elected from each of the three major cities in the state must still caucus to present the united front required to gain legislative assent to meet local demands. A whole series of formal and quasi-formal legislative procedures has been developed to deal with local matters, ranging from a scheme for classifying cities that approaches legitimation of local legislation, provided it is labeled as such and is approved locally, to procedures for expediting passage of legislation presented by unanimous county delegations.

THE LEGITIMACY OF POLITICS IN MINNESOTA

Another central feature of Minnesota's political culture is its implicit acceptance of the legitimacy of politics. This is reinforced by the values and attitudes of the moralistic political culture in at least two ways. First of all, the communitarian orientation of the political culture means that social action is considered legitimate. It is not difficult to move from acceptance of the principle of social action to the realization that social action in a democratic society must, by its very nature, be political action.

Second, the belief that politics is not necessarily dishonest makes it possible for the kind of people who in other political cultures would certainly avoid personal involvement in partisan political activity to use the political system to solve their problems—and even to devote a share of their time to party and other political affairs. The belief in the efficacy of politics remains strong among a substantial segment of the population, to an extent unmatched in states dominated by the individualistic political culture.

This conjunction of values and attitudes makes it possible for citizens to conceive of the possibility of social reform through political change. As in any political system, social change occurs only as a consequence of accumulated dissatisfaction. It certainly is not an end in itself, nor is it initiated for "light and transient reasons."

Minnesota has embraced social reform movements more frequently than most states, but there again, the dissatisfactions that have led to a demand for political change are rarely those that arise from popular disgust with the political system as structured but those that arise from a belief that the system is being perverted internally or threatened by external forces seeking to alter its essential ends. In such cases there tend to be temporary uprisings, designed to gain satisfaction on specific issues, rather than attempts to change the system's structure. It is no accident that Minnesota is still operating under its original state constitution despite the problems attendant on its adoption and occasional drives to rewrite it. Nor should it be surprising to discover that there has been relatively little change in the structure of local governments in Minnesota despite the almost nationwide tendency after World War II to try to cope with metropolitanization through structural change.

The Ventura vote in 1998 can be interpreted as an attempt at populist reform of the political system. Ventura's refrain that he was the only candidate who was not a professional politician resonated with the voters, as did his refusal to accept PAC money and his campaign slogan "Retaliate in '98." The candidates of the two major parties were perceived as sniping at each other while Ventura stood above the partisan fray. Of course, Minnesota bickering would not be recognized as such in other states where campaigns are more negative.

The achievements of local reform movements in Minnesota provide a particularly clear reflection of the basically political character of reform in the state. Local reform has not been apolitical. Even when nonpartisanship was the keynote for reform nationally, in Minnesota it rarely took on an antipolitical character. It was simply a device for overcoming the traditional Republican affiliation of the bulk of the local electorate, which frequently enabled anti-reform candidates to win elections by identifying with that party.

Nonpartisan elections were no less political, nor were they intended to be so. In fact, as soon as a competitive two-party system dominated by amateurs was established in the larger cities, the DFL developed an informal system of party endorsements covering the constitutional officers, as well as members of the legislature, plus city, county, and school board offices. As indicated previously, this endorsement system was eventually adopted by the Republicans as well. Because the change did not alter the state's basic political character, it met with little public interest. By the late 1950s Minnesota's formal system of nonpartisan elections had been effectively subverted on a statewide basis by both parties, without interfering with the unity of the state's political system or changing its fundamental orientation.

The final demonstration of the difference between political nonpartisanship in Minnesota and the apolitical nonpartisanship of many other states was reflected in Minnesota's general resistance to council-manager government, which had its heyday between World War II and 1960. Of the 106 incorporated cities in Minnesota in 1960, only 14 had adopted council-manager government. Commission government, a highly political form of nonpartisanship, was slightly more popular in Minnesota. In its day it was adopted by both Duluth and St. Paul, among other cities. Minneapolis, on the other hand, has retained its mayor-aldermanic system since its incorporation. In 1956 Duluth changed its form of government to an even more visibly political form.

The story is illustrative. When the abandonment of Duluth's commission government was first suggested, the council-manager system was proposed as the alternative. It was soon made clear that organized labor and the local DFL would strenuously oppose any effort to institute city-manager government. The local business community, whence the suggestion came, was really interested in improving the city's administrative structure in the hope that this would lead to greater economy in government and in its gaining better representation on the city council, which, under the "nonpartisan" commission system, had been dominated by the Labor-DFL coalition for a decade. Many in the business community had seized on the manager plan because it was the one called to their attention as the current reform panacea by the national organizations with which they were associated. Lacking any real commitment to the apolitical aspects of the plan, however, they were willing to accept a substitute establishing a modified "strong mayor-council" system. This gave them a mayor with strong executive powers, to be assisted by a professional administrative aide who would handle the day-to-day administration of city affairs, plus a fourteen-member council, part of which was to be elected from districts to ensure representation for all segments of the city and part at large. This plan was modeled in part after the state's device for combining administrative efficiency with political control, which has provided the governor with a commissioner of administration since 1939.

Minnesota's response to McCarthyism in the 1950s was characteristic of the state. When a few ultra-right-wingers attacked the freedom of speech extended to university professors, even the American Legion passed a resolution defending academic freedom. Just to make certain that matters were clear, the 1957 legislature passed three freedom-of-the-press bills sponsored by the Minnesota chapter of Sigma Delta Chi, the professional journalistic fraternity. One provided "that unless there is a specific law to the contrary, all meetings, including executive sessions of the governing body of any school district, unorganized territory, county, city, village, town, or borough and of any board, department or commission thereof, shall be open to the public."

Political culture should not be confused with political ideology. In terms of the American political debate, states of any of the three political subcultures can be conservative or liberal or some mixture of both. Utah, for example, is a moralistic state like Minnesota but is generally considered extremely conservative. Minnesota has a reputation of being very liberal.

Of all the states, none provides as pure and undiluted an example of the moralistic political culture as Minnesota. As in every human situation, culture changes very slowly, but its manifestations may shift more rapidly in tune with the styles of the times. That is the case in Minnesota as well. Minnesota in the late 1990s may not seem quite as moralistic as Minnesota fifty years earlier, when both public and private behavior in the United States was measured according to more stringent moralistic standards. But given the changed standards of the past thirty years, Minnesota remains strongly moralistic by American criteria, particularly in the public sphere, in some respects insisting on formal behavior far beyond that expected in earlier times.

CHAPTER 3

Minnesota's Constitution

In Federalist No. 1, Publius summarizes the three sources of all political organization:

> It has been frequently remarked, there seems to have been reserved to the people of this country, by their conduct and example, to decide the important question, whether societies of men are really capable or not, of establishing good government from reflection and choice, or whether they are forever destined to depend, for their political constitutions, on accident and force.

Force, accident, reflection and choice—these are the three ways in which humans have organized their polities over time. As models or ideal types, they seem to be the only three options available.

How many times in human history has political organization been imposed by force through the efforts of a conqueror or a coup d'etat? On the other hand, all too many civil societies have developed by accident; that is, they have evolved with no particular thought, plan, or grounds for existence other than convenience. Only a relatively few polities have their origins in reflection and choice, whereby their founders deliberately and democratically instituted government for their own common benefit. Modern democracy is based on the principle that legitimate government can only be a government instituted through reflection and choice. The principal means for doing so has been constitutionalism, the adoption by public and democratic procedures of a fundamental law that establishes the polity, defines and distributes the powers of its government, and provides for a proper relationship between the governors and the governed.

THE BEGINNINGS OF CONSTITUTIONALISM IN MINNESOTA

The discussion of American constitutionalism in the introduction to this book delineates six kinds of American constitutions, including the common-wealth pattern, which emphasizes Whig ideas of the constitution as a philo-sophic document, and the frame-of-government pattern, found frequently in the West and notable for its emphasis on the structure of state government and the distribution of powers within that state. Minnesota's constitution is a good example of the western variation of the commonwealth pattern, moder-ated by the frame-of-government tradition. Minnesota has had only one con-stitution, adopted in 1858 when it attained statehood. It is approximately 40 percent longer than that of Massachusetts but still ranks among the nation's shorter constitutions. The additional material in the Minnesota Constitution consists of more explicit delineations of the powers and duties of state offi-cers and clear provisions for schools, taxes, banking, highways, and legisla-tive apportionment, plus more extensive sections on natural resource conser-vation and progressive social policy.[1]

Despite periodic efforts to call a constitutional convention and write a new constitution, Minnesota retains its original documents. They have been modified through an active amending process to keep up with the times. Though Minnesotans do not pay particular attention to their constitution be-yond what is necessary and cannot be said to revere it in any way, they seem to respect the principle of constitutionalism sufficiently to be opposed to lightly changing the document as a whole.

At the same time, Minnesota's state government formally recognizes sev-eral constitutional documents as part of an overall constitutional package, beginning with the Constitution of the United States and including the Northwest Ordinance of 1787, the act establishing the Minnesota Territory (1849), the Statehood Enabling Act (1857), and the Act of Admission of Minnesota (1858), as well as the state constitution proper. All these are pre-sented as Minnesota's constitutional heritage in the state's official manual, published biennially by the secretary of state.

That part of Minnesota included in the original territory of the United States as determined by the 1783 Treaty of Paris ending the Revolutionary War came under the terms of reference of the Northwest Ordinance of 1787. The Northwest Ordinance was enacted by the Confederation Congress on 13 July 1787 to establish a government framework for the territory north of the Ohio and east of the Mississippi River. It abolished primogeniture (the pass-ing of an entire inheritance to the firstborn son); extended the principles of republican government to that area; guaranteed freedom of religion, habeas corpus, trial by jury, freedom of contract, fair judicial proceedings, and equitable bail; forbade cruel and unusual punishment; and prohibited deprivation of liberty or property except by law and with appropriate compensation. It provided for the public encouragement of education and promoted "religion, morality, and knowledge." It prohibited slavery and required that the Indian inhabitants be dealt with "in the utmost good faith." The ordinance established the principle that the public domain would be organized into new states to be admitted to the Union on an equal footing with the original states.

The ordinance is one of the great constitutional documents of American history, perhaps the one that most explicitly embodies the principles of the Declaration of Independence. Its most enduring section is explicitly presented as "articles of compact between the original states and the people and states in the said territory." As a political compact between the original thirteen states and the new states yet to be organized out of the public domain, it is to "forever remain unalterable unless by common consent."[2]

The state and federal courts have held that the Northwest Ordinance is the first constitutional charter of the state of Minnesota, but its full constitutional impact has never been totally clarified. The Minnesota Supreme Court, for example, has never decided whether the common law reached Minnesota automatically with the Revolutionary War or dates from its specific application in the ordinance of 1787.

In very few cases is a polity the result of the pure application of one or another of the three models of political organization: force, accident, or reflection and choice. Minnesota is a case in point. Its opening to European settlement was clearly a result of force, the conquest of territories and their indigenous inhabitants by the European powers—both France and Britain long before there was any government in Minnesota. Though the United States inherited territory nominally conquered by others, it, too, used force to coerce the indigenous inhabitants, the Ojibwe and Dakota tribes, to surrender their claims through treaties nominally among equals but actually imposed by the stronger part on the weaker.[3]

Minnesota's first European inhabitants came by accident; they followed the fur trade westward from Canada, and many of the first American civilians simply drifted into the territory seeking their fortunes. The first permanent American settlement, Fort St. Anthony (renamed Fort Snelling in 1825), was a forceful if unopposed implantation by the United States Army. But the civilians who settled around it came of their own accord. Nevertheless, the true organization of Minnesota as a polity and civil society came as a result of reflection and choice, the clear decision of the American settlers in the territory to erect a civil society.

In 1838 present-day Minnesota was divided between Iowa and Wisconsin territories. That part of the future state west of the Mississippi within Iowa Territory remained unorganized for the next eight years. Although dotted with tens of fur-trading posts, it was essentially unsettled by European Americans and thus did not require their civil government. After Iowa became a state in 1846, Minnesota reverted to unorganized territory with no difficulty.[4]

That part east of the Mississippi, however, had several hundred permanent American settlers, and in due course the Wisconsin territorial legislature established St. Croix County to provide them with civil government in a local government framework. Wisconsin was admitted as a state in 1848 with the St. Croix River its western boundary, thus leaving St. Croix County to its own devices. Eighteen of the region's leading men held preliminary discussions that led to their signing a call for a convention to be held at Stillwater, the county seat. They described themselves as "citizens of Minnesota Territory." They invited people from all the settlements east and west of the Mississippi to send delegates to the convention, whose main task would be to secure the organization of the territory, which was now a clear idea in their minds. On 26 August 1848, sixty-one delegates residing in all parts of what is today Minnesota assembled in convention in Stillwater.

This step was taken at the settlers' (embryonic Minnesotans') own initiative. The Stillwater Convention passed resolutions calling for Congress to establish a new territory to be named Minnesota. To strengthen their claim, one delegate came up with the ingenious idea that the parts of the Wisconsin Territory left out of the new state of Wisconsin still constituted Wisconsin Territory. The former governor of the territory had been elected as a senator from the new state, so, under this theory, the secretary of Wisconsin Territory, John Catlin, assumed the mantle of acting governor. In that capacity Catlin called an election to choose a new territorial delegate to Congress. The election was held on 30 October, and Henry Hastings Sibley was elected delegate to Congress for the territory in the making.

Once Catlin certified Sibley's election, he disappeared from the scene, but Sibley, who was already becoming recognized as the leading founding father of the state-in-the-making, went to Congress legitimated by two quasi-legitimate acts. To everyone's surprise, Congress seated him as delegate from Wisconsin Territory, in part because of his own impressive mien. They were not willing to do more than seat Sibley, however, and would not provide for the continuation of territorial government.

After a certain amount of lobbying and negotiation on Sibley's part Congress responded on 3 March 1849, hardly six months from the convening of the Stillwater Convention. Congress enacted An Act to Establish the Territorial Government of Minnesota, establishing Minnesota Territory, providing for its government, and applying the laws of the recently extinct Wisconsin Territory to it so that it would not be without law before its governor and legislature could act. Known as the Organic Act of Minnesota, which begins in Section 1 by defining the boundaries of Minnesota Territory, the act remains one of the constitutional documents of the state, reprinted in every legislative manual.

What is important to note is that the initiative for the founding of Minnesota came from the newly minted Minnesotans themselves, following the classic American theory that civil societies are established by covenant or compact among their members, who come together in convention to do so. As individual settlers, they may have reached Minnesota by accident, but their political community was established as an act of will and consent.

Once Congress acted, the new president, Zachary Taylor, who had once commanded Fort Snelling, appointed a fellow Whig, Alexander Ramsey of Pennsylvania, territorial governor on 19 March. Ramsey arrived in St. Paul by steamboat on 27 May 1849, and on 1 June proclaimed Minnesota Territory to be in operation. In addition to an appointed governor and secretary, the Organic Act provided for the establishment of a judicial system, also appointed, and for the election of a legislative assembly and a delegate to Congress. The legislative assembly consisted of a nine-member council and an eighteen-member house of representatives. Elections were held that summer, and the first session of the territorial legislature convened on 3 September 1849 in the Central House at the corner of Bench and Minnesota streets in St. Paul.

St. Paul became the capital of Minnesota from the very beginning. There was an attempt in 1857, on the eve of statehood, to transfer the capital to St. Peter. A bill to that effect passed both houses of the legislative assembly, but assembly member Joseph Rolette from Pembina, then in the far northwest corner of Minnesota Territory, managed to acquire the bill and hide it until the legislature adjourned. Since it could not be presented to the territorial governor for his signature, it never became law and St. Paul became the permanent state capital. One of the first acts of the new territorial legislature was to charter the Minnesota Historical Society, which was organized on 15 November 1849. As such, it is the oldest state institution.

The Organic Act served as the constitution of Minnesota Territory from 1 June 1849 until 11 May 1858, when Minnesota became a state. All its articles have been superseded. The boundaries of the Minnesota Territory included the eastern half of the Dakotas to the Missouri River. This area was subsequently detached when Minnesota became a state.

The structure of government provided in the Organic Act was modified by the new state constitution to reflect Minnesota's new political status as a state. The basic tripartite division of powers into executive, legislative, and judicial was already present in the territorial government and was carried over in sharpened form in the state constitution. The matter was never debated and was simply assumed, as it has been in every case of state constitution-making since the adoption of the federal Constitution. The legislative assembly, the judiciary, and the offices of governor and territorial secretary were continued with changes. The officers of the executive departments and judges were made elective under the state constitution.

The Organic Act provided from the first for the establishment of elected local governments. Section 7 of the act provided that "all township, district, and county officers, not herein otherwise provided for, shall be appointed or elected as the case may be, in such manner as shall be provided by the governor and legislative assembly of the Territory of Minnesota." Voting was restricted to free white males resident in the territory who were citizens or who under oath had declared their intention to become citizens. The provision defining who could vote prefigured the Fourteenth Amendment to the United States Constitution in language and intent. The legislative assembly was empowered to act with regard to "all rightful subjects of legislation, consistent with the Constitution of the United States and the provisions of this Act." Both the territorial governor and Congress had the right to veto acts of the legislative assembly. The governor's veto could be overridden by a two-thirds vote of each house of the assembly. Congress's veto could not.

The only limitation placed on the assembly was that "no law shall be passed interfering with the primary disposal of the soil; no tax shall be imposed upon the property of the United States; nor shall the lands or the property of non-residents be taxed higher than the lands or other property of residents." This reservation of the right of primary disposal of the soil to the federal government was common to all territories carved out of the public domain and remains in effect as a federal reservation even after statehood, resting on the property rights of the federal government as a landowner rather than its constitutional rights as a government. On the other hand, the Organic Act provided for reserving two sections of land, Sections 16 and 36 in every township, as a land grant to the state-in-the-making, to be used for establishing a universal system of education.

Establishment of the territorial government greatly stimulated the state's settlement and development. As late as the summer of 1849, there were fewer than 4,000 non-Indians in Minnesota (St. Paul had a population of 910;

Stillwater, the seat of government of St. Croix County, 609; and St. Anthony, later to become northeast Minneapolis, 248). The Organic Act mandated the taking of a census. In the federal census of 1850 Minnesota Territory had only 6,077 persons between the St. Croix and the Missouri. In 1852 the population had more than tripled and was estimated at 20,000. It had reached an estimated 40,000 by 1855, 100,000 the next year, and 150,000 in 1857 on the eve of statehood. Thus, we see once again how the state was a civil society and how the introduction of governing institutions made its growth possible.

One way in which government made a difference was that the territorial government pressed Washington to extinguish Native American land claims and enable the new settlers to acquire title to their lands. The first Indian cessions, land that is now Minnesota, were two tiny parcels along the southern border of the state, ceded in 1830. A somewhat larger segment covering the Mississippi–St. Croix region was ceded in 1837 and expanded a decade later. The Treaties of Traverse des Sioux and Mendota opened about half the future state to non-Indian settlement. Another third in the north and northeast was ceded by the Ojibwes in treaties of 1854 and 1855. More pieces were ceded in 1863 and 1866, and the last cession came in 1889. Between the establishment of territorial government and the achievement of statehood, approximately three-quarters of the state was opened to non-Indian settlement.

The next act of constitutional import was Minnesota's Enabling Act. Officially entitled An Act Authorizing a State Government, it passed Congress on 26 February 1857. It was the basis for the writing of Minnesota's own constitution. The act set Minnesota's final borders, lopping off the area to the west of the Red River of the North. It provided for calling a constitutional convention and established the basic system of federal land grants to the states for common schools, a state university, public buildings, and salt springs and provided that 5 percent of the proceeds of the sale of federal public lands in Minnesota be granted to the state for building public roads.

The Enabling Act has several provisions of enduring importance. For example, Section 2 provided that the state shall have "concurrent jurisdiction on the Mississippi and all other rivers and waters bordering on the state of Minnesota," and that its rivers and waters should be "common highways and forever free." The Enabling Act was just that; it enabled the people of Minnesota to decide whether they wanted to form a state through the election of a constitutional convention, the writing of a constitution, its approval by referendum, and its submission to the Congress of the United States as a ticket of admission to the Union. Since the days when the Israelites stood at Sinai and consented three times to a covenant with God as embodied in the Ten Commandments, it has been customary in republics for covenants, constitutions, and legislation to be approved in what we know today as three readings. The same was true in the founding of Minnesota. The Stillwater Convention can be seen as the first approval of Minnesota as a separate polity, the election of the constitutional convention as the second, and the ratification of Minnesota's constitution as the third.

The election for a constitutional convention was held on 1 June 1857. It was a partisan affair with the newly born Republican party contesting with the older Democratic party for control of the convention.[5] The Civil War was less than four years away. Kansas was in the throes of its own civil war, and Republicans were seen as a radical party advocating the abolition of slavery. The Democrats were trying to hold their party together in order to prevent its dissolution as a prelude to the dissolution of the Union. Tensions ran high throughout the United States, and every new state became a battleground for political control with an eye to the future shape of the Union.

THE ADOPTION OF MINNESOTA'S CONSTITUTION

The constitutional convention opened in St. Paul on 13 July 1857. The story of the writing and adoption of Minnesota's constitution is one of the extraordinary sagas of American constitutional politics. In the very same year, the United States Supreme Court was considering the case of Dred Scott, a black slave who had been brought by his master to Fort Snelling and who claimed his freedom on the grounds that Minnesota was free territory. In perhaps its most infamous ruling ever, the Court held that slaves were not persons in the meaning of the original Constitution but property and therefore could not claim protection of the laws, so could not sue for their freedom. This horrendous decision was the final catalyst that led so many northerners into the Republican party, gave Abraham Lincoln his presidential victory in 1860, and brought about the Civil War.

Not surprisingly, the tensions between the Democratic and Republican delegates were very high. In short order the two groups split apart over the convention's rules of procedure and began to meet separately, each claiming to be the authentic constitutional convention. Each wrote its own constitutional document. What is extraordinary is that despite the open hostility between them, the two products were extremely close. There were no major differences, and the minor ones were mostly stylistic. It is true that as both documents neared completion, certain members of the convention carried drafts back and forth between the two groups to assist in harmonization, but there were no serious problems of a constitutional nature involved in finding a way to harmonize them, except in connection with the amending process.

The problem came over the adoption of the documents. A conference committee was appointed to work out the differences between the two drafts. The Republicans accepted most of the Democratic proposals but held out for an easy amendment procedure in the hopes that they would later be able to secure amendments providing for Negro suffrage and prohibiting the sale of alcoholic beverages. In the end, the Democrats refused to sign the same document that the Republicans signed, so two documents were transcribed, with the one for the Democrats on blue paper and the one for the Republicans on white. Both were then submitted together to the voters of the embryonic state as required by the congressional enabling legislation. The vote for Minnesota's new constitution was essentially a vote for two separate documents, and the constitution as approved did not distinguish between them. Hence, both are the original constitutions of the state of Minnesota, and the Minnesota Supreme Court has had to rule on the differences case by case. This has never posed serious problems.

Substantively, the two documents are the same, but there are minor discrepancies in spelling, grammar, and style. The constitution consisted and consists of a preamble and fourteen articles outlining the structure of government, providing a bill of rights, and addressing a number of specific issues in the most concrete terms, including an amendment added just after World War I, detailing the routes of the public highway system. To the extent that they are conscious of its existence, Minnesotans are satisfied with their basic law and for the most part, because their politics has been so efficacious, have not sought to achieve ordinary political change through major constitutional revision.

There are periodic proposals for calling a constitutional convention; all have been rejected in the proposal stage. One of the reasons Minnesota's constitution is not especially revered, even though it has served the state for nearly 140 years, is because discussions of it have been couched either in the driest of terms, simply recounting its provisions, or very critically, enumerating its presumed defects. In other words, it has been of serious concern only to self-proclaimed reformers. Reform thought has varied from period to period but generally is based on a certain view of a constitution not as a charter reflecting the political compromises needed to enable different people with different interests to live together but as a document that is to be based on some abstract standard.

A Summary of the Current Constitution of the State of Minnesota

PREAMBLE

"We, the people of the state of Minnesota, grateful to God for our civil and religious liberty, and desiring to perpetuate its blessing and secure the same to ourselves and our posterity, do ordain and establish this Constitution."

ARTICLE I   BILL OF RIGHTS

Very similar to Bill of Rights of U.S. Constitution.

ARTICLE II   NAME AND BOUNDARIES

ARTICLE III   SEPARATION OF POWERS INTO THREE BRANCHES

ARTICLE IV   LEGISLATIVE DEPARTMENT

Provides for single-member districts, two houses, two-year terms for house and four years for senate. Limits legislative sessions to 120 days per biennium. No law to embrace more than one subject. Revenue bills to originate in house. Provides for veto, pocket veto, item veto, and veto override. A general banking law requires a two-thirds vote instead of the usual majority vote to pass.

ARTICLE V   EXECUTIVE DEPARTMENT

Provides for six executive officers elected by the people. Describes powers and duties of the governor. Specifies terms of office and line of succession of governor and lieutenant governor.

ARTICLE VI   JUDICIARY

Provides for a supreme court and district court and for the legislature to establish a court of appeals and other courts. Six-year terms of office for judges. Various provisions for retirement, removal, discipline of judges, and jurisdiction of the courts.

ARTICLE VII   ELECTIVE FRANCHISE

Sets qualifications for voting.

ARTICLE VIII   IMPEACHMENT AND REMOVAL

Impeachment by majority vote of the house and conviction by two-thirds of senators present. Determines impeachable offenses.

ARTICLE IX   CONSTITUTIONAL AMENDMENT

Initiation by majority of both houses; ratified by a majority of those voting at the next general election. Also sets procedures for constitutional conventions.

ARTICLE X   TAXATION

Sets exemptions from property tax. Allocates iron ore severance tax revenues.

Freezes taconite taxes until 1989. Authorizes legislature to permit pari-mutuel betting.

ARTICLE XI   APPROPRIATIONS AND FINANCES
Resricts state bonds to twenty years or less. Restricts indebtedness of local governments to aid railroads. Sets provisions for school fund and university fund.

ARTICLE XII   SPECIAL LEGISLATION: LOCAL GOVERNMENT
Sets conditions for special legislation for local governments. Provides for charter commissions and home rule charters.

ARTICLE XIII   MISCELLANEOUS SUBJECTS
Prohibits spending public money for sectarian schools. Allows farmers to peddle their products without a license.

ARTICLE XIV   PUBLIC HIGHWAY SYSTEM
Allocates highway users tax (that is, gasoline tax and license tab) revenue; 62 percent to state trunk highway fund; 29 percent to county highway fund; 9 percent to municipal street fund.

AMENDMENTS
Minnesota's constitution has been amended 116 times as of 1998. Unlike federal constitutional amendments, Minnesota constitutional amendments are incorporated directly into the text of the constitution itself. For this reason, there is no need to list the amendments separately.

In the case of American state constitutions, that standard usually has been some combination of the expectations set by the federal Constitution (for example, that it should be short, whether or not such expectations are appropriate to state documents) and the expectations prevalent in the business community at any given time. Thus, efficiency and economy have always ranked high on the scale of constitutional desiderata among reformers. In the twentieth century, at least until relatively recently, this has meant desiring more executive power and control, greater hierarchy, and the subordination of the "messiness" of politics to the "cleanness" of administration.

The people of Minnesota, like the people of most states, have had different ideas and more common sense. They have accepted only a few of the more sensible proposals put forth by reformers, either through the amendment process or through one of the constitutional commissions that is periodically convened to propose changes in the document. This is not to suggest that reformers' recommendations have all lacked merit. Their basic premise that constitutions should concentrate on the fundamental principles of government and not become bogged down in too many specific details that would be better left to statutory law is congruent with the American idea of constitutionalism.

AMENDING MINNESOTA'S CONSTITUTION

Most of the constitutional amendments adopted were added before 1913. Since then a majority of those submitted to the voters have been rejected. One of the reasons that the incidence of constitutional amendments dropped so substantially after 1913 was that Minnesota's 1857 constitution had the easiest amending clause of any American constitution. A proposed amendment had only to be passed by simple majorities in both houses of the legislature in one session and ratified by a simple majority of the voters voting on the proposition in the next general election. In 1898, believing that this was too easy, the legislature proposed and the voters approved a clause requiring that voter approval involve a majority of the total votes cast in the general election, a much more difficult goal to achieve. The result was an immediate drop-off in the number of amendments approved.

Between 1858 and 1998, 211 constitutional amendments were proposed, 116 of which were adopted and 95 rejected. Between 1858 and 1898, 66 amendments were proposed, 48 accepted, and 18 rejected. Between 1900 and 1952, when the voters changed the formula for ratification to 60 percent of those voting on the question rather than a majority of those voting at the election, thereby making the adoption of amendments easier, 92 constitutional amendments were proposed, 30 adopted, and 62 rejected. From 1956 through 1998, under the new rules, 53 amendments were proposed, 38 adopted, and 15 rejected. In other words, in the first and last periods ratios were about 3 to 1 in favor of adoption, whereas in the middle period the ratio was 2 to 1 in favor of rejection.

There have been two comprehensive efforts to revise the constitution through commissions. The first such effort to bear any success was in 1948, when the Minnesota constitutional commission made extensive recommendations and urged that a constitutional convention be called to consider them. In order to undercut support for a convention, legislative leaders initiated extensive constitutional reform through the amendment process. Pro-constitution forces, realizing that this was the best they would get, worked hard to secure adoption of the amendments, so a good part of the commission's report found its way into the constitution.

In 1972 a second constitutional commission produced another series of significant changes. The year before, a similar commission did not even recommend a constitutional convention because there was little public enthusiasm for any major changes. Rather, it proposed a series of changes, a number of which were also adopted by the voters through constitutional amendment. The most important involved the rewording and restructuring of the constitution itself, reducing the number of articles from 21 to 14 and the number of words from 20,000 to about 9,500 but making no substantive changes. The revision did not become the state's constitution but became its public version. Hence, Minnesota has three authoritative constitutional documents for one constitution.

The only substantive change the 1971 constitutional commission succeeded in moving forward was placing the establishment of a court of appeals on the agenda, although it did not come about until later. Nevertheless, there has been much reform through legislative action. For example, when the public wanted a nonpartisan legislature, the legislature provided for it in 1913; then, after public opinion shifted, the legislature returned itself to partisan designation in 1972.

Voters gave the executive and legislative branches of the government more flexibility, including the removal of obsolete language from the constitution (1964), introducing greater flexibility in approving or disallowing legislation at the end of the session (1968), empowering the legislature to define or limit categories of tax-exempt property (1970), and allowing flexible legislative sessions (1972). In 1970, in the wake of congressional legislation upheld by the U.S. Supreme Court, voters amended the constitution to reduce the voting age requirement from twenty-one to nineteen years, while introducing an age requirement of eighteen years to hold public office.

Still, most of the amendments were fairly narrow in scope and there were those who thought that broader constitutional revision was still necessary. Governor Wendell Anderson took the lead in reopening the issue by sending a special message to the legislature on 3 March 1971, calling for a constitutional convention on the ground that it was necessary for state government to "reassert its assigned role in the federal system." The governor sought annual flexible legislative sessions, a reduction in legislative size, and party designation for the legislature; elimination of special tax provisions in the constitution and empowering the legislature with total tax responsibility; and introduction of an environmental bill of rights and reexamination of dedicated funds so as to give the legislature "the broadest possible discretion in the appropriation of state funds." Finally, he called for an easier method of constitutional revision.

In response, the legislature established the Constitutional Study Commission of 1972. Governor Anderson appointed former governor Elmer L. Andersen, a Republican, chairman and another former governor, DFLer Karl Rolvaag, vice-chairman. David Durenberger, later to be elected U.S. senator from Minnesota on the Republican ticket, was appointed the commission's executive secretary.

The commission reported that "the original document as amended since adoption is an adequate statement of the relationship between the people of this state and their government." All that was needed was a series of amendments to simplify the constitutional language and make constitutional amendment easier. They supported amending the reapportionment and finance articles to remove the reapportionment power from the legislature and give it to a bipartisan districting commission, to allow the state to levy income taxes computed as a percentage of federal income tax, to repeal the gross earnings tax paid by railroads in lieu of other taxes, and to allow the legislature to set the rate of taxation on railroads as it does for other industries. The adoption of a new constitutional document with simplified language was accomplished in 1974, after passage by the legislature and ratification by the voters.

The preamble remained the same, but the bill of rights was restored to its original form. The rest of the constitution was rearranged, rewritten, and shortened so as to make the document more readable. Although the new text is now the one in general use, the meaning of the constitution has not been altered and in constitutional law cases the original documents remain the final authority. In other words, Minnesota now has three constitutional documents saying essentially the same thing.

The most often cited problems of state constitutions are (1) too long and too detailed, (2) too many legislative restrictions, (3) fragmentation of the executive branch, (4) fragmentation of the judicial branch, and (5) a hamstringing of local government. In truth, none applies to Minnesota's constitution. It is not very long and, since its streamlining, has much less detail than before. The legislature is not that restricted because it has never wandered too far from public expectations, as has happened in many other states, and most of the restrictions that evoked complaints in the past have been eliminated or substantially weakened.

One of the more profound changes proposed in the Minnesota Constitution narrowly failed passage in 1980. The proposal to establish the initiative and referendum received the support of 53 percent of those voting on the issue, but 60 percent was required for ratification. Until 1996, in fact, Minnesota had remained aloof from the various forms of "direct democracy." In that year's election, voters approved a recall provision that, in practice, is so difficult to initiate that it may never be used.

The so-called fragmented executive branch represents an approach to government found in the states, which is different from that found in the U.S. Constitution. Those state constitutions emerging out of the Whig doctrine are essentially committed to a plural executive, whereby the governor presides over a group of significantly independent colleagues, each of whom has specific tasks assigned but all of whom must work together to establish basic executive-branch policies. Under this doctrine, power is deliberately not concentrated in the hands of the governor, but the governor is to be in a position where he or she can bring together all the elements to wield the power that is necessary to govern the state.

The record in Minnesota suggests that this has been the case. Governors have not been seriously limited by so-called fragmentation. There are more limitations on the governor because of the norms of Minnesota politics than in the state constitution itself. Thus, the state provides no limit on gubernatorial terms, but unwritten rules limit governors to a maximum of eight years in office (though Rudy Perpich served ten years, two of which resulted from his moving from lieutenant governor to governor). Nor does the constitution limit the numbers of people the governor can appoint, but Minnesota's moralistic political culture has placed almost all state employees under the provisions of civil service, so that the governor has few opportunities to appoint people responsible to him personally in carrying out policy.

Minnesota began with a divided judicial authority but has moved toward a unified judiciary through legislative action, entirely acceptable under the state constitution. Here, indeed, Minnesota has an excellent record. So, too, the constitutional situation in state-local relations simply recognizes the degree to which the state and its localities are tied together. Localities have the opportunity to acquire home rule but are still closely integrated into the network of state public policy.

Minnesota's constitution is a clear expression of the state's moralistic culture. It establishes a government with considerable latitude to act in furtherance of the common weal. Minnesotans respect but do not revere their basic organizational document, perhaps not surprising since there are, in fact, three versions of the one constitution. At bottom, the state's residents expect their constitution to permit efficacious government. If that purpose is thwarted, they will change the constitution.

CHAPTER 4

Public Opinion, Political Participation, and Lobbying

Minnesotans are renowned for their interest and activity in politics and public affairs; they routinely turn out at the polls in greater proportions than do most states' citizens. Minnesota supports a greater number of interest groups than most other states as well; and, the state still uses the caucus nominating system, which demands a higher level of energy than the primary system. This proclivity toward participation is often said to be due to the liberalism of Minnesotans, to their fondness for "big government." But although residents of the North Star State participate actively, they are not necessarily more liberal than citizens in other states. Rather, their civic participation is rooted in the moralistic political culture. In this chapter we describe Minnesotans' patterns of participation in politics, both individually and collectively through interest groups. We also discuss the lobbyists who work for interest groups and how they are regulated in a moralistic political culture. And we outline the structure of the active public affairs community in Minnesota.

PATTERNS OF INDIVIDUAL POLITICAL PARTICIPATION

Minnesotans are accustomed voters: Figure 1, showing the percentage of the adult population that votes, demonstrates this fact clearly. Minnesota has consistently been about 20 percent above the nation's average, whether in presidential years or nonpresidential years (data not shown). The most recent study of state voter turnout showed that Minnesota ranked fifth in turnout percentage, behind Montana, South Dakota, Maine, and Wyoming (weather is obviously not a deterrent to voting).[1] States at the top of the turnout rankings, Minnesota included, tend to have more highly educated citizens, to have close electoral competition between the two political parties, to

Figure 1: Voter Turnout in Presidential Elections Years, 1952–96 (%)

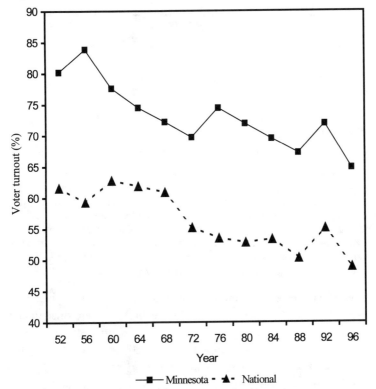

Sources: *Statistical Abstract of the United States*, 1996, p. 290;
Minnesota Secretary of State Office.

have laws making it easy to vote, and to be moralistic in their political culture. Minnesota exemplifies each of these characteristics; for example, it has
long had same-day voter registration at the polls. A citizen can register with
proof of residence (such as a driver's license or a piece of mail with the cor-
rect address) or with the vouching of a neighbor. In the 1990s Minnesota introduced several other mechanisms to make it easy to vote—so-called mo-
tor-voter registration, generous absentee-voting rules, and preliminary
experiments with conducting elections by mail ballot.

The 1998 gubernatorial election was a graphic demonstration of the significance of high turnout and the laws facilitating it. Minnesota voter turnout
was 60.4 percent, the highest nonpresidential showing since 1982; nationally, the turnout was 36 or 37 percent by unofficial estimates.[2] An important

Table 1: Participation in Community Activities: Minnesota vs the United States (%)

	Minnesota	*United States*
Attended meetings	45	37
Volunteered time	49	36
Held office	16	3
Contributed money	77	66

Source: Minnesota data adapted from "Divided We Stand: A Minnesota Poll Report on Shared Values, Social Tolerance, and Community Attachment" (Minneapolis: *Star Tribune*, 1995), p. 6. The question referred to activities in the community or in charitable organizations in the 12 months before April 1995. United States data from Sidney Verba, Kay Lehman Schlozman, and Henry E. Brady, *Voice and Equality* (Cambridge: Harvard University Press, 1995), pp. 51, 76. Three of the questions asked in 1989 were about participation in nonpolitical organizations; one (held office) asked about community activities.

factor fueling Minnesota's turnout was the option of same-day registration: 15.7 percent of voters registered at the polls, the highest figure since 1974.[3] Same-day registrants were thought to be primarily supporters of the ultimate election victor, Jesse Ventura, whose campaign targeted those who hadn't been voting, such as students and the disaffected.

Voter turnout has an effect on public policy; Kim Hill and Jan Leighley calculated the extent to which a state's gubernatorial turnout is equally distributed among income classes or biased toward the upper classes and against the lower classes.[4] Every state overrepresents the upper classes and underrepresents the lower classes, but New Jersey and Minnesota were the least biased against the lower classes. In these two states the rate of turnout and the socioeconomic structure underlying it mean that they have balanced electorates. So Minnesota comes closer to achieving the ideals of participatory democracy than most states.

Participation data outside the electoral realm are more elusive, but public opinion polls give us some insight into Minnesotans' patterns of participation in community affairs. In 1995 the Minnesota Poll (sponsored by the Minneapolis *Star Tribune*) asked about citizen participation in community affairs (seemingly combining political and nonpolitical organizations). Table 1 compares Minnesotans' responses with data from the most recent national academic poll on the same topic. As seen in the table, Minnesotans at-

Table 2: Minnesotans' Interest in Politics (%)

Very interested	32
Somewhat interested	43
Slightly interested	19
Not at all interested	6

Source: Adapted from "Divided We Stand: A Minnesota Poll Report on Shared Values, Social Tolerance, and Community Attachment" (Minneapolis: *Star Tribune*, 1995), appendix, p. 15.

tended meetings of community groups in higher proportions than the national average. Similarly, more Minnesotans volunteered their time to such groups, held office in them, and gave them money. Thus, Minnesotans' participation goes well beyond voting on election day. The moralistic political culture makes participation a community norm.

POLITICAL IDEOLOGY AND PUBLIC OPINION

The most common explanation outsiders give for Minnesotans' excessively participatory nature is a "pro-government" one; Minnesotans are alleged to be liberal, trusting of government, interested in politics, and so forth. In this section we investigate some of these characteristics. First, political interest is often a precursor of participation, and Minnesotans are indeed interested in politics, as demonstrated in table 2. In 1995 nearly one in three were very interested in politics, while four in ten were somewhat interested.

Second, Minnesotans supposedly embrace big government, one measure of which might be the extent to which they identify themselves as liberals. Figure 2 displays the trend over the last thirty years in self-identified liberalism and conservatism, comparing Minnesota with the national average. Minnesota was indeed above the national average, often by a considerable margin, until the late 1980s, when liberalism plummeted. By 1994 Minnesota's score was slightly below the national average; only 15 percent of Minnesotans admitted to being liberal while 18 percent of all Americans did so.

As one writer characterized the state: "Image, culture and lifestyle also

Figure 2: Political Liberalism: Minnesota vs National Percentage

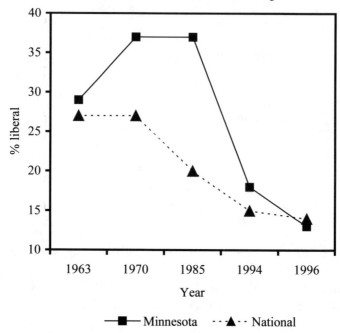

Sources: Minnesota Poll as reported in *Star Tribune;* Gallup
Organization as reported in *Gallup Poll Reports* and *The Gallup Poll;*
Lloyd A. Free and Hadley Cantril, *The Political Beliefs of Americans: A
Study of Public Opinion* (New York: Simon and Schuster, 1968), p. 204.

belie the reputation of liberal Minnesota. Newcomers are often surprised by
the state's essentially conservative personality. Minnesotans, it turns out,
are frugal, disinclined to faddishness and outlandish behavior, taciturn, re-
pelled by extravagance or waste, and leery of crazy new ideas. Liquor stores
are closed on Sundays. Churches often are full on Sunday. The denizens tend
to stare down their noses at you if you smoke, swear, talk loudly, wear bright
colors or too much make-up."[5]

This conservative strain is especially visible among the state's leading
(and wealthiest) citizens. As a general, though perhaps changing, rule, the
state's most elaborate and expensive homes—many around Lake Minnetonka, west of Minneapolis—are not visible from the road. It has always
been considered acceptable for Minnesota business leaders to build and live
in very expensive homes, but it was thought gauche to show off in front of
those less fortunate. That ethic may be changing, however. In 1994 Minne-

sota was presented with its first "gated" community, that is, a residential en-
clave surrounded by a fence and guarded by security personnel. The idea of
the wealthy protecting themselves from others was considered shoddy, but
the community prevailed and continues to exist.

Third, we turn to faith in government. Minnesotans rather consistently
place their confidence in their own government. For example, in 1995, when
asked if "things are going in the right direction" at different levels of government, only 33 percent agreed with this proposition when applied to the
federal government, 55 percent when applied to Minnesota, and 72 percent
when applied to the local level.[6] Thus, Minnesotans are inclined to trust
those governing close to home. Perhaps because of this high level of trust,
they are more inclined to participate.

Fourth, Minnesotans feel attached to their communities. For example,
four in five agreed with the statement, "I feel very much that I belong to this
community."[7] Only about a third agreed with the statement, "This used to
be a better community to live in"; about half disagreed. When asked if they
would like to move (unclear whether to another state or just another part of
town), an amazing 79 percent wanted to stay right where they were! Thus,
the level of satisfaction with the community is very high. Again, the strength
of attachment to community may be a factor in motivating participation. For
example, in 1990 the Church of St. Charles Borromeo, which has served
northeast Minneapolis since 1940, celebrated its fiftieth anniversary. A committee was formed to hold a special celebration for the first class whose
members went all the way through St. Charles's grade school—the class of
1948, whose members began kindergarten in 1940. There were 31 students in
that 1948 grade-school graduating class. The committee discovered that 25
of those 31 people still lived within three miles of the church.

Fifth, Minnesotans want a positive role for government. In 1996 the Minnesota Poll asked citizens who should solve a series of problems. The results
are reported in table 3. For five of the eight problems, people thought the
government should bear the most responsibility. For two issues—job security and job retraining—private organizations were thought to be the major
solution, but government was a close second in each case. Individuals were
thought to be the major solution for race relations, with government a more
distant second. Thus, for every problem except race relations, government
was thought to be either the solution or one of the major solutions. Although
we don't have comparable data for other states, this attribution of responsibility to government would seem to be stronger than most.

Table 3: Main Locus of Responsibility for Solving Problems (%)

	Government	Private Organizations	Individuals
Juvenile crime	43		
Race relations			50
Poverty	51		
Welfare	64		
The economy	67		
Job security		35	
Middle class's economic situation	50		
Retraining people for new jobs		36	

Source: Adapted from the Minnesota Poll, *Star Tribune*, 12 May 1996, p. A14.

The election of Jesse Ventura in 1998 was seen, by some, as a reversal of Minnesota's willingness to look to government for solutions. Though Ventura's postelection rhetoric was more libertarian than communitarian, during the gubernatorial campaign his statements were not specific enough to allow attribution of his election to a major shift in feelings about government.

In summary, several factors appear to be related to Minnesota's relatively high level of political participation—factors that are known to be related to participation in general. These include keen interest in politics, high attachment to community, and strong faith in state and local government. Minnesotans also believe in a positive role for government in solving problems, although they do not think of themselves as liberals. We believe Minnesotans are closer to the communitarian position; that is, they want to balance individual rights with community responsibilities. They take public service seriously. Minnesota also exhibits the socioeconomic characteristics associated with high participation—above-average income, above-average levels of education—though it is far from the highest state in either category. Finally,

Figure 3: Number of Registered Interests in Minnesota

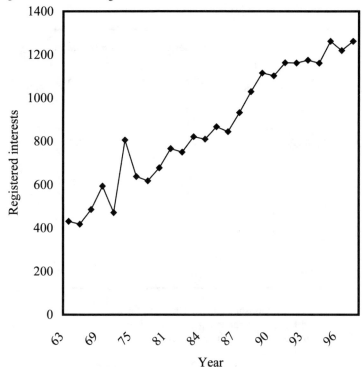

Source: Unpublished data collected by Virginia Gray and David Lowery.
Note: Data are biennial from 1963 to 1977, 1979 is missing, and the data
are annual after 1980.

Minnesota exhibits the legal and political characteristics associated with
high participation—facilitative registration laws, moralistic political culture, and intense party competition. All these factors together seem to produce the Minnesota ethic of participatory citizenship.

COLLECTIVE PARTICIPATION: INTEREST GROUPS

In addition to participating as individuals, citizens can band together to pursue common goals. Such organizations are called interest groups; they are
organized bodies of individuals who have goals in common and who try to
affect public policy. Like other forms of participation, they tend to appeal
more to people in the upper socioeconomic stratum.

Table 4: Organized Interests by Sector: Minnesota vs the
United States, 1990 (%)

	Minnesota	*United States*
Business	59.8	61.6
Labor	5.7	4.2
Professional	8.0	8.5
Government	10.4	11.3
Farm	1.6	1.0
Social	14.0	12.6
Unknown	0.4	0.6

Source: Unpublished data by Gray and Lowery.
Note: Entries are percentages of all registered interest
organizations that are in each sector.

The Growth in Organized Interests

It is not clear how many Minnesotans have belonged to interest groups in recent years, but it is clear that Minnesota has an extensive and active group
life. In 1990 it ranked eighth in the number of organized interests registered
to lobby the legislature; considering Minnesota's medium population size of
4.5 million people, that is a lot of interest organizations.[8] This count includes interest groups that individuals join, associations of organizations
(for example, the AFL-CIO), and an array of institutions that lobby, such as
corporations, universities, and hospitals. An analysis by Virginia Gray and
David Lowery showed that in 1997 18 percent of the registered organizations
in Minnesota were membership interest groups, 21 percent were associations
of organizations, and 58 percent were institutions.[9] Minnesota has proportionately more associations and fewer institutions than most states, and the
number of associations is growing faster than other types of organizations.

The number of registered interests has moved steadily upward over the
years, as seen in figure 3. By 1997 1,199 organizations had registered with
the state for the purpose of lobbying the legislature. Minnesota, like other

states, has a majority of its organizations representing the business sector (nearly 60 percent). Its overall array, as shown in table 4, is quite similar to the national average.

One factor leading to growth in the number of organizations is the fragmentation of interests into narrower and narrower groups. For example, Minnesota for many years had an association representing municipalities, the League of Minnesota Cities. During the past twenty years the league has been joined by the Association of Metropolitan Municipalities, the Coalition of Greater Minnesota Cities, the Municipal Legislative Commission, the League of Small Cities, the North Metro Mayors Association, and the Range Association of Municipalities and Schools. The Minnesota School Boards Association has been joined by the Association of Metropolitan School Districts, the Rural Education Association, and what used to be called the Association of Stable and Growing School Districts.

One reason for the splintering of interests is fiscal stress. One Minnesota lobbyist said in a phone survey conducted by Gray and Lowery: "The fragmentation is caused by the general economy. It is easy to have an umbrella organization when there is a lot of money to go around. When dollars are tight, it is hard to generate consensus to hold the group together. So fragmentation occurs. So, for example, first Minneapolis and St. Paul split apart from the other cities, then the suburbs and the small cities. So the Coalition of Greater Minnesota Cities was formed."[10]

Several contract lobbyists (those who lobby for multiple clients) mentioned that their desire for more lobbying business contributed to the splintering of interests, because they got individual companies to leave umbrella business organizations. One lobbyist in the Gray and Lowery survey alleged that as much as 20 percent of firms engage in unnecessary lobbying business that is motivated solely by profit for the lobbyist: "There is no question that lobbying firms encourage fragmentation. The lobbying industry is very competitive; they are always trying to splinter groups off and are always stealing clients from one another."[11]

Lobbyists who have been involved in this splintering process defend their actions with this retort: years ago members were willing to join and support general-interest organizations simply because they operated "in the best interests of the industry" (or local level of government, or whatever). But more and more organizations don't accept that general "good of the industry" argument any longer. Now organizations want to know what specific benefits they receive from lobbying. When the request for benefits is specific, the drive for fragmentation is pervasive.

Among local governments this drive for fragmentation has been augmented by technology. In the 1970s changes were made to the incredibly complex local government property tax system on the basis of estimates by a few people with knowledge of the system. The first computer program that could rapidly assess what proposed changes meant for individual taxpayers in individual districts was developed around 1980 by the Minnesota Department of Revenue. Legislative staff soon duplicated the feat, so now there were two predictive programs, but all the knowledge about who would pay how much in property taxes was in the state government. Minneapolis developed its own program in the early 1980s, and local government lobbying was transformed. Any proposal could be run through the city's computers, and Minneapolis legislators would know within days what would happen specifically to their homeowners. Not surprisingly, armed with this knowledge, they tended to resist proposals that cost their constituents money.

Soon a lawyer named Tim Flaherty saw that knowledge, in the lobbying sense, was indeed power. He had developed a computer program for the client he created, the Coalition of Greater Minnesota Cities, and the coalition's knowledge became a powerful lobbying tool. The norm in local government lobbying became "the war of the runs," that is, each organization would come up with computer runs detailing what a proposed change would cost voters in their district. The widespread availability of all these runs made it more difficult to shift taxes from one type of property to another, even though such a shift seemed appropriate in terms of equity. Legislators were reluctant to vote for a bill that required their constituents to pay a little more.

Gray and Lowery discovered in their fifty-state study that the number of organized interests does not grow without bound over time; rather, each state seems to have a natural "carrying capacity" for interest organizations, based on its economic structure.[12] One reason for a natural limit on interest organizations is that their mortality rate is quite high. For example, about 63 percent of Minnesota's interest organizations left the lobbying scene between 1980 and 1990. The lobbying community is very fluid, with new organizations constantly being created and old ones dying or temporarily disappearing.

Some Minnesota institutions, instead of dying a permanent death, tended to withdraw temporarily from politics, but membership groups and associations were more likely to stop lobbying because the organization died altogether: 79 percent of membership groups and 84 percent of associations dissolved by decade's end. Institutions are a high proportion of all lobbying organizations because they both enter and exit the lobbying scene at higher rates than other organizations, but the entry rate is about twice as high as the exit rate.

Another possibility is that organizations that withdraw from lobbying support political action committees (PACs) instead of lobbying; that is, they use multiple means of political action. In 1995, however, fewer than one in ten had PACs, about the same as a decade earlier.

The Range and Influence of Organized Interests

Scholars of interest groups rate Minnesota as having a rather weak interest-group system. The latest Thomas-Hrebenar ranking in 1998 places Minnesota among the bottom four states; that is, its groups are constrained in their effect by other political actors, the political culture, the party system, and so forth.[13] Chapter 5 notes that Minnesota's campaign-finance system places less reliance on special-interest money than any other state's, and this gives credence to thinking of interest groups as weak. Few people in Minnesota would agree with that proposition, however: most are liable to say that interest groups are too powerful and ought to be restrained even more.

Minnesota's group structure is quite similar to the rest of the country's, with business being the largest sector. This sector includes numerous single firms such as Northern States Power, a utility, which was the top lobbying spender in 1994 (about $1.4 million was spent lobbying on the storage of nuclear waste from its power plant at Prairie Island). Other businesses frequently on the list of lobbying influentials are Dayton-Hudson, the retail giant that fought a hostile out-of-state takeover in 1987; Northwest Airlines, which successfully sought a state subsidy in 1991; and tobacco manufacturer Phillip Morris, which fights smoking regulation.

The business sector also includes a range of associations such as the Minnesota Chamber of Commerce, always among the top spenders. Umbrella organizations such as the Minnesota Business Partnership and the Minnesota Agri-Growth Council pursue ambitious agendas of legislative activity. Other top business associations are the Minnesota Retail Merchants Association and the Minnesota Association of Realtors, both of whose executive directors/lobbyists were listed among the eight most influential lobbyists in 1995.[14] Closely related are the array of professional associations representing people with considerable clout—the trial lawyers, the dentists, and the doctors.

It is important to remember that the business sector includes large and small businesses, firms that are very competitive with one another. So business is rarely a unified lobby. On those rare occasions when it does unite, however, the results are an impressive show of strength. The two overarching business issues in the 1990s were reform of the workers' compensation system, which was accomplished in 1993, and a commercial and industrial property tax overhaul, which resulted in a permanent rate reduction in 1997–98. Both were significant achievements for business.

Among unions, the AFL-CIO is important in representing traditional labor, but also weighty are the organizations representing teachers—the Minnesota Education Association (MEA) and the Minnesota Federation of Teachers (MFT)—and public employees—the American Federation of State, County, and Municipal Employees (AFSCME) and the Minnesota Association of Professional Employees (MAPE). The conventional wisdom among those involved in lobbying at Minnesota's capitol is that the public employee unions are the most powerful interest groups in the state; their membership totals 48,000 for AFSCME and 9,500 for MAPE. We would place teachers second in influence. The MEA is a perennial among the top-spending lobby groups and also has a top-spending PAC. In fact, in 1990 the PAC expenditures of the teachers and the public employees dwarfed those of all other special interests.[15] In September 1998 the two teachers' organizations, MEA and MFT, merged. The resulting organization—Education Minnesota—will be the largest, best-funded lobbying group in Minnesota, with 65,000 members. Nonetheless, the combined power of teachers could not stop the expansion of school-choice legislation in 1997, thus verifying Minnesota's classification as a weak interest system.

The AFL-CIO has probably declined in power a bit over time, but it is still a force to be reckoned with. An identifiable subset of labor, the building and construction trades, has proved formidable in protecting its most cherished policy position, prevailing wage, which essentially establishes union wages as the norm for all government-funded construction jobs.

The power of labor groups stems from their large membership size, their geographic dispersion across all legislative districts, and their ability to get their members involved in working on campaigns, attending "lobby days" at the capitol, and making sizable campaign contributions. Incidentally, labor leaders can allocate political contributions to candidates without members' specific consent, a prerogative that has sometimes been an issue in other states. Labor leaders have also generally been skillful in extracting labor-friendly votes from legislators.

Local governments and government associations are also a major force at the state capitol, but they are rarely a unified force, as they are often lobbying against one another. Nearly 250 people lobbied for localities in 1998.[16] The top spenders typically include the City of Minneapolis, the Hennepin County Board of Commissioners, the League of Minnesota Cities, the Coalition of Greater Minnesota Cities, and the Minnesota School Boards Association. The amount of local government lobbying raises a lot of eyebrows because it is erroneously characterized as "using state money to lobby state government for more state money." In fact, local governments use local property tax money to pay lobbyists, but that doesn't make critics of the practice any happier. Symbolic of these concerns was the grousing by Governor Arne Carlson about a very handsome and well-appointed new building right across the street from the capitol erected by the League of Minnesota Cities in 1994.

A wide variety of social groups represent issues of the day. Environmental groups are particularly influential in Minnesota; for example, in 1994 the Clean Water Action Alliance was second on the list of top spending on lobbying. Abortion groups are very active on both sides, with the lobbyist for Minnesota Citizens Concerned for Life being one of the capitol's most powerful people. There are active groups with prominent lobbyists on the right—the Family Council—and especially on the left—Minnesota Alliance for Progressive Action, the Children's Defense Fund, and Citizens Organized Acting Together (COACT). Religious groups, such as the Joint Religious Legislative Coalition, are often active on issues affecting the disadvantaged, such as housing and welfare.

The Lobbying Community

Minnesota has approximately twelve hundred people in its lobbying community. It includes contract lobbyists (those who work for several clients at a time), in-house lobbyists (those who work full-time for one organization or company), legislative liaisons for state agencies, citizen lobbyists (unpaid volunteers representing their organization), and hobbyists (private individuals lobbying for their pet project without compensation or significant financial interest). As in most states, Minnesota's lobbying community has made the transition from a "good ole boy" network to a more sophisticated operation relying on information and credible arguments. As one lobbyist put it in the Gray and Lowery survey: "People used to sell themselves on being old boys, having relationships, being in a network. Now we pride ourselves, sell ourselves on information and advocacy."[17] Lobbying has become professionalized, with the contract firms offering their clients research, legal ex-

Profiles of Minnesota's Most Influential Lobbyists, 1995

Judy Cook is the only woman among the top eight lobbyists. Now in her own firm, she previously lobbied for the Minnesota Retail Merchants Association and exemplifies the changing face of lobbying. Cook's style is no-nonsense and low-key, reminiscent of an academic. At hearings she straightforwardly presents facts and figures in support of her clients' views, and she is a master of organizing clients to do grassroots lobbying.

Ron Jerich, in contrast, represents the "old school" of lobbying. Before the 1994 gift ban Jerich routinely spent thousands of dollars per year entertaining legislators, arguing that "people want to have a little fun." A large man, he is garrulous and gossipy, the type of person central casting would pick to play the role of lobbyist. He rarely testifies before committees, relying on talking to legislators behind the scenes and "schmoozing" in the halls of the capitol.

Wy Spano, one of the authors of this book, also made the "top eight" list. Spano's style lies somewhere between those of Cook and Jerich: he gathers facts and figures to make his case for his clients, but he also had a habit of socializing with legislators and staff, especially on the golf course, before the 1994 gift ban trimmed back his activities. His power is enhanced by his media positions: he is one of the publishers of *Politics in Minnesota*, a newsletter for political junkies; a frequent panelist on "Almanac"; and a regular contributor to the op-ed pages of the newspapers. In his spare time he is a Ph.D. candidate in political science at the University of Minnesota.

Glenn Dorfman is the main man for the Minnesota Association of Realtors. He eschews the "good ole boy" school of lobbying for a more "in your face" style, described as "preachy and provocative." This more confrontational approach is referred to as a "New York City" style, definitely not a "Minnesota" style. Still, he enjoys close relationship with senior leaders in both political parties and is highly influential.

Source: Sixty members of the Minnesota legislature were asked to name five to ten lobbyists they considered "most influential or effective" (Dane Smith, "The Lobbyists," *Star Tribune*, 4 May 1994, pp. 1A and 18A, and 5 May 1995, pp. 1A and 20A).

pertise, fiscal analysis, political newsletters, fax alerts to grassroots members, and media relations, along with the traditional core services of monitoring legislation, drafting bills, contacting legislators, testifying, and rounding up votes.

The most recent survey of Minnesota interest groups' tactics was done in 1984 by Virginia Gray. It showed that lobbying the legislator in person was the most frequently used tactic; there is no substitute for human contact in making one's case.[18] At the bottom of the hierarchy were filing a lawsuit and engaging in a protest or demonstration. Few groups relied on these tactics in the mid-1980s, and almost no groups do today. There is no interest group we know of that relies exclusively on litigation to pursue its cause. Demonstrations do occur, but they are rarely effective, in our experience. One tactic that has increased in usage is the so-called grassroots lobbying, whereby the lobbyist gets members of the group to write or visit their legislator; whereas in 1984 only 39 percent of lobbyists regularly organized their members, today a majority of lobbyists do so, we estimate. Legislative interns report that legislators routinely ignore correspondence that does not emanate from the constituency.

The power structure of Minnesota's lobbying community has become more diversified, although contract lobbyists continue to dominate it. We have provided profiles of some of the most influential lobbyists named in a 1995 newspaper survey of legislators. Interestingly, about 140 lobbyists were mentioned by someone, and no lobbyist was mentioned more than twelve times.[19] Thus, lobbying clout is diffused among many different people; influence does not reside just in a few lobbyists or in one or two firms.

Lobbyists who work in a number of states often marvel at the strength of Minnesota's "do-good" lobbying core, and even of some so-called hobbyists. A long-term example of the "do-good" genre was Louise Brown, who represented Family and Children's Service for many years. Brown's agency was funded largely through the United Way and private giving; little of her legislative work involved trying to get state money. Nonetheless, she was a trusted advocate for family and children legislation and often played a major role in helping craft programs. Among the hobbyists, Richard Neumeister was perhaps the best known in the 1980s and 1990s. Neumeister says he grew up in public housing projects and became incensed at the violations of privacy his family faced there. Neumeister's long, flowing hair and drooping mustache are considered normal adornments to meetings of the Judiciary Committees when privacy matters are discussed. No bill on privacy or related issues leaves the Minnesota legislature without his considerable input.

The Regulation of Lobbying

Legislation regulating lobbying typically follows a scandal or crisis; in most states such legislation was passed in the mid-1970s after the Watergate scandal in Washington DC and again in the 1990s. Minnesota started early, requiring lobby registration in 1963, but otherwise has followed this general pattern. In 1974 the legislature passed a comprehensive ethics bill that included regulation of lobbying activities; it created the Ethical Practices Board, now called the Campaign Finance and Public Disclosure Board, to police lobbying and campaign-finance activities. Amendments were added over the years, and in 1994, following the "Phonegate" scandal (members of the legislature used government phones for personal business), another round of significant reform came about, which included a ban on gifts of any size to legislators by individuals or organizations registered to lobby.

Minnesota statutes define who is a lobbyist (anyone who is engaged for pay and who spends more than five hours a month or more than $250 per year in attempting to influence legislative, administrative, or metropolitan action). Lobbyists must register with the Campaign Finance and Public Disclosure Board and disclose their employers, the issues on which they are lobbying, and their expenditures on lobbying. The employer (or "principal," in statutory language) who spends more than $500 per year on lobbyists or more than $50,000 in any effort to influence official action must also register. The main purpose of these laws is to put lobbying activities into public, and media, view.

Statutes also regulate the nature of relationships between public officials and others, including lobbyists. Lobbying contracts on a contingency basis have long been forbidden. In 1994, amid the sweeping reform package adopted, a ban on gifts of any kind was enacted, thus outlawing a lobbyist's buying a meal or even a cup of coffee for a legislator. These laws are intended to prevent public officials from profiting from their public positions—a goal consistent with Minnesota's moralistic culture.

Finally, Minnesota law regulates campaign finance, which affects the electoral efforts of interest groups and their PACs. Since 1990 legislators have not been allowed to hold campaign fundraisers during the legislative session; they are restricted in the amount of money they can accept from PACs and interest groups (described in more detail in chapter 5). Overall, Minnesota's regulations are among the most stringent in the country; in a ranking of the laws on the books in 1993, Minnesota was among the ten toughest states.[20] Minnesota has since tightened up its laws even more.

Still, ethically questionable practices do occur. The 1998 tobacco trial (described in chapter 8) forced the disclosure of twenty-six million pages of heretofore secret industry documents. Newspaper reporters have been plowing through them and have discovered the use of various shady lobbying practices by Big Tobacco. For example, more than one Minnesota labor leader failed to disclose on his lobby registration form that he was also being paid secretly by the tobacco industry. Thus, labor support of tobacco industry positions over the years, supposedly based on potential job loss, was called into question. Also, documents revealed that the tobacco industry had its own unique way of making legislative contributions: tobacco lobbyists asked for the name of the legislator's favorite charity and then sent a handsome donation to it. Such an exchange is not recorded or reported to the state.

THE PUBLIC AFFAIRS COMMUNITY

Minnesota has a set of public affairs institutions that affect public policy. The Citizens League is the best-known, having been active for fifty years. It uses volunteer research committees of members to study public problems in depth and to issue reports containing policy solutions. League staff then lobby the legislature for adoption of these solutions. For example, several recommendations from a 1992 study were included in the legislature's reform of campaign-finance legislation. Among the Citizens League's better-known proposals are the creation of the Metropolitan Council and a two-decade-long insistence on what it first called "public service options," the ability for public bodies to go outside themselves, including to the private sector, for service delivery. Since 1990 Minnesota has had a newer and conservative think tank—the Center of the American Experiment—which has, with great skill, popularized the conservative agenda.

Also in the public affairs community are a number of private foundations whose grant-making influences the course of public policy. These include the Minneapolis Foundation, the St. Paul Foundation, the Northwest Area Foundation, the McKnight Foundation, and the Bush Foundation. They fund research and demonstration projects and sponsor various programs in different sectors of public life, For example, the Bush Leadership Program sponsors "emerging young leaders" for study at top universities. Many of the state's political leaders have benefited from this program. The Northwest Area Foundation focuses on the economic development of an eight-state region; McKnight encompasses human services, rural development, housing, the disadvantaged, the environment, and the arts. In a crisis the collective will of the foundations can be impressive. In 1997 more than thirty Minnesota foundations contributed to a joint fund, matched by the legislature, to enable nonprofit organizations to plan for federal budget cuts and the end of AFDC. The fund was the brainchild of the Minnesota Council of Nonprofits, an organization that brings together the public affairs clout of the nonprofit sector.

No discussion of the public affairs community would be complete without examining the role of the mass media. It is important to know that the state capitol and the major media market are in the same place. Therefore, state government affairs get the kind of sustained media attention that is not possible in capital cities such as Sacramento or Springfield, located far away from the media centers of California and Illinois. State government reporters have offices, albeit somewhat grungy ones, in the basement of the state capitol and hence ready access to legislators and executive branch officials. Camera crews are a frequent sight in the capitol's galleries and in the rotunda.

Also unusual is the fact that the Twin Cities community supports two major daily newspapers, the *St. Paul Pioneer Press* with a daily circulation of 207,624 and the Minneapolis *Star Tribune* with a circulation of 343,729. The *Pioneer Press* is owned by the Gannett chain, and the *Star Tribune* was owned by the Cowles family for sixty years until its sale in 1997 to the McClatchy Company, a California newspaper chain. Although highly competitive with each other, both papers have long histories of involvement in and influence over public policy. For example, the *Pioneer Press*'s 1992 series "Bankrolling the Legislature" was partly responsible for the campaign-finance and lobbying reforms adopted in 1993 and 1994. The *Star Tribune* was instrumental in covering the legislative "Phonegate" scandal (described in chapter 6), which led to Speaker Dee Long's resignation in 1993. Both papers take an active role in electoral politics as well, endorsing candidates, conducting polls before the election, and monitoring campaign advertising.

The Minneapolis paper is a national leader in the civic or public journalism movement, which seeks to involve more citizens in meaningful ways in their communities. In 1997 the *Star Tribune* and KTCA (public television) experimented with a Citizens Forum in which focus groups of citizens were convened to study certain issues for several months; at the end of the legislative session the "citizen experts" rated the legislature on how well it did on each issue. Citizen panels were also used to guide coverage of the 1998 election. Many residents worry that the *Star Tribune*'s new owner will not be as committed to civic endeavors.

The easy access of print reporters to the capitol works both ways; legislators can easily get information from the media. The University of Minnesota student newspaper, the *Minnesota Daily*, is dropped off each day so any interested legislators can read about the machinations of the university. Legislators especially follow the *Star Tribune*. In a 1997 survey conducted by Virginia Gray 73 percent of members said they regularly read editorials in the *Star Tribune*, whereas 56 percent regularly read editorial opinion in the *Pioneer Press*.[21] Legislative staff are even more avid readers of the two newspapers' editorial pages: 87 percent regularly read the *Star Tribune* and 80 percent the *Pioneer Press*.

Outstate newspapers are plentiful too, from small-town weeklies to well-regarded dailies, such as the Rochester *Post-Bulletin*, the Mankato *Free Press*, the St. Cloud *Times*, and the Duluth *News-Tribune*. Among the most widely read political columnists outstate is John Sundvor, who writes for the Forum chain of newspapers in west-central Minnesota. Among outstate editorial writers, former governor Elmer Andersen stands out; until the age of eighty-nine Governor Andersen was still composing elegant and insightful editorials for his chain of nineteen newspapers, headed by the *Princeton Union*.

The importance of the local newspaper in the community was amply demonstrated by the magnificent performance of the *Grand Forks Herald* during the spring floods of 1997. Though located on the North Dakota side of the border, the *Herald* is read throughout the Red River Valley and was the lifeline of western Minnesota and eastern North Dakota as the Red River crested, flooding cities and towns on both sides of the river and covering valuable farmland for a hundred miles or so. The *Herald*'s headquarters was first isolated by floodwaters and then burned to the ground in the fire that further destroyed downtown Grand Forks. Despite these calamities, the paper never missed a day of publication; it was composed on computers in a local school, e-mailed to the *Pioneer Press* in St. Paul (both papers are part of the Gannett chain), where it was printed overnight, and then flown back to Grand Forks for distribution the next morning. For this accomplishment, the *Herald* was awarded a Pulitzer Prize in 1998.

The Twin Cities has television stations affiliated with each of the three major commercial networks plus a Fox network station, along with an independent station and two public television stations. Of the network stations, wcco, the cbs affiliate, and kare, the nbc station, have regular political reporters who provide substantial coverage of state government. kstp, the abc affiliate, is remembered for its major role in bringing about the downfall of a house Speaker in the "Phonegate" scandal. The commercial stations also provide election polling and extensive election-night coverage and commentary.

In addition, public television station ktca provides in-depth political reporting and analysis every evening on "News Night Minnesota." On Friday night it offers a popular public affairs show called "Almanac," avidly followed by policy wonks. In 1994 "Almanac" was watched by seventy-one thousand viewers, the fourteenth largest audience in its Nielsen market. The show, hosted by Eric Eskola and Cathy Wurzer, sponsors candidate debates, furnishes commentary by local experts on emerging political developments, and provides a forum for informed exchange on controversial issues. The show is available throughout Minnesota on seven nonmetro public television stations. In addition, the public television stations in Duluth and Grand Rapids carry "Almanac North," which focuses on issues of northeastern Minnesota.

Commercial television stations in Duluth, Rochester, and Mankato provide complete news shows daily with extensive focus on local and regional issues; two stations in Alexandria, designed to cover the western and northwestern parts of the state, are satellites of Twin Cities stations with short local news inserts.

Minnesota also has an extensive array of radio stations, both commercial and public. Of the commercial stations, the CBS affiliate WCCO offers the most sophisticated political coverage, with reporter Eric Eskola of "Almanac" fame. Minnesota News Network provides the basis for an all-news commercial station, WMNN, plus state-oriented newscasts for commercial radio stations all over the state. The highly regarded Minnesota Public Radio network consists of twenty-nine stations around the state. It offers extensive public affairs programming, analyzing public policy developments and dissecting election returns. And of course millions of listeners around the country know Minnesota through native-son humorist Garrison Keillor and his show "Prairie Home Companion." His mythical "Lake Wobegon" symbolizes rural culture everywhere.

Finally, talk radio, mostly of the conservative stripe, has come to Minnesota. Former wrestler Jesse "The Body" Ventura had to quit his "shock jock" radio show in order to run for governor in 1998. Similarly, Minneapolis mayoral candidate Barbara Carlson gained notoriety by conducting radio interviews with political candidates while sitting with them in a hot tub.

All in all, the public affairs community in Minnesota offers considerable information and policy analysis to interested citizens.

Minnesotans are in the habit of participating vigorously in public affairs. They are among the nation's hardiest voters, coming out in large numbers in snow and sleet to elect candidates in November of even-numbered years. Minnesota's facilitative voter-registration laws help boost voter turnout, as do its high socioeconomic status, moralistic political culture, and keen interparty competition. Minnesotans also participate in a range of community activities in higher proportions than citizens of other states. Minnesotans, as compared with citizens elsewhere, are very interested in politics, have faith and confidence in government (especially in their own government), are closely attached to their communities, and want government to be involved in most problems. In short, they are positive about an activist government and possibly communitarian in orientation. Minnesotans do not necessarily think of themselves as liberal, however; they have shied away from this label in recent years, just as most Americans have.

Minnesota is richly endowed with opportunities for collective participation. It has more organized interests than forty-one other states; both the number of interest organizations and the number of lobbyists have grown over time. However, the interest-group universe is quite fluid: groups wax and wane over time, moving into and out of the lobbying mode.

Among the organized interests, business is especially well represented, with about 60 percent of the registered interest organizations. Labor organizations, particularly those representing teachers and public employees, are very influential, as are local governments and their associations. Minnesota also has a variety of social or cause groups plus an array of think tanks, foundations, and media organizations, all of which provide policy input and advice. Among the lobbyists themselves, contract lobbyists seem to be more powerful than other types of lobbyists. Lobbying is becoming more professionalized and more diversified in terms of gender, age, and so forth. Minnesota regulates its lobbying activities more than most states, particularly since the 1994 ethics reform package. Minnesotans take pride in maintaining good clean government.

CHAPTER 5

Political Parties, Elections, and Campaign Finance

If money is the mother's milk of politics, Minnesota is the home of the lowest-fat political milk in the United States.

In keeping with its overwhelmingly moralistic political culture, which dictates that politics is not considered a legitimate realm for private economic enrichment, Minnesota has fashioned a system for choosing its political leaders which is less influenced by private economic interests than in any other state. That candidate selection and campaign system features (1) strong political parties, dominated by issue-oriented activists, whose preprimary endorsements of candidates have been all-important in attaining political office, and (2) a state campaign-financing scheme that places limits on campaign spending in exchange for extensive governmental funding of campaigns: taxpayers provide more than half the money spent on the elections of Minnesota candidates for the legislature and for the five statewide offices.

Federal candidates do not participate in Minnesota's state campaign-financing scheme, but they benefit from the strong political parties that make it possible for Minnesotans without significant personal resources to be nominated for and elected to Congress. Indeed, in Minnesota significant personal wealth is thought to be as much a handicap as an asset for a candidate. In line with the tenets of the moralistic culture, politics is not considered a legitimate realm for generating private economic enrichment; moreover, Minnesotans have been ambivalent concerning whether or not they want to elect wealthy officeholders. Federal candidates also are subject to Minnesota's strictures against campaign contributions from corporations, another practice that limits private economic participation in campaigns.

Candidates for major local offices do not receive the kind of government funding that state candidates do, but they are subject to the same corporate campaign restrictions, and the major cities and counties have passed ordinances that tend to limit the ability of single economic interests to dominate campaigns.

Thus, as we shall see, Minnesota has devised a system for electing its leaders of which it was accurately said in the 1990s, "Money doesn't matter," at least not very much. The system is under serious challenge, however, for two reasons: The gubernatorial election of 1998, won by Reform party candidate Jesse Ventura, appeared to be an antiparty election. Voters rebelled against the Republican and DFL candidates, who were seen as too readily espousing the positions of what were thought to be their parties' extremists. Ventura's Reform party had been a surrogate for the electoral choice "none of the above" before 1998, and many thought it continued that role with a candidate who had sufficient name recognition to win a three-way race. If the previously strong, ideologically oriented parties lose their say in the election process, their role will probably be replaced by money. Second, the money to do the job is available because of federal judicial rulings relative to soft money, independent expenditures, and issue advertising.

This chapter does not attempt to demonstrate a connection between Minnesota's egalitarian election process and the state's high tax–high service status or its national leadership in liberal policy innovations (see chapter 10), but such a connection seems commonsensical. It is reasonable to assume that the additional money that would come into Minnesota campaigns, were the election system in the state less well insulated, would represent more conservative, antitax, low-service interests and that their wishes would eventually find themselves represented in policy.

THE PARTIES IN MINNESOTA POLITICS

Through its first eighty-seven years Minnesota's Democratic party, hampered by its Civil War image as the party of the South, never could achieve parity with the Republicans. Beginning about 1890 and continuing until 1944, Minnesota often had three and sometimes four parties contending for elective posts. Through the 1920s Republicans continued to win elections, but with pluralities considerably under 50 percent. A new organization, the Farmer-Labor party, won two U.S. Senate and three congressional elections in the 1920s and by the 1930s had became the plurality leader in the state, though its leadership was short-lived. Finally, in 1944 Minnesota entered an era of two relatively equal major parties when the Democratic-Farmer-Labor party was created through a merger of the Democrats and the more militant

Farmer-Laborites.[1] That two-party era was ended in 1998 with the election of Reform party gubernatorial candidate Jesse Ventura.

Minnesota: The Liberal, Democratic State?

Both inside and outside its borders Minnesota has usually been characterized as a Democratic stronghold, a liberal state. Hubert Humphrey had a major role in creating that image. He was the founder of the DFL party, one of the most influential U.S. senators of his or any time, vice-president and almost president, clearly the dominant figure in Minnesota politics for three decades. As the pater familias of the DFL party, Humphrey, true to Minnesota moralistic tradition, did not operate as a boss. He was not known for keeping the troops in line or punishing dissidence. His leadership, rather, was exercised through rhetoric and, particularly, enthusiasm.

Those who insist that the characterization of Minnesota as a liberal, Democratic state remains accurate offer as proof the fact that, since 1960, Minnesota has voted Republican for president only once, in 1972; or the fact that the Minnesota senate has been in DFL hands since 1972 and the house has been controlled by the Republicans for only one two-year period during the 1980s and one more at the end of the 1990s.

The picture is not so monochromatic, however. From 1974 through 1998 Republicans won half of the gubernatorial elections and two-thirds of the U.S. Senate elections. And Minnesota's presidential voting has clearly been affected by the frequent presence of Minnesotans on national Democratic tickets—Hubert Humphrey in 1964 and 1968 and Walter Mondale in 1976, 1980, and 1984. For five of the ten presidential elections between 1960 and 1996, there was a favorite Minnesota Democratic son on the ballot.

A substantial portion of the seeming DFL dominance in the legislature can be attributed to favorable redistricting. In both 1971 and 1981, redistricting was eventually accomplished by federal judge Gerald W. Heaney, among other things a former DFL national committeeman and one of the founders of the DFL party. Although the plans adopted were compact, contiguous, and within very small population variances, they were also favorable to DFL control, a fact Republicans were quick to assert and Democrats would admit, but only privately. In 1991 Republican governor Arne Carlson failed to veto the DFL legislature's redistricting plan properly, so it became law. Thus, for three decades, Democrats had favorable districting arrangements that helped them win legislative majorities.

In Minnesota "independent" is by far the largest partisan designation chosen by citizens responding to poll questions. That situation is true every-where in the 1990s, but it became a reality in Minnesota in 1980, eight years before it happened nationally. The 1998 election of Governor Jesse Ventura is the most striking example of Minnesota's spirit of political independence, but there were harbingers of this reality before that election. In 1992 Minne-sota gave Reform party candidate Ross Perot 24 percent of the vote, five per-centage points higher than the national average and the ninth highest per-centage among the states.[2] In 1994 and again in 1996 Minnesota Reform party founder Dean Barkley ran for the U.S. Senate, gathering 5 percent of the votes the first time and 7 percent the second.[3]

Minnesota's Political Geography

In statewide and legislative elections the DFL has a firm hold on the cities of Minneapolis and St. Paul and on St. Louis County, a large area in the north-eastern corner of the state that includes the port city of Duluth and the Iron Range, home of the iron mining industry. Republicans are predictable win-ners in the more affluent western and southern suburbs of the Twin Cities and in the area surrounding Rochester in the southeastern part of the state. Al-though Democrats dominate the big cities and Republicans the suburbs, it is the Reform party that has the most support in Minnesota's exurban region— those parts of the state growing most rapidly. In 1998 Jesse Ventura had more votes than the Republican and DFL candidates combined in a swath of coun-ties that form a semicircle northeast and northwest of the Twin Cities.

THE PARTIES IN ELECTIONS

There are 18,870 elected officials in Minnesota, but only 218 of them appear on the ballot with party designation. These 218 include the president and vice-president, two U.S. senators and eight congressional representatives, the 201 members of the legislature, and the six state constitutional officers: governor, lieutenant governor, attorney general, auditor, treasurer, and sec-retary of state. Another 100 or so positions in the state, though officially non-partisan, are in fact politicized, that is, they attract formal endorsements from the political parties and contributions from interest groups and parti-sans. Generally, these 100 include the mayors and councils of the largest cities, the county attorneys and county boards in the largest counties, and school boards in the largest cities. When we discuss partisan offices in the election system, we include these 100, even though they appear on the ballot without party designation.

Preprimary Party Endorsements

For all the jobs with party designation on the ballot and the extra 100 "partisan" jobs that are on the ballot without party designation, both Minnesota's Republican and DFL parties have engaged since 1958 in preprimary endorsements, convention-voted blessings of candidates at various levels. Minnesota adopted primary elections during the Progressive era (1913 for state offices). Primaries are "semi-open," that is, voters receive ballots with the list of contenders for all parties' primary nominations, but they may vote for the candidates of only one party per primary election. Naturally, such a system invites crossover voting. More important, it permits Minnesota's many independents to participate in the partisan selection of candidates. Minnesota is one of only eleven states with a party-controlled endorsement system and one of only four where the system is informal (that is, not prescribed in law).[4] In some states party endorsement is the means to get on the ballot. In Minnesota, ballot access is open to all, endorsed or not, through either payment of a modest filing fee or gathering of petitions. Candidates may not display the fact of their endorsement on the ballot, nor do they receive favorable ballot positions because they have their party's imprimatur. Despite these drawbacks, candidates have, in the past, fought hard for endorsements, because endorsed candidates usually won the primary election.

It was the Farmer-Labor party that caused preprimary endorsements to become the norm in Minnesota. The Farmer-Labor party was constructed on the European political party model, with membership associations that collected dues, held debates on issues of the day, and endorsed candidates for office.[5] After the 1944 merger the DFL adopted the practice of preprimary endorsement, and Republicans discovered the utility of the practice in 1958.[6]

Sarah Morehouse, who has extensively studied preprimary endorsements in the eleven states in which it exists, has affirmed categorically that preprimary endorsements significantly reduce the impact of money in the political system.[7] The assertion makes sense. Primary elections are generally low-turnout elections. In order to win, candidates must dig out voters and get them to the polls. When there is a party apparatus with lists and workers and some money, and that apparatus has been harnessed for one candidate, the endorsed candidate can have a significant advantage in a primary contest. Without the activation of the party apparatus in a primary election, the only way to motivate voters is to buy their attention. As Morehouse puts it: "If a candidate aspires to be governor in a state where the primary is the only point of decision, he or she must outspend the opponent."[8] Money is the determining factor in a primary-only state. In a state with preprimary endorsements the party's blessing can overshadow a candidate's available financial resources.

Minnesota's political parties were and still are astonishingly egalitarian in their management of the endorsement process. Caucuses are held every two years, and anyone can participate as long as they are willing to say they belong to the party. Delegates are elected to intermediate-level and state conventions, at which the appropriate-level candidate is endorsed with a vote of at least 60 percent. The system is so open that it is difficult for party leaders to control. As a consequence, Minnesota has no modern tradition of political bosses, even when that word is used in its most benign sense.

From 1960 through 1978 Minnesota's Republican (and alternately named Independent-Republican [IR]) party and the DFL party were almost always successful in their endorsements of gubernatorial candidates, that is, the candidate endorsed by the party was the candidate who survived the primary and was the party's standard-bearer in the general election. During that eighteen-year period there were five gubernatorial elections and ten endorsed candidates, only one of whom failed to move on to the general election (in 1966; see chapter 7). Between 1982 and 1998, however, the success of the endorsement process at the gubernatorial level deteriorated. There were five gubernatorial elections with ten endorsed candidates, only five of whom made it to the general election.

For legislative candidates, endorsement was and continues to be even more important than for statewide candidates. A study of the 1986 Minnesota election showed that only 4 of 377 legislative endorsees from both political parties lost in the primary, a 99 percent success rate.[9] We estimate that the percentage remained about the same for the elections of the 1990s. In genuinely competitive districts both parties almost always endorse candidates. In districts heavily tilted toward one party or the other the party that's sure to win always endorses, whereas the one that's sure to lose sometimes doesn't bother. With few exceptions, the road to a seat in the Minnesota legislature goes through the local political party's endorsing convention. Not only is partisan endorsement for legislative candidates a necessary cause for election, it can also be a sufficient cause, especially in districts where one party dominates.

Controversies about the Role of Political Parties in Selecting Candidates

Through the 1970s and even the 1980s there was general recognition in Minnesota among political activists that the preprimary endorsement by a political party added political value to the candidate who received that endorsement, even though there was not agreement on whether such a system was harmful or helpful to the political process. By the 1990s, however, there were more and more voices suggesting that not only were partisan endorsements for statewide office not good for the political process but they could also be damaging to the candidates receiving them. Despite their open and egalitarian caucus/endorsement structures, both Minnesota's Republican and DFL parties came to be seen as representing extreme special interests. The rhetoric surrounding the 1998 election of Reform party candidate Jesse Ventura made it clear that the vote for Ventura was seen by many as a vote against the larger two parties. Within days after the election, activists in both those parties began a long series of agonizing, soul-searching discussions, attempting to figure out what to do next.

In part, the debate about political parties and preprimary endorsements is an aspect of the larger debate concerning representative as opposed to direct democracy.[10] Generally, Minnesota has clung to a more representative style. There is no initiative or referendum, and the first modern recall provision, passed in 1997, has yet to be used. In candidate selection Minnesota has been structurally committed to the dominance of primaries (the direct democracy model) while permitting party endorsements that can, especially at the local level, obviate the need for the primary (the representative model). Criticism of Minnesota's caucus-endorsement-primary system comes from both those with experience in the system and those who view it from afar.

Many active in the Republican and DFL caucus and preprimary endorsement system fault the system's growing inability to ensure successful endorsements at the statewide level. They believe that the timing of the caucuses (usually in February), party statewide endorsing conventions (in early June), the primary (mid-September), and the general election (early November, six weeks after the primary) gives candidates who did not receive the party's endorsement too much time to challenge, in the primary, those who were endorsed, while giving the eventual winner of the primary too little time against the other party in the general election.[11]

Those who are concerned about the intermediary role of political parties in the selection of Minnesota candidates raise a number of issues to challenge the validity of the endorsement system. The most common challenge is based on the assertion that Minnesota's caucuses are not representative of the state's voters. There aren't many people there, it is alleged, and all the people who do attend are (depending on the party) right-wing or left-wing ideologues. The question of how many people attend caucuses is not as simply answered as one might think. Both parties routinely cooked their attendance numbers, responding to a desire to outdo the other side and prove that caucuses were alive and well. We do know that in 1996, combined caucus attendance for the two major parties was 71,057, approximately 16 percent of the participants in the subsequent primary election but only 3 percent of those voting in the general election. Whether these numbers are "enough" is, of course, open to question. From the standpoint of party building, there seem to be enough people at precinct caucuses to renew the parties' leadership and to provide sufficient people power for successfully supporting candidates.

From the standpoint of representativeness, of course, caucuses do not measure up. The number of attendees is considerably larger than the number required for a representative sample of the state, but caucus attendees are decidedly unrepresentative. They are self-selected and are considerably more liberal (DFL) and conservative (Republican) than the average voter in the state.

Many former caucus participants in both the DFL and Republican parties think that the unrepresentativeness of the current system has led to a shift in political parties from candidate orientation to cause orientation. Jewell and Morehouse, who have surveyed state-convention delegates in the states that grant preprimary endorsements, note that in Minnesota and elsewhere party delegates gathered to make statewide preprimary endorsements are, in the 1990s, "less concerned about picking an electable candidate than picking one with the 'right' stand on issues."[12] In Minnesota the shift from candidate-centered to cause-centered party conventions has been accompanied by a polarization of major party ideologies.

Much of the impetus for that polarization seemed to stem from the issue of abortion. Before the U.S. Supreme Court's 1973 *Roe v. Wade* decision,[13] Minnesota's DFL party, with its heavily Roman Catholic base, was vaguely antiabortion in its platforms, while the Republican party was assertively in favor of birth control and sex education in the schools.[14] In 1974 the DFL reached agonizing ambivalence about abortion. One plank in that year's platform declared support for a constitutional amendment recognizing "equal protection under the law to all human life from the moment of conception." Two minority reports were filed with the "Human Life Amendment" statement, one affirming support for *Roe v. Wade*, the other suggesting that abortion was too volatile for Democrats to talk about. Thus, in 1974 the DFL party's position on abortion was "Yes," "No," and "Don't talk about it."[15] Eventually, the ongoing stand of the Minnesota Republican party was firmly pro-life,[16] whereas the DFL was just as firmly pro-choice.[17]

Generally, it became impossible for a statewide candidate to be an endorsed, pro-choice Republican or an endorsed, pro-life Democrat. It was estimated at the 1996 DFL state convention that about 100 delegates, 8 percent of the 1,246 total, were pro-life.[18]

The 1994 and 1998 Gubernatorial Endorsements

It took the DFL party seven ballots in 1994 to give its endorsement to state senator John Marty instead of to the person deemed by most observers to be more electable, Hennepin County attorney Mike Freeman. Marty appealed to cause-oriented party delegates with his calls for increasing taxes to provide more social services and his promise to accept no PAC money and no contributions greater than $100. Marty barely survived a four-way primary with 38 percent of the vote compared with 36 percent for his nearest challenger. Freeman was not a participant in the primary, having pledged to abide by the convention's decision. Marty lost the general election nearly 2 to 1, at that time the most lopsided loss ever suffered by a DFL gubernatorial candidate since the party's founding in 1944.

If anything, Republicans had an even bigger problem in 1996. The incumbent governor, Arne Carlson, was from their party, reasonably popular, and seeking reelection—usually considered positive elements by partisans. But Carlson could muster only 31 percent of the 1994 Republican convention delegates. Carlson had what most Republican delegates considered the wrong position on abortion—he was pro-choice. Many delegates also recalled resoundingly rejecting Carlson in their convention four years earlier; he went on to lose the 1990 primary, then was placed on the general election ballot by the state supreme court when the Republican-endorsed candidate and primary winner withdrew from the race because of allegations that he had acted inappropriately with teenaged friends of his daughter's in a swimming pool some eleven years earlier.

Republicans in 1994 easily endorsed for governor social and religious conservative Allen Quist, a former state legislator. Unlike Marty, however, Quist had only one opponent in the primary, Governor Carlson. Although Carlson's moderate positions on abortion and other social issues made him anathema to the party's delegates, he was more acceptable to the electorate. Carlson beat Quist in the primary by a 2-to-1 margin and then went on to defeat John Marty for his second term.

In 1998 Minnesota's DFL party had a wealth of prominent candidates seeking the governor's chair being vacated by Republican Arne Carlson.

Among them were three referred to in many national stories about the race as "My Three Sons": Attorney General Hubert H. ("Skip") Humphrey III, son of the former vice-president, senator, and founder of the DFL, Hubert H. Humphrey II; Mike Freeman, Hennepin County attorney, whose father, Orville Freeman, had been Minnesota governor and U.S. secretary of agriculture in the Kennedy administration; and Ted Mondale, son of the former Minnesota attorney general, senator, vice-president, and ambassador to Japan Walter Mondale. The three were joined originally by the 1994 endorsee, John Marty; by Mark Dayton, heir to a prominent retailing name in Minnesota; and by state senator Doug Johnson, for seventeen years one of the state's most powerful legislative figures as chair of the senate Tax Committee.

Of the entire group, Freeman was the only one who agreed to "abide by the endorsement," that is, who stated publicly he would not run against an endorsed DFL candidate in the primary. Freeman had made the same pledge in 1994 and had honored it. The June 1998 convention endorsed Freeman after ten ballots. His principal opposition came from Humphrey, who did not promise to abide by the endorsement but who was perceived by many as more electable than Freeman because his name was better known and because, as attorney general, he had just won a $6.1 billion judgment for the state against the tobacco industry. Freeman's candidacy became a test of the endorsement process, which failed, since Humphrey won the primary.

Many Democrats were distraught at the results of the 1998 endorsement, primary, and general election, but for varying reasons. There were those thoroughly disgusted with the reality that the party's state convention had been presented with what seemed to be the ideal candidate—a career public servant with a distinguished record as a state senator and attorney general, who was the son of the party's founder and who thus bore the most famous and recognizable name in Minnesota politics—and nonetheless failed to endorse that candidate. There were others equally disgusted that this same Humphrey would not "honor" the endorsement and election system that his father had so skillfully put in place.

On the Republican side, in 1998 there was a striking movement by party delegates toward pragmatism and an apparent desire to endorse a candidate who could win. The change came from the party chairmanship of William Cooper, the CEO of a large financial institution, who put electability back on the party's agenda. The party's 1994 endorsee, Allen Quist, again sought the party's endorsement in 1998, as did Lieutenant Governor Joanne Benson. But the clear favorite of Cooper and, eventually, the convention, was Norman Coleman, the DFLer-turned Republican mayor of St. Paul. Coleman had energized St. Paul's business community and had transformed the moribund capital into what seemed to be a city on the move. Traditional business/ wealthy individual support for the Republican party, which had dwindled during the cause era when religious conservatives were in ascendance, returned in force for the 1998 election. All three candidates for Republican endorsement agreed to abide by that endorsement, so that, after winning the endorsement, Coleman was unopposed by serious opponents in the primary.

The 1998 Election and Its Implications for the Republican and DFL Parties

The Republican and DFL parties faced the November 1998 elections with arguably the best candidates they could muster. Although a new Republican, Norm Coleman had excited his party and convinced Republicans they had a good chance to have their endorsed gubernatorial candidate prevail for the first time since 1978. Skip Humphrey was the best-known, and one of the best-liked, politicians in the state, the son of the founder of the DFL. He had not been endorsed, but he was still clearly of the DFL party, and his lack of endorsement was quickly forgotten in the general election.

Coleman finished second and Humphrey a distant third. Both ran technically sound campaigns. Coleman stressed his experience and success as St. Paul mayor and his promise to cut taxes; Humphrey spoke of his victory as attorney general against Big Tobacco and said that he, too, would cut taxes but that he would also "invest" in a few programs, particularly in early childhood education. The winner, Jesse Ventura, represented the Reform party on the ticket. Ventura made few promises. Voter commentary after the election seemed to indicate that Ventura's success was predicated on his image as an outsider, a nonpolitician who spoke honestly and was clearly not scripted and cautious, like the other two.

In the aftermath of Jesse Ventura's gubernatorial victory, there were many explanations offered. The most salient relative to this chapter asserted that the election was a repudiation of the two other major political parties, the Republicans and the DFL. Parties were seen to be "tools of the special interests," a phrase usually used, in the case of the Republicans, as a surrogate for right-wing and conservative groups and, in the case of the DFL, as a surrogate for labor unions, minorities, and gays. "Each party's endorsing convention has become an outpost of exotic and extreme politics," said the chair of the political science department at Carleton College.[19]

Although there was agreement on the problem relative to political parties—except among the "extremists" who allegedly controlled their activity—there was no agreement on what should be done about it. The extremist problem differed for the Republican and DFL parties. In the case of the Republicans, the selection of delegates had always been on a winner-take-all basis, but before the era of abortion politics and the involvement of religious fundamentalists it was common for Republican caucuses and local-level conventions to allocate proportional numbers of delegates informally to various competing candidates, thus rewarding party loyalists even though they had chosen to support the "wrong" candidate. By the mid- to late 1970s, however, such ecumenism was put aside. All Republican delegates had to meet strict issue-support criteria, and the task for candidates came to be convincing delegates that they were most committed to those same issues.

For a time, the DFL party thought it had a way to avoid the Republicans' winner-take-all problem. Responding to the national reforms of its party in the 1960s (reforms, by the way, often crafted by then Minnesota congressman and later Minneapolis mayor Don Fraser), the DFL used a proportional system for choosing delegates based on issues and candidates and enforced strict gender-balance rules, thus presenting the face of open-armed inclusion. The result, however, was eventual balkanization. DFL conventions became a left-wing idea bazaar where activists favoring this or that position would scramble to round up enough people so that their position would be "viable," that is, would have enough supporters to permit naming "their" delegate to the next-level convention. Candidates at each succeeding level saw as their only alternative supporting all the various ideas so as to obtain 60 percent of the delegates for endorsement. The DFL exacerbated its problem by officially balkanizing its governing state central committee—literally assigning seats to various interest groups.

The results of the 1998 gubernatorial election left Minnesota political activists in a muddle. Activists in the Republican and DFL parties had, for fifty years, participated in what seemed to them to be an open and honorable process. The process would begin with a completely open neighborhood meeting where people would discuss ideas, seek positions as delegates to their local, regional, and state conventions, and act as intermediaries, holding candidates who sought the party's support accountable to a unified body of beliefs. The election of 1998 made clear a painful reality: while the activists thought they were behaving in the best Minnesota moralist tradition, participating in an open process to ensure that capable, issue-centered candidates were elected to public office, the public had come to see the conduct of political activists as antithetical to Minnesota moralism, an attempt by a few to control the state's government. The Republican and DFL parties in Minnesota had crossed a line. The 1998 election made it obvious that the public no longer trusted them as intermediaries.

CAMPAIGN FINANCE

Beginning in 1974 Minnesota's legislatures have systematically reduced the importance of private and special-interest money in state politics. In the 1994 election for constitutional officers and members of the house, direct and indirect public funds accounted for 54 percent of the total campaign spending. In 1996 61 percent of the money spent on senate and house races in Minnesota was public money. Public funds combined with preprimary endorsements made the Minnesota of the late 1980s to the mid-1990s a place where money simply was not very important in state politics. Whether this situation will continue depends to a great degree on whether candidates for Minnesota's partisan elected offices are willing to abide by the current system. As of mid-1998, Minnesota led the nation in terms of the percentage of campaign expenditures paid for by public funds. Maine's legislature, however, had voted for total public funding beginning in 2000.[20]

Minnesota's campaign financing system uses tax check-offs and direct appropriations for funding. The system began with check-offs only, but appropriations were soon required because the percentage of Minnesotans willing to designate that some of their tax money be used for campaigns, even though the designation costs the taxpayer no more, had peaked at 27 percent in 1977, then dwindled to an estimated 9 percent in 1998.[21]

Public dollars are distributed to candidates who sign pledges to limit their campaign expenditures. In 1994 and 1996 combined there were a total of 721 legislative candidates with campaign committees registered with the state's Ethical Practices Board. The act of registering a committee signals that the candidate will at least try to raise some money and mount an effort to be elected. Of those 721, only 3, all in 1994, failed to participate in the public financing/expenditure limit system. Of those 3, only 1, an Independent candidate for the house running against a popular incumbent in Minneapolis, actually raised and spent more money than the expenditure limit would have allowed—about $50,000 as opposed to the $21,000 maximum in that year. Despite the spending, she was defeated, 54 percent to 46 percent.

The Popularity of the Campaign Financing System

There are three reasons why Minnesota's campaign financing system is used by virtually all candidates:

(1) Most important, the spending limit is sufficient to run a competitive race. The limit is adjusted upward each election, and it is calculated to make extra money available to those on the ballot for the first time and those who face a primary. Minnesota's 134 state house districts produced 4,000 to 15,000 voters each in 1998's general election, depending on that area's turnout. To woo those voters, candidates could spend between $24,083 (the base amount, for experienced candidates without primaries) and $31,791 (for first-time candidates with contested primaries). State senate limits are twice those in the house, since each senate district encompasses two house districts.

(2) The second reason the public funding scheme has been popular is that so much of the money a candidate spends is public money—in 1996, as indicated, the average candidate had 61 percent in public dollars. Two-thirds to three-fourths of that public money is received by candidates in a lump sum after the primary. A quarter to a third of the public money comes to candidates through a unique Minnesota refund program paid for through the state's general fund. Individual contributors who give $50 ($100 for a couple) to a candidate or political party simply send a receipt from the candidate or party to the state and receive a check in return for the full amount. Contributors can tap this system only once a year. Nonetheless, its original intent, to encourage small givers so as to reduce reliance on the traditional sources of money, has been admirably met. Every candidate seeking funds through the mail—and that's just about every candidate—makes prominent mention of the rebate program in his or her solicitation. A number of candidates are so adept at finding contributors who will "loan" them $50 or $100 until the state pays it back that their entire campaigns are paid for with public funds. Widespread contributions are further encouraged by the fact that Minnesota candidates who participate in the campaign-finance system are prohibited from accepting more than 20 percent of their spending limit from PACs, lobbyists, and large givers combined.

(3) Finally, public financing is popular among candidates because the penalty for nonparticipation is severe. If a candidate elects to, as the parlance would have it, "blow the limits," that is, to raise and spend more than the spending limits would allow, he or she is not eligible for any public money. All funds must be raised privately. That candidate's opponent, however, presuming he or she agreed to sign a spending limit agreement, not only is released from the spending limit but also is eligible for the state payments.

The Political Impact of Special-Interest Money

A primary reason for introducing public financing in Minnesota was to re-

Table 5: Minnesota State Campaign Spending and Public Subsidies, 1982–96

Year	Up for election	Campaign spending ($)	Public funds in campaigns ($)	Public funds as a % of total
1982	H, S, S-W .	10,229,000	1,577,000	15
1984	H	3,104,000	702,000	23
1986	H, S, S-W	11,359,000	2,390,000	21
1988	H	4,276,000	1,110,000	26
1990	H, S, S-W	17,674,000	4,427,000	25
1992[a]	H, S	9,587,000	4,803,000	50
1994	H, S-W	12,224,000	6,625,000	54
1996	H, S	10,353,000	6,335,000	61

Source: Annual Campaign Finance Reports, Minnesota Campaign Finance and Public Disclosure Board (formerly known as the Ethical Practices Board).

[a] 1992 was the first year of the campaign contribution rebate program for persons giving party units or candidates $50 ($100 for joint filers). In that year the state refunded $3.2 million but did not track whether the money went to candidates or to political parties or caucuses, called party units in Minnesota law. In 1994 the small giver program yielded $3.8 million, $2.6 million to campaigns and $1.2 million to party units. $4.5 million was returned in 1996, of which $2.4 million went directly to campaigns and $2.1 million to party units. We estimated that two-thirds of the 1992 contribution, or $2.2 million, was contributed directly to candidates and that amount was added to public funding for the year.

H = House, S = State Senate, S-W = Statewide Candidates

duce the impact of special-interest money. Has that happened? Table 5 shows the campaign spending for each election from 1982 through 1996, together with the amount of public funding and the growing percentage of that funding. As can be seen, direct public financing as a percentage of candidate spending has grown significantly if somewhat erratically.

In Minnesota in 1982, 85 percent of that year's campaign spending for state offices came from nonpublic funds. In 1996 39 percent of the total state-level campaign spending came from nonpublic funds. That does not prove a

Table 6: Total Contributions to Minnesota's Four Legislative Caucuses, 1990–96

Year	DFL House caucus	State Senate DFL campaign committee	House Republican campaign committee	Senate Republican election fund
1990	$218,382	$152,558	$467,894	$169,475
1992	$321,689	$203,342	$469,307	$278,121
1994	$577,265	$118,336	$1,129,559	$56,686
1996	$763,908	$501,878	$921,513	$556,201
Increase '90–'96 (%)	250	229	97	228

Source: Annual Campaign Finance Reports, Minnesota Campaign Finance and Public Disclosure Board (formerly known as the Ethical Practices Board).

diminution of the impact of special-interest money on the Minnesota legislature or on the state's elected constitutional officers. It does prove that there is less than half the opportunity for special interests to finance campaigns directly and through that vehicle to have an impact on policy. Minnesota legislatures have consciously decided to curb the flow of special-interest money and they have succeeded. And, as previously noted, in any one campaign no more than 20 percent of the spending limit may be contributed by the "usual suspects," PACs, lobbyists, and big givers.

Although the possible impact of special-interest money has been dramatically curbed for state races in Minnesota, there are other areas in the campaign financing system where control mechanisms do not exist. There are no limits on what may be given to "party units" under Minnesota law. A party unit may be a local, regional, or state party or a legislative caucus. Table 6 shows the rapid growth of contributions to legislative caucuses from 1990 through 1996. Clearly, PAC and lobbyist money, which used to go directly to candidates before the limitations on those contributions, is now filtered through the legislative caucus.

The fact that party units, like legislative caucuses, are receiving more and more special-interest money is often cited by reformers as an indication that Minnesota's campaign-finance system is not working well and that special interests are still "buying elections," though both sides of many controversial issues contribute to both caucuses. The decision on which candidates are helped with caucus funds rests with the caucus leadership; "earmarking" by the special interest, that is, attempting to designate which candidate should receive help from a particular contribution, is illegal. Thus, though party units are receiving increasing amounts of special-interest money, the money is combined so that the intent of the givers is blunted by the time a candidate receives the funds. Nevertheless, some special interests—trial lawyers, for example—give much more money to one caucus (the DFL) than to the other; concomitantly, tort reform advocates give much more to Republicans.

Independent expenditures are one of two categories of campaign spending created by federal court rulings, expenditures that, though being made during a campaign period, have been interpreted as not being subject to campaign-finance spending restrictions because they are seen to be expressions of free speech. Independent expenditures are defined as spending by individuals or groups during the campaign period which may address the issues involved in the campaign dialogue but which are not coordinated with a candidate. Independent expenditures are so named because they are supposed to be independent of any candidate. For state campaigns, the ratio of independent expenditures to total campaign expenditures has been relatively small, 4.6 percent in 1996. There are no limits on how much individuals can give to groups making independent expenditures, but Minnesota law is interpreted to prohibit corporate contributions for independent expenditures. Also, groups making independent expenditures are required to report those expenditures and the sources of their funds.

The other free-speech category defined by U.S. courts is called issue advocacy, defined as expenditures by individuals or groups which can be coordinated with candidates but which may not specifically urge the election or defeat of a candidate. There has been little if any use of issue-advocacy advertising in Minnesota. It is thought that issue-advocacy ads may be coordinated with candidates. It is also thought that Minnesota may not be able to prohibit corporations from participating in issue-advocacy ads.

There are two areas concerning candidates' raising and spending funds where special-interest money has not been curbed in Minnesota. One involves federal campaigns. Minnesota's members of Congress have to grub constantly for money just as members of Congress do all over the country. Minnesota received a distinction of sorts in the 1994 election. DFL candidate Bill Luther won the open Sixth Congressional District seat and became a Washington rarity: a 1994 Democratic freshman. Luther raised and spent $1.1 million in his campaign, one of only three freshmen in the nation to raise more than a million dollars in that election. The other area where special-interest participation in campaigns is not well curbed is in major local elections—mayors, city councils, county boards. Disclosure is required in nearly all such elections, and there are contribution limits, but PACs and lobbyists are not limited in the aggregate amounts they can give.

BEYOND THE TWO PARTIES IN MINNESOTA POLITICS

Since the state's founding, gubernatorial candidates have presented Minnesotans with thirty-seven different political parties. Of those, only seven have actually won, the Republicans and the Independent-Republicans (the Republican party's name from 1975 to 1995), the Democrats, the Farmer-Labor party and the merged Democratic-Farmer-Labor party, the Democratic-People's ticket (actually a fusion effort that elected John Lind governor in 1898), and now the Reform party. For most of the period since 1944, the year that the DFL was formed and became one of Minnesota's two major parties, "third" parties have not had a significant impact on electoral outcomes. There are exceptions, however. Third-party impact has grown recently, eventually resulting in a third-party gubernatorial victory in 1998.

The gubernatorial election of 1962 was so close—the eventual victor, Karl Rolvaag, had an official margin of 91 votes out of 1.2 million cast—that the 7,234 votes amassed by William Braatz on the Industrial Government party ticket can be said to have affected the outcome even though he polled a mere 0.006 percent of the vote. Braatz's total for the year was typical of third-party candidates through the 1940s, 1950s, and 1960s. Their combined gubernatorial tally was always less than 1 percent.

Nineteen seventy-four was different. Third parties garnered more than 5 percent of the vote, but Governor Wendell Anderson's victory was so one-sided that third-party votes could not be said to have materially impacted the eventual outcome.

After 1974 third parties generally continued a more robust presence on the Minnesota ballot. In the 1990 and 1994 elections third-party candidates tallied more than 3 percent of the gubernatorial votes cast. The Ross Perot–inspired Independent and then Reform party movements led to the most significant third-party showing in Minnesota for sixty years when Reform party candidate Dean Barkley garnered 7.6 percent of the vote in the 1996 U.S. Senate campaign. He had captured 5.4 percent in 1994. Barkley's 152,333 votes in 1996 was larger than the difference between the two major-party candidates, U.S. senator Paul Wellstone, the DFLer, and former senator Rudy Boschwitz, the Republican.

Obtaining more than 5 percent of the vote in an election became a major goal for the Reform party. Minnesota's campaign-finance law defined any party that received more than 5 percent in the last election as a "major" party and made it eligible to participate in public financing. In 1998 the Reform party candidate, Jesse Ventura, the former mayor of Brooklyn Park, Minnesota, but better known as professional wrestler Jesse "The Body" Ventura, would receive approximately $350,000 in public funds for his gubernatorial campaign because the Reform party had attracted more than 5 percent of the votes in 1996.

Lost in the publicity surrounding the 1998 election of a third-party candidate in Minnesota was the reality that another "third" party had qualified that year as a major party under the state's election law. Called the Taxpayers party, the group identified itself as a "Christian, conservative" party. The party's candidate for state auditor, Patricia Becker, garnered just 5 percent of the votes and received at least one vote in every county, thereby meeting the major-party qualifications. What long-term impact the fourth Minnesota party will have is unknown. According to the *Star Tribune*, Becker was a delegate to the state Republican convention in 1998 and then ran under the Taxpayers party label as a protest against the Republican endorsement of the state auditor, Judy Dutcher, who has a pro-choice position on abortion. The Taxpayers party chairman told the newspaper that the group was opposed to the use of public funds by political parties in elections. That would probably make it more difficult for the party to obtain 5 percent of the vote again— something that parties in Minnesota have to do every two years in order to retain their "major" designation. Another problem for the Taxpayers party: the only statewide election in 2000 is for the U.S. Senate seat held by Republican Rod Grams, whom most of the Taxpayers party's adherents support.[22]

THE FUSION DECISION

One of the small political parties operating in Minnesota and eleven other states, the New party, attempted unsuccessfully to change the rules concerning "fusion" candidates. Most states no longer permit candidates to be on the ballot as the candidate of more than one party. New York is an exception, and multiple ballot tracks are an accepted part of that state's political landscape. A liberal DFL state lawmaker, Rep. Andy Dawkins of St. Paul, agreed, in the 1994 election, to be the candidate of both the DFL and the Twin Cities New parties. The New party was self-described as progressive. Multiple ballot endorsements were clearly prohibited by Minnesota law, but since both parties and the candidate agreed to the endorsements, a test of the constitutionality of Minnesota's prohibition ensued. The New party lost at the federal district court level, won in the Eighth Circuit Court of Appeals, then lost in the U.S. Supreme Court. The Eighth Circuit worried that New party members had to choose between voting for candidates who couldn't win or not voting at all, whereas the Supreme Court agreed with the state's argument that fusion gave candidates the opportunity to associate themselves with popular catchphrases and causes, thus turning the ballot into a billboard.[23]

Minnesota has crafted an election system for its state-level candidates which features (1) the opportunity for political parties to endorse candidates, (2) the opportunity for those candidates to receive a majority of their funding from the taxpayers, and (3) as discussed more fully in chapter 4, the opportunity for the broadest possible participation in elections because of widespread use of same-day registration.

This combination of factors is what made the election of Reform party candidate Jesse Ventura possible in 1998. The public had turned against the endorsement contests in the Republican and DFL parties, and even though Ventura was endorsed by the Reform party, he was clearly seen as an outsider and not a professional politician. Because Ventura represented what is called, in Minnesota, a major party, he had access to approximately $350,000 in state funds with which to conduct his campaign. The Republican and DFL candidates received considerably more than Ventura, about $1.2 million, but the smaller amount of public money, combined with Ventura's outsider, celebrity appeal, proved to be enough to win the election. Finally, it was clear to election judges on 4 November 1998 that many of the 332,540 voters who registered that day—15.8 percent of the total voters—had come to the polls for the express purpose of voting for Ventura.

What the 1998 election will do to Minnesota's election system is open to question. Endorsement by the Republican and DFL parties, at the statewide level, will clearly no longer always be the goal of candidates seeking election, though it will probably continue to be of paramount importance at the legislative level. As for campaign financing, Minnesota devised a campaign-finance scheme based on the moralistic concept that the dialogue of political campaigns may and should be controlled by the community at large so that no particular interest is allowed to dominate that dialogue. But federal court rulings see financial participation in campaigns differently, not as a community dialogue but as an expression of free speech. Independent expenditures, especially political-party independent expenditures, are growing in importance in Minnesota political campaigns; issue-advocacy ads are still relatively uncommon.

Whether Minnesota will settle into a three-or even four-party normalcy is currently unknown. Immediately after the 1998 election the Reform party announced that it would arrange to manufacture and sell Jesse Ventura action figure dolls. The prototype of these dolls had been used with great effect in Ventura's election ads. The Reform party planned to use the proceeds from the dolls to begin to build a major-party infrastructure, identifying voters, hiring field workers, and so on. Eventually, the Reform party hoped to be able to field candidates in many legislative districts and to have a full slate for statewide office. Early indications did not bode well for the Reform party. In two Senate special elections held in early 1999, Reform party candidates ran third. Whether a new party can be created to be competitive with the Republicans and DFL across the entire political landscape, or whether the Reform party is simply a vehicle for well-known outsiders to provide Minnesota voters a credible "none of the above" option, is the major question facing Minnesota's party system.

CHAPTER 6

The State Legislature

The Minnesota legislature is a capable body. It has produced a myriad of innovative legislation, ranging from the nation's first antismoking law in the 1970s, to the first school-choice program in the 1980s, to comprehensive health-care reform in the 1990s. In a national study of state legislatures in the early 1970s the Minnesota legislature was ranked tenth;[1] in the 1990s the foremost scholar of state legislatures labeled it "strong and effective."[2] A recent analysis by the National Conference of State Legislatures placed the Minnesota legislature in the "hybrid," or middle, category of professionalization.[3] Neither an amateur, part-time body like those found in small, rural states nor a full-time, "congressionalized" body like those found in California or New York, the Minnesota legislature meets for a total of 120 days over a two-year period.

Yet Minnesotans are never satisfied that their legislature is good enough; indeed, the legislators themselves are never satisfied. In 1984 they appropriated $16,000 to the University of Minnesota's Humphrey Institute for a study of the legislature. Legislative leaders said the institution was "pretty good" but probably could be better.[4] This study resulted in a series of scholarly working papers and in Royce Hanson's definitive book *Tribune of the People*. At the time of the study various bills were introduced to reduce the size of the legislature (its 67-member senate is the nation's largest and its 134-member house is the nation's twelfth largest) and to make it a unicameral body. More than a decade later, in 1999, the unicameral option was once again on the legislative agenda. Minnesotans like to talk about tinkering with their government.

THE LEGISLATURE AT WORK

Since 1973 the Minnesota legislature has had flexible sessions in which the body meets for 120 days during each biennium. In practice, this means a long session during odd-numbered years and a short session during even-numbered years. The long session of approximately 90 days begins in early January and extends to roughly 22 May; the budget and major policy initiatives are considered. The short session of about 30 legislative days begins in late January or early February and extends to about Easter; the capital budget is adopted, and a few pressing policy matters are considered. Special sessions are called to deal with items deemed to need immediate action. The house holds minisessions in the fall of odd-numbered years, although these are just for informational purposes.

The Minnesota body is deluged with about six thousand bills per biennium, which places it among the more prolific state legislatures. Minnesota has coped with the flood of legislation by establishing certain deadlines. By the first deadline day a bill has to have cleared the relevant policy committees in the house of origin; by the second deadline the bill has to have cleared the relevant policy committees in the other house. Money bills are not subject to these deadlines but have their own later deadlines.

At the beginning of the session the pace is almost leisurely as the governor gives the state-of-the-state address, committees hold overview hearings, and bills are introduced. As the first deadline approaches, the pace intensifies: committees work more assiduously, interest groups lobby, and a few floor sessions are held. After the first deadline some ideas have died, and the remaining ones receive more serious attention; some bills are passed by one house and sent to the other. The bargaining begins in earnest over the budget—whether it is the operating budget or the capital budget—and over the tax bill and key policy initiatives. Eventually, activity shifts from the original committees, which have nothing left to consider, to the floor; sessions are held daily, and the maneuvering centers on the agenda and the time required for debate.

As bills are adopted by each house, conference committees are appointed to begin ironing out differences. Before 1993 conference committees would often have marathon sessions around the clock. Since then leaders in both the house and the senate have usually enforced midnight rules (that is, no meetings after midnight). Conference committees go on all day, however, fitted in around daily floor sessions, caucus meetings, and meetings of other conference committees. Leaders set a target for adjournment, and the frenzied race begins in which legislators, staff, and lobbyists work from eight or nine o'clock in the morning until midnight every day. Staff often work after midnight, processing the day's agreements into language so that work can continue the next morning. Usually, after a few false tries, the critical legislation is passed, and adjournment is reached by the deadline. Before the flexible sessions Minnesota leaders often would cover the clock in the legislative chamber in order to complete business. Recently, there have been a few examples of clock ignoring, but covering is no longer used. And though the covering could go on for hours and sometimes days, the clock ignoring usually extends sessions only fifteen minutes or so. It has happened just once in the past ten years.

RECRUITMENT

Minnesota is divided into sixty-seven senate districts, each having more than 60,000 people. Each senate district is further divided into two house districts, each of which has about 32,000 to 33,000 people. Therefore, the scale of campaigning for the legislature is still rather modest compared with a state such as California. Minnesotans can run for the legislature on shoe leather, expended by going door-to-door, and friends and neighbors form the campaign committees. Public financing made up 61 percent of the total campaign-related spending in 1996, so campaign finances are a relatively low barrier. Minnesota legislators are well paid, earning $29,675 in 1997 plus $56 per diem and a housing allowance during the session; this puts Minnesota thirteenth among the states in legislative pay. Both factors—salary and campaign costs—influence who is attracted to run for the legislature. Lower pay is less attractive than high pay, and higher campaign costs screen out women, minorities, and lower-income people disproportionately.

The trends in the composition of the Minnesota legislature have paralleled the trends in most states toward diversity in gender and occupation— there are more women, fewer attorneys, and more full-time legislators (that is, those with no outside occupation). At the same time, there is stability in membership from year to year as the electorate returns incumbents at a high rate. As in most states, concern is sometimes expressed about the caliber of members and whether the barriers to entry are too high for many candidates, especially women and minorities. More than most states, Minnesota has sought to "level the playing field" through providing public financing for legislative (and gubernatorial) campaigns. In 1994 99 percent of the legislative candidates accepted the spending limits and restrictions that go along with public financing.

The number of women in each legislative chamber has gradually increased, as shown in figures 4 and 5. In the house (figure 4) the numbers have generally gone up every year, though there were some exceptions. In the

Figure 4: Number of Women in the Minnesota House

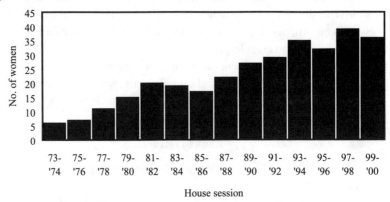

Source: Minnesota Legislative Reference Library, *Legislative Subject Notebooks: Legislators–Women.*

Figure 5: Number of Women in the Minnesota Senate

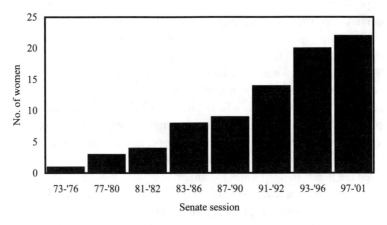

Source: Minnesota Legislative Reference Library, *Legislative Subject Notebooks: Legislators–Women.*

senate the numbers have gone up every year. By 1999 Minnesota had 36 women in the lower house and 22 in the upper house, amounting to 29 percent overall. Women have served in significant party leadership positions: Connie Levi (*R*) and Ann Wynia (*D*) served as majority leaders and Dee Long (*D*) as Speaker of the house. The record on minorities is worse. Only an occasional member of a minority group has served in the Minnesota legislature: in 1997, for example, there were two Hispanics, one African American, one Asian American (the first ever), and no American Indians serving in

St. Paul. Minorities thus made up 3 percent of the Minnesota legislature, compared with 5.9 percent in the state's population.

The transition away from an attorney-dominated body began with the shift from biennial sessions to annual sessions in 1972. As table 7 shows, the number of lawyers who served in the house in 1971 was 32; by 1981 the number was down to 9, though later it rose again. In the senate (table 8) there were 22 attorneys in 1971–72; in 1973 the number dropped to 13 and has remained at that level ever since. This diminution in legal talent occurred in most states because lawyers could no longer afford to be away from their practices. For a variety of reasons, the legal career has changed so that it is less compatible with full-time public service. The composition of the lawyer corps in the legislature has also changed since 1971. One-fourth of the lawyers in the lower house in 1995 worked at public sector jobs rather than in private practice. Another 15 percent were listed as attorneys, but their sole job was legislator. Interestingly, the number of Minnesota farmers shrank, but the number of farmers is still more than in the average state legislature. The number of businesspersons has fluctuated, but often they are the largest group, as is true in most states. The number of educators is higher than in most states. Educators are numerous because teachers and professors can arrange leaves from their jobs and because the state's teachers' unions have long encouraged their members to seek legislative seats.

Tables 7 and 8 also show how the number of full-time legislators has changed over the years, gradually creeping up and settling at fifteen in the house and seven in the senate in 1999. The presence of full-time legislators is generally thought to be an indicator of the professionalization of the legislature, the movement from a part-time citizen body to a full-time professional body. Minnesota has resisted this trend more than some states; it is about average in the percentage of full-time legislators. The statistics on this category are somewhat suspect, however, as members are loath to report that they have no other occupation. Minnesota has a number of legislator-consultants who would be hard-pressed to describe their last consulting assignment. The reluctance of legislators to admit to full-time status may be seen as a tribute to Minnesota's work ethic and the fear government officials have of being perceived as full-time politicians.

In Minnesota, as in many states, the ease with which incumbents are reelected has led some people to advocate term limits. Twenty-one states have enacted this reform since 1990, but in all but one case it was done through the initiative, a process not available in Minnesota. Therefore, it seems unlikely that Minnesota will enact term limits, although the concern will still be voiced.

Table 7: Occupations of House Members

Session	Attorney	Legislator	Educator	Farmer	Business	Other
1971	32	0	17	35	37	20
1973	25	0	16	31	30	32
1975	19	4	24	24	33	30
1977	11	3	25	18	34	43
1979	12	1	21	21	37	42
1981	9	0	21	23	43	38
1983	11	11	28	25	39	20
1985	11	11	19	23	50	20
1987	12	14	21	27	42	18
1989	16	19	20	23	36	20
1991	17	22	15	19	35	26
1993	16	17	20	16	34	11
1995	18	19	20	14	36	27
1997	17	18	22	11	39	27
1999	15	15	22	8	41	33

Sources: Data from 1971 to 1987 come from Royce Hanson, *Tribune of the People* (Minneapolis: University of Minnesota Press, 1989), p. 54. Data for 1989 to 1999 have been compiled from the *Minnesota Legislative Manual,* supplemented with unpublished data compiled by Sarah Janecek.
Note: There may be some discrepancies between the data sources for various reasons. For example, legislators often list more than one occupation in their biographies.

Table 8: Occupations of Senate Members

Session	Attorney	Legislator	Educator	Farmer	Business	Other
1971	22	0	6	12	24	3
1973	13	0	8	13	29	4
1977	12	0	8	13	24	10
1981	12	0	9	18	12	16
1983	11	1	8	17	14	16
1987	10	4	9	14	19	11
1991	11	10	7	14	19	6
1993	13	9	8	10	21	6
1997	14	7	8	9	21	8

Sources: Data from 1971 to 1987 come from Royce Hanson, *Tribune of the People* (Minneapolis: University of Minnesota Press, 1989), p. 54. Data for 1991 to 1997 have been compiled from the *Minnesota Legislative Manual.*
Note: There may be some discrepancies between the data sources for various reasons. For example, legislators often list more than one occupation in their biographies.

As in most states, a high percentage of Minnesota incumbents choose to run again, and of those, a high proportion are reelected. Since 1972 about 85 percent of members of the house have chosen to run again, on average; on average, 77 percent of all races were won by incumbents. Normally, the re-election rate goes down the next election after reapportionment, as some incumbents choose not to run in unfamiliar territory and others who do run are not welcomed by their new constituents.

In the senate about 78 percent of members chose to run again over this time period; on average, 71 percent of all races were won by incumbents. Thus, the senate is a bit more volatile than the house. One reason might be that the quality of challengers is higher in senate races than in house races. Former house members often challenge senators, for example. For the 1996 elections, the number of house members who filed for reelection was 86 percent, about the same as the historical average. In the senate in 1996, 90 percent of the incumbents filed for reelection, considerably higher than the 78 percent average. In both houses the proportion of elections won by incumbents was higher than usual, 82 percent in the lower house and 87 percent in the upper house.

We can also look at legislative turnover, the problem the institution of term limits is intended to solve. In general, turnover has declined over time in both houses and has been slightly lower in the senate than in the house. The only exception to this rule is that in the year immediately following reapportionment, turnover is greater. In the period 1972 to 1998, 18 percent of senate seats turned over, and an average of 25 percent of house seats turned over. How would term limits affect this rate of turnover? According to a recent study by the Citizens League, these rates of turnover are *higher* than could be expected if the state had a mandatory limit of, say, ten years.[5] Such a result is common in states of low to medium levels of professionalization, as they have natural rates of turnover higher than would be imposed by statute.

Along with this degree of stability in membership, the legislature has exhibited stability in party control in the modern era. It has been controlled by the DFL most of the time, whereas in earlier times it was dominated by rural conservatives. From 1914 to 1973 the legislature was officially nonpartisan, though the liberals and conservatives each organized a caucus. In the senate, the mostly Republican conservative caucus consistently held the majority of seats; in the house, conservatives dominated except during the governorships of Floyd Olson and Orville Freeman. The reapportionment revolution that began in the mid-1960s, plus the switch to party labels on the ballot and

Figure 6: Party Control of the Minnesota House

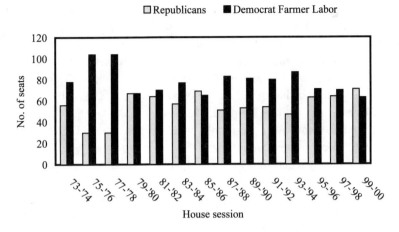

Source: Minnesota Legislative Reference Library, *Legislative Subject Notebooks–Caucus Statistics*.
Note: Figures are for the first day of the legislative term.

Figure 7: Party Control of the Minnesota Senate

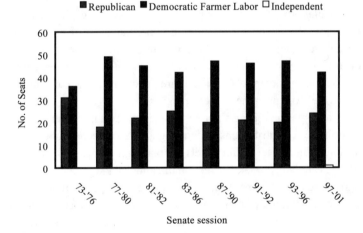

Source: Minnesota Legislative Reference Library, *Legislative Subject Notebooks–Caucus Statistics*.
Note: Figures are for the first day of the legislative term.

the Watergate fallout of the early 1970s, brought the DFL faction to power in both houses.

Figures 6 and 7 show the partisan divisions in the house and senate since 1973. As indicated, the DFLers have controlled the Minnesota senate each session, often by a wide margin. But in the house the Republicans and Democrats were tied once (in the session beginning in 1979), and the Republicans held the majority in 1985–86 and again in 1999–2000. The party division was also close at other times. Thus, the Republicans have always held relatively more power in the house than in the senate. Still, the overwhelming DFL advantage in the legislature in modern times is what has given the state its Democratic and liberal image. This is despite the fact that, since 1974, Republicans have won three-fourths of the elections for the U.S. Senate and half the elections for governor.

Periodically, concern is expressed that the legislature does not contain a broad cross-section of citizens; it underrepresents women, persons of color, blue-collar workers, low-income people, and so forth. The Republican party feels underrepresented as well. Recently, the problem of representation was studied by the Citizens League; its 1992 report *Reform the Election Process, Restore the Public Trust* discussed the major barriers to running for office in Minnesota.[6] It noted that incumbents have advantages in fundraising and staff support that their opponents don't have, which scares away challengers. Moreover, campaigning and serving is very time-consuming and poses a particular problem for single parents and those who can't take leave from their jobs. Parents of young children living hundreds of miles away from St. Paul are reluctant to run for the legislature. Being a stockbroker or a partner in a major law firm has become nearly incompatible with a legislative career. Finally, some potential candidates are put off by the fact that single-issue groups are more prominent in campaigns.

Partially in response, the legislature in 1993 imposed a limit on PAC, lobbyist, and big giver contributions to campaigns at 20 percent of the candidate's spending limit. The ceiling levels the playing field, as both new and old candidates are likely to take the maximum allowed PAC money. All four of the legislative caucuses insist that, given the level of public funding and the spread of PAC money, their candidates have little difficulty raising enough money to wage a decent campaign, as long as the district is reasonably competitive politically. Although the financial barriers have been addressed, the staff advantage incumbents possess and the presence of single-issue groups in campaigns continue.

The difficult and time-consuming nature of campaigning is also a continuing reality. The norm for legislative candidates seeking office in Minnesota is to "door knock" the entire district personally, going house to house or farm to farm and chatting with constituents. Savvy incumbents and hungry challengers typically begin door-knocking in late June or early July of election years and devote about four hours a day, seven days a week, to the activity. A handful of incumbents actually door-knock their districts in the off-election years, just to keep in touch with constituents. Running for a competitive legislative seat in Minnesota is a full-time job during July through November of an election year. Once the seat is won, legislative service is a full-time job during the period the legislature is in session, five months in odd-numbered years after the election and three months in even-numbered years. Legislative service is not a responsibility to be taken lightly.

One person who looks forward to the rigors of the campaign season is DFL representative Henry Kalis. Before the filing date in the summer of 1998, as he has done thirteen times before, Representative Kalis slept on the marble floor outside the secretary of state's office so he could be the first candidate to file for office. Kalis says his act is a symbol of what a privilege it is to serve in the legislature.

THE POLITICAL PARTY AND ITS LEADERSHIP IN THE LEGISLATURE

The principal organizational features of American legislatures are the party system and the committee system. The Minnesota legislature is no exception. Although many Minnesotans will tell you that political parties are in decline in Minnesota, actually the party in the legislature is strong, at least as compared with other states. A recent study by Malcolm Jewell and Marcia Whicker examined ten state legislatures with respect to several dimensions of partisan strength, cohesion, and leadership.[7] On their combined scale, Ohio scored highest, followed by Wisconsin; then came Minnesota and Connecticut. These scholars argued that leaders in the Minnesota legislature had significant ability to influence public policy, through both party cohesion and their leadership tools. Because the two chambers operate somewhat differently, we discuss them separately.

The House Party System

The caucus is the basic organizational unit of the party in the legislature; the caucus simply is the members identified with the DFL party or with the Republican party in the house or senate. Thus, there are four distinct party caucuses.

In the house the caucus decides how to vote on pending bills in its caucus meetings; the parties decide on their nominees for house leadership positions in caucus meetings; and caucus meetings are used for the discipline of way-ward members. The caucus position is not necessarily the same as the party platform, adopted in the state convention. The caucus position is usually more centrist than the respective party platforms. Each party caucus has its own staff, whose members conduct research, perform constituent casework, and offer media services, all so that their caucus legislators can get reelected.

Voting with the caucus is generally expected on all procedural matters, on rules, on organization of the house, and sometimes on substantive policy matters.[8] But it is understood that members will occasionally depart from the caucus position because of their district or their personal convictions. Party caucuses meet frequently, even daily during the busiest part of the session.

Discipline within the caucuses varies by party and over time. Generally speaking, the Republican party has exhibited more discipline, because it has usually been the minority party. Once caucus positions were defined, Re-publican members tended to stick to them. As in other legislatures, the over-whelming percentage of roll-call votes in Minnesota are nearly or actually unanimous. Caucuses talk about and take positions on the few, but impor-tant, tough political issues. Generally, the Republican caucus, when in the minority, offered alternatives, which it knew would not pass. The caucus al-ternative to the DFL program was offered to make "talking points" for Re-publican candidates at the next election. In this context, cohesion was rela-tively simple to put together and maintain because there were few consequences.

The DFL caucus has, with three exceptions, been the majority party in modern times, often by a wide margin. Thus, it has been hard to enforce dis-cipline within its ranks because discipline wasn't needed. Whatever the caucus was doing could actually become law. DFL legislators often felt they didn't have the luxury of "talking points." Further complicating matters for the DFL caucus is the clear demarcation between the liberals, generally coin-ciding with the urban delegation, and the conservatives, roughly coinciding with the outstate representatives. This split made it difficult to enforce disci-pline across the range of issues on which the party caucus took stands. Re-publican caucuses were usually more ideologically homogeneous than DFL caucuses.

The ability to form a cohesive party caucus also varies according to who is the party leader. David Jennings, who was Speaker during the Republi-cans' sole period of majority control in the 1980s, was effective in holding his ranks together. Partly because Republicans were new to majority status and partly because of his forceful personality, Jennings exerted control over his troops. Among modern DFL Speakers, Martin Sabo, now a U.S. congressman, is remembered as a model Speaker who held the respect of partisans and opponents alike. Sabo had a more relaxed style than Jennings and commanded his caucus through respect and being interested in producing legislation. Other DFL Speakers have had less success in knitting together diverse elements of the party and have seen some of their members desert the caucus position from time to time.

Important among the Speaker's powers is the right to appoint committee chairs and members. Historically, the Speaker has exercised his or her discretion in making appointments, though seniority is an important norm, as are geographical and ideological balance on the committee. Still, these are only general guiding principles, and Speakers frequently ignore them when putting together the committees. Through this power, which was not shared with anyone else, as it is in the senate, the Speaker was able to command personal loyalty from committee chairs. In 1997 Speaker Phil Carruthers chose to share his appointive power with a committee on committees. In 1999 Speaker Steve Sviggum returned to the previous practice. The Speaker and his or her committee also appoint members of conference committees.

Another power is the right of the Speaker to preside over house sessions. At one time this power in Minnesota was more important than it is today because Speakers could choose not to recognize certain members, thus better controlling the flow of the debate in their favor. Today it is expected that any member who wishes to speak on the floor may do so, though the Speaker still has the ability to make obstreperous members wait. More important is the Speaker's ability to rule on parliamentary points of order, particularly the question of germaneness, which comes up often and can be a key factor in whether the minority can force embarrassing votes on the majority. While the Speaker presides, the majority leader acts as the field general of the majority caucus, making necessary motions and supervising the presentation of the majority's position.

A third power is the authority of the Speaker to appoint key personnel and to assign office space and facilities. These perks again reinforce the loyalty of staff and members to the Speaker. A fourth power is the authority to set the agenda. The Speaker assigns bills to committees; through the majority leader's control of the Rules and Legislative Administration Committee, the Speaker controls the floor agenda; and the Speaker coordinates the conference committees and the budget deliberations. He or she is in a key position to shape the agenda and thus the outcome of the legislative process. When these formal powers are used in concert with political acumen, the Speaker can lead his or her party effectively.

One of the most interesting tests of the party system came in 1978 when an equal number of DFLers and Republicans were elected to the house; recall that the membership of 134 allows for the possibility of an evenly divided membership. For two months, the house was not organized; the two party caucuses, led by Irv Anderson (DFL) and Rod Searle (Republican), negotiated over how to share power. The outcome was that Searle got to be Speaker in 1979, but the DFL got three of the four important committee chairmanships—Rules, Taxes, and Appropriations. This arrangement lasted only one year. The Minnesota Supreme Court convicted a Republican member of election fraud; the DFL caucus then unseated him on a straight party-line vote (the Republican being unable to vote on his own case); then, in a special election, he was replaced by a DFLer, giving the DFL the majority again in the 1980 session.[9]

The Speakership has exercised a powerful magnetic attraction for many members of the house—none more than a recent Speaker, Representative Irv Anderson. First elected in 1964, Anderson had been Martin Sabo's majority leader, and when Sabo was elected to Congress in 1978, Anderson fully expected to become Speaker. But former governor Wendell Anderson's self-appointment to the U.S. Senate in 1977 soured voters on Democrats, and the year of the tie kept Anderson from his goal. When the Democrats took control in 1980, Anderson was thwarted again when an urban Democrat, backed by a bipartisan coalition, was elected Speaker. Another Democrat was chosen Speaker in 1981. In 1982 Anderson was defeated in a primary, then lost to the same man in 1984 and 1986. Finally, in 1990, Anderson prevailed with the electorate and returned to the house. After Speaker Dee Long was forced to resign her position in 1993, Anderson finally achieved a goal he admitted harboring since the first day he arrived at the legislature thirty years before. He was reelected Speaker in 1995, but his triumph was short-lived because he was toppled by party rival Carruthers after the 1996 elections.

The Senate Party System

Like the U.S. Senate, the Minnesota senate is more of a club than "the lower body"; it is more sedate than the house, more formal in decorum, smaller in size, and more stable in composition owing to the four-year term and lower turnover. Although historically controlled by the Republicans, since 1973 the senate has been comfortably controlled by the DFL and since 1981 has been led by the same majority leader, Roger Moe. As a result of these factors, partisanship in the senate is less important than in the house; senators act more as individuals than as partisans. Members of the minority party have more impact than in the house. By the same token, the senate majority leader has less formal power than the Speaker of the house. He is "first among equals" but shares power with others in the leadership group.

The senate majority leader does not appoint committee chairs directly; rather, such appointments are made by the Rules and Administration Committee, which the majority leader influences but does not control. Thus, committees behave more autonomously in the senate than they do in the house. Another key difference is that the majority leader does not preside over the senate; there is a separate presiding officer, the president of the senate, who is chosen by the steering committee of the majority caucus. Usually, the president is among the most senior members of the senate. He generally presides in a less partisan manner than does the Speaker of the house and is not as much an agent of the majority party.

One of the majority leader's significant formal powers is to chair the Rules Committee, which structures the agenda for the floor. (In fact, at the capitol there is no parking space designated for the majority leader, only for the chair of the Rules Committee.) For most majority leaders, the formal powers inherent in the position have been less important than the person's informal powers, such as his ability to build consensus within the party caucus, his leadership on the floor, and his gaining the respect of members of both political parties. The present majority leader, Roger Moe, is a master of these traits and has gradually built up considerable legislative clout beyond his formal powers. His longevity alone—1981 to 1999—is testament to his skills.

The portrait of the senate as having muted partisanship must necessarily be tentative. The senate has been governed by the DFL since 1973 and has had only two majority leaders in that quarter century. Thus, what we may be describing is the "DFL senate" or the "Roger Moe senate," one that might have evolved differently if the Republicans had been more dominant or if the DFLers had been more factionalized.

THE COMMITTEE SYSTEM

In most state legislatures, where party is important (often in competitive states), committees are less important; where party is unimportant (in one-party states), committees are key. But political scientist Wayne Francis determined that Minnesota is among those states that are the exception to this rule. Here party leadership, the party caucus, and committees are judged equally important both in the house and in the senate.[10] Thus, power in the Minnesota legislature is dispersed among several centers.

Committees in the Minnesota House

As in most state legislative chambers, the committee structure has evolved in the Minnesota house. In the 1950s there were committees on Temperance and Liquor Control, State and County Fairs, and Dairy Products and Livestock; in the 1990s there were committees on International Trade and Economic Development, Environment and Natural Resources, and the Gambling Division of Governmental Operations. Until 1992 the traditional division of authorization and appropriations committees was maintained, but then the responsibilities were fused so that now there is a finance division of the parent substantive committee.

When this change was made, however, most of the chairs of the key divisions of the Appropriations Committee had considerably more clout than the chairs of the substantive committees under which they were supposed to toil. Enormous power struggles broke out. As a result, the relationship between the finance division and the "parent" committee varies from case to case and depends on negotiations between committee chairs and the Speaker, which are revisited every year. For example, some finance divisions have the authority to receive bills from the full committee, attach the necessary money, and then send the bills directly to the floor or to another committee without returning through the parent. In other cases, the parent committee reviews all the work of the finance division before sending it on.

One result of the new fused system was the elimination of the Appropriations Committee, considered, with the Tax Committee, one of the two most powerful. A new Ways and Means Committee attempts to coordinate what is passed in the various finance divisions, but so far Ways and Means does not redo the work of the finance divisions, as the old Appropriations Committee could do with its various divisions. In 1999 the house had sixteen policy committees and ten budget divisions. Each member serves on three or four committees.

As mentioned above, the Speaker traditionally had considerable authority over committees; he or she sets the number of standing committees and their areas of responsibility. But the 1997 Speaker was an exception; he relied on a committee to name the chairs, vice-chairs, and members of each committee, after considering requests from each member concerning his or her preferences. Minority members' requests for assignment go through the minority leader, though the Speaker is not required to (and does not) always honor what the minority wants in terms of committee assignments. Committees are balanced with respect to party (generally but not always reflecting the party breakdown in the chamber) and geography. Seniority is an important norm for committee-chair appointment. In 1995, with the proliferation of finance divisions, almost every majority party member with ten years of service got to be chair of a committee or a division—but it is not an absolute. Unlike the case in the U.S. Congress, seniority accrued within a specific committee is less important than seniority in the chamber. In Minnesota it is not uncommon for a legislator to be appointed to chair a committee that he or she hasn't served on.[11]

The real work of the house takes place in its committees, where bills are dissected and amendments are added. Committee chairs have great importance. An unfriendly chair can keep a bill off the agenda; a friendly chair can expedite a bill. Chairs have a largely free hand in running the committee, though an open and regular process must be observed in today's committees. Each committee has a regular meeting time and place; agendas are published in advance; all meetings are open to the public; and copies of the bills are available. The chief author of the bill testifies before the committee, as do the opponents and any other interested parties.

Committees in the Minnesota Senate

Ideally, both chambers would use the same committee structure, but that would be too easy. In fact, in 1999 the senate had thirteen policy committees, as compared with the house's sixteen, plus ten budget divisions and four tax and finance committees. For example, the house has a Capital Investment Committee; this is not found in the senate. The senate has some committees not found in the house: for example, Children, Families, and Learning. Thus, anyone shepherding a bill through the legislature must learn two different committee systems.

As in most legislatures, the most powerful committees are the Tax and the Finance committees. Their chairs are among the most powerful senators and are heavily involved in budget negotiations and in all substantive policies that have financial implications. They usually work closely with the majority leader, and together they run the senate's business. The senate's Finance Committee had always been analogous to the house's Appropriations Committee. Like the house, the senate in 1992 adopted a system that fused policy and financial committees. Like the house, the relationship between the finance division and the "parent" committee varies according to circumstance. Unlike the house, the senate kept its Finance Committee until 1997, when it was divided into several finance committees.

In many respects the senate committee system operates like the system in the house, but there are a few key differences. Committees tend to be less partisan in their operation in the senate than in the house; minority senators can and do make important substantive contributions. Senators serve longer terms than house members and have less frequent turnover; thus, they have an opportunity to develop expertise in various policy areas. Some believe that the senate also has a longer time horizon, acting as a "cooling chamber" for the more quick-to-act house. One practical application of the difference between the senate and the house is that lobbyists often ask minority senators to carry their legislation. If the minority member happens to be well versed in a particular field, his or her advocacy can be just as effective as that of a majority member. In the house it is less typical that a member of the minority is asked to carry a bill someone actually wants to pass.

Committees in Operation

Committees used to be more important in Minnesota. If a bill failed in committee, it was dead. In the last few years failure in committee has often done nothing more than signal that the bill's proponent needs to find a new committee home for his or her idea. For example, a proposal that the state purchase drugs for senior citizens was defeated in committee two years in a row but reemerged in another committee's conference report. Generally, in the past, if a controversial bill passed through committee and to the floor, members of the majority and particularly majority members of the committee that worked on the bill were expected to support the committee's product, regardless of their own beliefs. That norm has been changing rapidly, however, and it is common to see members of the majority party attempting to amend bills on the floor which have been crafted by the majority's own committees.

Minnesotans have unusual access to their legislature's deliberations; in fact, Minnesota ranks first in a study of legislatures' public information strategies.[12] In each body there is a weekly newsletter during the session, distributed free to anyone who subscribes; a telephone hotline describing daily committee agendas; and beginning in 1996, access to committee schedules, bills, and so on via the World Wide Web. There is a computerized bill tracking system, which anyone can access via the Internet. Since 1995 floor ses-

sions and some committee meetings have been carried live on cable television. Beginning in 1996, floor sessions and an expanded schedule of committee meetings were moved from cable to an over-the-air television station.
Thus, anyone interested can find out what is happening in the legislature.

Committee operation is greatly facilitated by the extensive complement
of legislative staff, numbering 652 in 1997, plus about 200 session-only employees.[13] Each senator has a secretary; in the house members usually share a
secretary. The permanent staff is of two types: nonpartisan and partisan. The
nonpartisan complement includes attorneys, fiscal analysts, researchers, li-
brarians, media and public education people, and those performing administrative functions such as payroll, clerical, and auditing. The partisan staff,
on the other hand, is selected by party leadership or committee chairs. It includes committee administrators, secretaries, researchers, and those in media and constituent services. In total, the Minnesota legislature has a formidable policy analytic capacity: a recent study classified 179 of the staff as
doing policy analysis or research, nearly one researcher per member.[14]

The Conference Committee

No discussion of the committee system would be complete without mention
of the conference committee. The conference committee, made up of equal
numbers of members from each house, is the formal mechanism used to re-
solve differences in the language of bills on the same topic produced in different chambers. Much of the time, identical bills pass the two bodies and
are sent to the governor. Often, however, different versions of the bill are
passed. If the differences are minor and the authors can agree, one house accepts what the other has done, and the bill then goes to the governor. For controversial or complex legislation, substantial differences between the house
and senate versions are almost always present as the bills pass their respective chambers. When that happens, the house that acted first, on notification
that the other body had passed something different, formally "refuses to
concur," and a conference committee is formed.

The Speaker in the house and the Rules and Administration Committee in
the senate appoint conferees, typically three or five members from each side,
to arrive at a mutually acceptable bill. The conferees are normally the chair
and senior members of the relevant committee, the author of the bill, and
others deemed to have expertise on the matter. Though members of the minority serve on conference committees, a disproportionate number of conferees are members of the majority caucus.[15] Appointment to a conference

committee is a mark of distinction and an opportunity for influence for individual members; thus, such service is highly prized.

It is thought that Minnesota makes heavier use of conference committees than other states and that such committees have broader latitude in Minnesota.[16] Certainly our research demonstrates that Minnesota makes substantial use of this device, and usage has increased over time. In the 1960s the number of confereed bills averaged 47 per session; in the 1970s the average jumped to 112 per session, and in the 1980s it jumped again to 141 per session. In the 1990s the average diminished a bit to 130 per session. Almost all major legislation is produced through the conference-committee process; thus, oftentimes what happens in conference is more important than what happens in either body.

The biggest criticism of conference committees in Minnesota has centered on their willingness to wander far afield from their house's position as expressed in the bill. In the early 1980s conference committees became virtually de novo legislative chambers, inserting items regardless of whether they were germane to a bill's subject and whether they had been heard or passed anywhere in the legislative process. Indeed, some provisions were inserted in conference committee reports which had been defeated by both houses, either in committee or on the floor. Conference-committee reports became magnets for controversial proposals that couldn't stand on their own, because a conference-committee report cannot be amended or changed in any way. At that point in the process, it's take it or leave it.

The product of these freer times came to be called "garbage bills" and were subjected to severe criticism. For example, an analysis of the 1985 omnibus appropriations act found that only one-third of the 323 sections was actually related to appropriations.[17] The result of this logrolling was deemed to be a perversion of the democratic process. Since then both houses of the legislature have tried to adhere to the Joint Rules, which specify that nothing may be added to conference-committee reports which has not been approved by one or the other house. Controversy concerning legislative overreach has not ended with the virtual elimination of proposals never passed by either chamber, however. In 1998 a Ramsey County district judge and later the Court of Appeals declared a 1997 law unconstitutional because it failed to meet the constitutional requirement that all laws deal with a "single subject." If the Minnesota Supreme Court uses the case to attempt a definition of the single-subject rule in the state's constitution, and that definition is more restrictive than has been used by legislators in recent years, it could become more difficult to add provisions seemingly unrelated to their parent proposal.[18]

Outside evaluators have generally placed the Minnesota legislature among the top group of state legislatures. Minnesota residents over the years have rated the legislature in public opinion polls. From the 1940s to the 1970s a little over a quarter of the respondents called the Minnesota legislature good to excellent (various polls of the *Minneapolis Tribune*). The *Star Tribune*, successor to the *Minneapolis Tribune*, no longer does polls on general satisfaction with the legislature. In the Hanson study, *Tribune of the People*, legislators themselves "ranked their workplace, like all the children in Minnesota's mythical Lake Wobegon, as somewhat better than average, but far short of excellent."[19]

Among the problems facing the legislature, the Hanson study stressed the need for a competent minority, especially in the house of representatives. Another problem is leadership style. In 1996 the house was confronted with a revolt led by female legislators against the alleged autocratic style of its Speaker, Irv Anderson. This revolt demonstrates the tension in legislatures around the country between a command leadership style identified with men and a more consensus-based approach associated with women. As Jewell and Whicker assert in their study of legislative leadership, "Today's legislators want to participate actively in the decision-making process, in committee, in caucus, and on the floor. They want to bargain and negotiate, to mobilize support for their legislative proposals, rather than simply following instructions from the leadership. They are likely to react negatively to leadership pressures or to a strategy of rewards and punishments."[20] Minnesota legislators, especially its women, are no different. They replaced Anderson with someone more committed to sharing power and reaching consensus.

Overall, the 1990s has been a decade of diminished reputation for the Minnesota legislature, especially the house, as its members got in trouble for unauthorized phone use, drunk driving, shoplifting, and spouse abuse. Even the respected leader of the senate, Roger Moe, was subjected to a staffer's accusation that he made her do political work on state time; he was ultimately cleared of the charges. In 1997 the legislature was the subject of an unflattering portrait in a national magazine; the story was entitled "The Sick Legislature Syndrome and How to Avoid It."[21] Its thesis was that professionalism and partisanship are the root of all evil. In the face of both national and local criticism, the legislature has attempted to "reinvent" itself. As noted, in 1994 it strengthened its already strict ethics laws. In the 1997–98 session, leaders of the two parties managed to set and maintain a tone of bipartisan civility unmatched in recent years. Welfare reform in the post-AFDC era was swiftly accomplished on a bipartisan basis, for example.

In 1999 lawmakers entered the uncharted territory of triparty government, with the DFL still controlling the senate, the Republicans taking over the house, and Reform party newcomer Jesse Ventura occupying the governorship. During the campaign when Ventura, the former wrestler now clad in size-fifty suits, was asked how he would work with the two chambers, he would flex his enormous biceps and growl, "I'll show 'em these."

Early on, Ventura was expected to side with the Republicans on limiting the size of government and giving all of the budget surplus back to the taxpayers. He was also expected to side with the Democrats in opposing abortion restrictions. The latter expectation was realized; the former was not. The end result was a legislative session seen as generally very positive by most Minnesotans. A good economy generated massive budget surpluses, and money began rolling in from the tobacco trial settlement (see chapter 8). Ventura, despite early protestations that he would not "make deals," brokered compromises that satisfied all sides except those favoring abortion restrictions. Rebates and tax cuts returned $2.9 billion to taxpayers; general spending was allowed to increase modestly. Despite Ventura's continued use of macho rhetoric vis-à-vis the legislature, the first tripartisan legislative session in Minnesota's history ended with remarkable amity.

CHAPTER 7

Minnesota's Governors and
the Executive Branch

Orville Freeman served as Minnesota's governor from 1955 until 1960, when voters rejected his third reelection bid. But Freeman didn't go long without an executive job. President-elect John F. Kennedy asked Freeman, who had nominated Kennedy at the 1960 Democratic convention, to be his secretary of agriculture. It was an exhilarating time for Freeman. He was arguably the most influential secretary of agriculture in the nation's history. Freeman served as secretary for eight years, governor for six; yet today he will admit readily that, if he could have had only one of the two jobs, governor of Minnesota would be the one he would choose: "When you're in the cabinet, you have to be a team player, you have to dance to the president's tune. When you're governor, you make the music."[1] This chapter is primarily about the music makers of Minnesota's political life, the governors. We begin, however, by discussing briefly the other state officials elected by all the people.

THE CONSTITUTIONAL OFFICERS

Minnesota has six elected executive-branch officers: governor, lieutenant governor, attorney general, auditor, secretary of state, and treasurer. All were enumerated in the state's first constitution, but the duties and responsibilities are generally set statutorily.

Until 1972 Minnesota's lieutenant governors were elected separately from the governor and had the task of presiding over the senate. A constitutional amendment passed that year allows governors and lieutenant governors to run together on the same ticket. What a lieutenant governor gets to do (or not do) depends almost entirely on the governor with whom she serves (from 1983 to at least 2002, Minnesota lieutenant governors have been women. No woman has yet served as governor). Lieutenant governors do have one statutory job: they chair the capitol area architectural and planning board.

For the first hundred years of statehood, Minnesota's attorneys general were primarily legal counsels. Politically, the attorney general was similar to the auditor, treasurer, and secretary of state, with largely ministerial functions carried on outside public view. In 1955 Miles Lord was elected attorney general and ushered in a new era. Lord, a part of the DFL founding establishment who eventually became a populist federal judge, saw that, properly used, the attorney general's office could have political benefit. The attorney general quickly became not Minnesota's legal counsel but "the people's lawyer," with sweeping power to investigate antitrust violations, unfair business practices, consumer fraud, and the like. Lord was succeeded by Walter Mondale, who was soon appointed a U.S. senator. Since then all attorneys general have subsequently run for governor, though none has succeeded.

Attorney General Hubert H. ("Skip") Humphrey III (1982–99) continued and expanded the tradition of activism in the attorney general's office, especially pursuing consumer fraud, a role that, longtime attorney general staffers insist, was pioneered by Minnesota attorneys general. Indeed, Humphrey carried the overall activism to a new level when he pursued and eventually won, in 1998, a $6.1 billion settlement against the tobacco industry (see chapter 8).

Minnesota's state auditor has, as a primary responsibility, auditing local units of government, an activity that generates little public interest unless a problem is discovered. Minnesota governor Arne Carlson was auditor for twelve years before his election as governor in 1990. He proved to be especially adept at using the powers of the auditor's office to gain publicity about his role as local government watchdog. Minnesota has had only sixteen state auditors. Once attained, the job tends to be held for a long time.

The secretary of state's office has a disparate group of activities: it supervises election administration in the state, registers corporations and other business and nonprofit entities, enrolls bills signed by the governor, and keeps the state's great seal. A former legislator, Joan Growe, was secretary of state from 1975 through 1999. She achieved national recognition for her innovative encouragement of voter participation. A staple in Minnesota's political life has been the turnout prediction by the secretary of state's office before every statewide election.

The state treasurer "receives and issues receipts for all monies paid into the state treasury."[2] It is an important ministerial function, but probably not one that needs an elected official to perform it. During the tenure of a particularly controversial treasurer the legislature attempted to transfer all the functions of the office, leaving the treasurer with nothing to do. The supreme court ruled the attempt unconstitutional.[3] In 1998 the legislature authorized placing before the voters a constitutional amendment that would eliminate the treasurer's post. The amendment passed, and the treasurer's job will end in 2002.

Many argue that one of the desirable features of the separate constitutional officers is that the positions are a training ground for higher office. Unfortunately, not one secretary of state, treasurer, or attorney general has become governor in Minnesota's history. One auditor and ten lieutenant governors have made that transition.

Minnesota's constitution stipulates that all the constitutional officers, save the lieutenant governor, sit on the State Board of Investment. The board is responsible for the investment, purchase, and sale of securities for statewide pension and trust funds. An advisory council and a professional executive director guide the decisions. The board's deliberations are little noticed except when proposals for "social investing" are made, that is, to divest of all stocks in companies doing business in South Africa during apartheid days, or of all companies engaged in selling tobacco more recently. The statutory Executive Council, which includes all the constitutional officers, has a grab bag of responsibilities, including approving depositories, approving mineral and timber permits and leases, and acting as a disaster relief board in times of emergency.

THE FORMAL POWERS OF MINNESOTA'S GOVERNORS

Generally, the stronger the formal powers a governor has, the more impact he or she is likely to have on policy making. An index of formal gubernatorial powers puts Minnesota in the upper half of all the states, so Minnesota governors ought to have sufficient institutional ability to do their jobs.[4]

One factor used in assessing gubernatorial authority is the relative strength of the veto powers. Minnesota governors can veto entire bills or individual appropriations in financial bills (that is, the line-item veto). Both actions can be overridden by two-thirds majorities in the legislature. Governors can also pocket veto at the end of legislative sessions. Vetoes were used sparingly until the administration of Arne Carlson. Table 9 shows the number of vetoes issued by the last seven governors.

Table 9: Use of the Veto by Minnesota Governors, 1961–98

Governor	Years served	No. vetoes
Andersen	1961 through March 1963 (2 1/4 years)	4
Rolvaag	March 1963 through 1966 (3 3/4 years)	22
LeVander	1967 through 1970 (4 years)	9
Anderson	1971 through 1976 (6 years)	19
Perpich	1977 through 1978 (2 years)	0
Quie	1979 through 1982 (4 years)	31
Perpich	1983 through 1990 (8 years)	20
Carlson	1991 through 1998 (8 years)	179

Source: "The Veto Book," a compilation of all vetoes maintained by the Legislative Reference Library, 6th Floor, State Office Building, St. Paul; also available at <http://www.leg.state.mn.us/leg/vetogov.htm>.

Before 1938 Minnesota's governors were part of what can be called the Whig tradition in executive leadership. Other constitutional and administrative officers were more central to a greatly reduced scope of government; department heads were often appointed by independent boards for fixed terms that extended beyond the governor's term. The governor played the role of presider and consensus builder among those with whom he shared administrative responsibility. The thrust toward making the governor *the* administrator was begun by Governor Harold Stassen (1939–43), who created the Department of Administration and charged it with budgeting. Because dedicated funds and independent commissioners remained the norm, though, the budget was more an accounting sheet than a policy document, but it was the first time that the entire state operation had appeared in one fiscal document. In 1955 Arthur Naftalin, Governor Orville Freeman's commissioner of administration, changed the budget to its current policy-oriented focus, a major development in administrative practice.

Commissioners were shifted to terms coincident with the governor in 1971 and began to serve at the pleasure of the governor in 1975. Slowly, the practice of treating departments as independent fiefdoms came to an end. Yet until the early 1990s it was still standard practice for the legislature to receive from the governor an "agency request" as well as the "governor's recommendation." Now there is only a governor's recommendation. Departments can no longer formally let the legislature know they want something different from what the governor has recommended, though they still do it informally.

THE BUREAUCRACY

Minnesota's bureaucracy, which the governor is supposed to administer, is highly professional and of reasonably moderate size when compared with those of other states. In 1881 the state government consisted of five departments: the Railroad Department, the Department of Public Instruction, Department of Insurance, Department of the Public Examiner, and Department of Public Property, puny by modern standards but exceedingly active by the standards of the time.[5]

Table 10 shows the size of state government in terms of the number of departments for the past one hundred years and in terms of the number of employees since 1941. Departments, of course, are not the only type of government unit. Minnesota has 121 agencies, boards, and commissions, from the Arts Board to the Zoological Board. Though Minnesota's state workforce has shown impressive gains in numbers over the past five decades, it is not especially large compared with that of other states. In 1995 Minnesota ranked twenty-third in the total number of employees, just about average.[6] On another frequently used measure, the number of employees per ten thousand residents, however, Minnesota is below average, tied for thirty-third in 1995.[7] So Minnesota is reasonably efficient in its complement of state workers.

In keeping with its moralistic political culture, Minnesota gives its governors relatively few opportunities to appoint people directly or indirectly to jobs, outside judgeships. According to a survey by the authors, out of 36,589 full-time executive-branch employees in October 1996, the governor would have had the opportunity to appoint only 225: the commissioners in the departments, about six political jobs in each department, and the members of the governor's staff.

Table 10: Size of the State Government, 1881–1991

Year	No. of departments	No. of other agencies	No. of employees
1881	5	14	
1891	4	24	
1901	8	36	
1911	7	42	
1921	7	54	
1931	6	60	
1941	11	56	12,046
1951	13	76	26,013
1961	16	75	35,465
1971	21	94	59,765
1981	20	104	72,084
1991	24	121	83,842

Sources: The Book of the States (1992-93, p. 315; 1984-85, p. 275; 1974-75, p. 192; 1964-65, p. 185; 1954-55, p. 186). Statistical Abstract of the United States (1943, p. 301). Minnesota Secretary of State, 1881, 1891, 1901, 1911, 1921, 1931, 1941, 1951. The Legislative Manual of the State of Minnesota (St. Paul: State of Minnesota, 1961). Legislative Manual (St. Paul: State of Minnesota, 1971, 1981, 1991).

Although patronage jobs that pay actual salaries are few, the governor appoints about fifteen hundred people to the 121 boards and commissions. A number of these positions—especially those that govern a profession or industry, such as the Board of Accountancy or the Chiropractic Examiners Board—are eagerly sought after, despite the fact that Minnesota law sets the daily compensation for these time-consuming positions at only $55, plus mileage and child-care costs.

Minnesota state employees rank high on various indicators of professionalism, including years of education and salary. For example, in 1995 Minne-

Table 11: 1964 Ranking of Minnesota Governors

Ranking	Governor	Total Points
1	Floyd B. Olson, 1931–36	60.5
2	John S. Pillsbury, 1876–82	46
3	Alexander Ramsey, 1860–63	45.5
4	John A. Johnson, 1905–09	43
5	Harold E. Stassen, 1939–43	39
6	Luther W. Youngdahl, 1947–51	38
7	Henry H. Sibley, 1858–60	20.5
8	John Lind, 1899–1901	16
9	Orville Freeman, 1955–61	8
10	William R. Marshall, 1866–70	7
11	Adolph O. Eberhart, 1909–15	6
12	Lucius F. Hubbard, 1882–87	5
13	Knute Nelson, 1893–95	5
14	Theodore Christianson, 1925–31	4.5
15	J. A. O. Preus, 1921–25	1

Source: Russell Fridley, "Evaluation of Governors," at JK 6151.F7, Minnesota Historical Society.
Note: The twenty-three evaluators were historians and political scientists. Some cast tie votes.

sota state salaries were seventh among all states, the same ranking as the governor.[8] Pay for department heads and commissioners is quite low, however, and subject to constant egalitarian sniping. Minnesota commissioners went from 1988 to 1997 without pay increases, and the increase finally granted them in a special session of the legislature merely brought them back to about the midpoint of the states.

Despite inadequate pay for its top policy leaders, Minnesota state government has won awards for its performance. In 1993 it was third in *Financial World*'s ranking of state government management, on the basis of its ability to exercise fiscal responsibility, set goals, and measure agency efficiency and effectiveness.[9] Minnesota state government has been innovative in a number of areas, examples of which are provided in chapter 10, and has been a leader in the "reinventing government" movement. In recognition of fiscal competence, Minnesota in 1997 joined five other states that had AAA credit ratings from all the major government-rating organizations.[10]

RANKING MINNESOTA'S GOVERNORS

In 1964 the Minnesota Historical Society undertook the task of evaluating Minnesota's first twenty-nine governors, those serving from 1858 to 1961. Thirty-two historians and political scientists were asked to rank the top five governors in the state's history. The fifteen governors who received any votes, their rank, scores, and the years they served are in table 11. As can be seen, Floyd B. Olson, Minnesota's colorful depression-era Farmer-Labor party governor, was considerably ahead of all the others.[11]

This chapter picks up where the historical society evaluation ended, with the governorship of Elmer L. Andersen. We describe and briefly evaluate the last eight governors of Minnesota, through 1999, without formally attempting to place them in the society's ratings. As an organizing rubric, we examine Minnesota's governors in terms first suggested by Daniel J. Elazar in a study of the Illinois governorship: a five-part analysis of how governors expanded their roles and exercised power through (1) the leverage of federalism, (2) the leverage of crisis, (3) the leverage of personal executive ability, (4) the leverage of the political party, and (5) the leverage accruing to the head of state.[12]

Elmer L. Andersen, 2 January 1961 to 25 March 1963

Elmer Andersen did not have much chance at gubernatorial success. He served two years and not quite three months, in limbo his last five months in office because the 1962 gubernatorial election was so close that a recount eventually gave the victory to his opponent, Karl Rolvaag. Yet many Minnesotans count Andersen among Minnesota's greatest governors. The appellation comes, in truth, not for what he accomplished as governor but for the service he gave Minnesota afterward, as chair of the University of Minnesota Board of Regents, chief proponent of the Voyageurs National Park, founder of the Andersen Horticultural Library, environmental activist, and adviser to all subsequent governors. In 1998, at the age of eighty-nine, Andersen ended his practice of writing weekly editorials for a chain of newspapers he purchased long after his governorship was over, though he still did periodic pieces to indicate his continuing interest in public affairs.

The campaign between Elmer Andersen and his predecessor, Orville Freeman, featured the first televised debates in Minnesota's election history.[13] Andersen won with the narrowest of margins in 1960, 22,879 votes out of 1,550,000 cast, but two years later that margin would look like a landslide.

Despite considerable political party background and ten years of experience in the legislature, Elmer Andersen may have done less with the leverage of his titular leadership of the Republican party than any other governor. He simply refused to take politics into account when performing essentially political acts, such as making appointments or promoting policy. His disregard for the political affiliation of appointees was so thorough that his chief detractors came to be Republicans who lamented his appointment of prominent DFLers to key posts. (Minnesota's legislature was nonpartisan until 1974. Legislators divided into the liberal and conservative caucuses, roughly, but not entirely comprised of DFLers on the one hand and Republicans on the other.)

Andersen's policies, like his appointments, had a distinctly unconservative, un-Republican flavor. It was Andersen who willingly signed income-tax withholding during his first year in office—something his DFL predecessor had spent six years trying to pass. Spending during Andersen's one term increased 19 percent. Taxes were increased as well. In his role as governor, Andersen's "exceptionally high degree of both intellectual and sympathetic comprehension of the other fellow's point of view,"[14] as one columnist put it, left him looking indecisive.

As his first term came to a close, Andersen was adjudged as something of a failure. He had no major crisis to provide him leverage; he was not perceived as a forceful executive; he was clearly out of step with his own party; and new federal programs were being enacted by the Kennedy administration, but at nothing like the pace that would ensue in the later 1960s, and thus the lever of federalism was not as important as it would become.

The 1962 election, the first for a four-year term, pitted Andersen against Lieutenant Governor Karl Rolvaag, the DFL-endorsed candidate. With just eight days to go in the campaign, Andersen was accused of improperly taking advantage of a traditional federalism lever, rushing construction on Interstate 35 so that he could cut the ribbon on the road before the election. The charges were false, but that wasn't apparent until after the election.

The 6 November 1962 election for governor of Minnesota was not decided until 21 March 1963. After the first canvass of the 1,246,661 votes, Rolvaag led by 58 votes. Andersen was 142 votes ahead after the amended returns were counted again. Finally, after a recount of all the votes, Rolvaag won by 91 votes, a 0.007 margin, the closest ever in Minnesota and apparently the closest gubernatorial election in our nation's history. The so-called Highway 35 scandal surely had caused enough people to vote against Andersen to cost him the election.[15]

Karl F. Rolvaag, 25 March 1963 to 2 January 1967

When he returned from World War II with a Purple Heart and a Bronze Star, Karl Rolvaag was immediately recruited as a candidate by the newly formed Democratic-Farmer-Labor party. He ran for Congress three times and then succeeded Orville Freeman as DFL party chair. When Freeman became governor in 1954, Rolvaag was elected lieutenant governor, in which position he served the six Freeman years and two more with Elmer Andersen.

Years after his gubernatorial term was over, Rolvaag began to admit publicly what many had suspected, that during his service as governor he suffered from alcoholism. Both the political and policy stories of the Rolvaag era are best understood as manifestations of the denial that inevitably results from chemical dependency.

Rolvaag, although the first governor elected to a four-year term, actually had only one legislative session that dealt with his proposals and his budget. His first session, in 1963, was better than half over when he finally took office. Conservatives controlled both legislative chambers throughout his term.

Rolvaag participated in enough of the 1963 session to veto a number of bills, most notably one involving workers' compensation rates and benefits. The bill was alleged by the conservatives to be mild reform. Rolvaag's veto irritated the business community, and workers' compensation reform would be an issue in every election for the next three decades. After the 1963 session Rolvaag unilaterally cut state spending 5 percent, a very unpopular move once it became clear he had miscalculated revenues and expenditures and the cuts were not necessary.

After the 1965 legislative session Rolvaag claimed credit for a small school funding increase and a 36 percent increase in mental health spending.

Rolvaag also admitted that not much else had been done, blaming the conservatives. He called the "creation of public awareness and attention of the problem of mental retardation" his "single most important accomplishment" in the 1965 session. He also cited the passage of the taconite amendment as one of his accomplishments, though in truth Democrats, Rolvaag included, opposed the taconite amendment when Elmer Andersen first proposed it.[16] The amendment essentially guaranteed low taxes to the iron mining companies deciding to invest in the technologies required to mine and process taconite with a low iron content. Minnesota had depleted its high-grade ore.

Rolvaag would have to be ranked low in terms of his use of our five leverages. Federalism was expanding in importance, but Rolvaag apparently paid little attention to the subject. There was no crisis, and he definitely was not a forceful administrator. His basic inarticulateness made his use of the bully pulpit of the governorship all but impossible.

In terms of using his political party as a lever, Rolvaag's major trouble as a governor came not from opposing conservatives or Republicans but from his own DFLers. In July 1965 the DFL leadership gathered at a northern Minnesota resort where they reached a consensus that Rolvaag could not be re-elected in November 1966. Rolvaag challenged the party leadership's choice, Lieutenant Governor A. M. ("Sandy") Keith. After twenty ballots at the state DFL convention, Keith was endorsed for governor, but it wasn't too difficult for Rolvaag to mount a successful primary campaign with the slogan "Let the people decide." Minnesota's open primary system allowed Republicans and independents to join Democrats casting their votes against the move to "dump" Rolvaag. Rolvaag easily won the primary, then easily lost the general election.

After his defeat Rolvaag was appointed ambassador to Iceland, where he served for ten months. He returned to Minnesota and lived quietly, eventually becoming a quite public member of Alcoholics Anonymous and a sought-after AA speaker all over the state. He died in 1990.

Harold LeVander, 2 January 1967 to 4 January 1971

Harold LeVander is the only true nonpolitician to become governor in our list of seven, though the governor elected after these seven, Jesse Ventura, was spectacularly nonpolitical. Though a member of a prominent law firm and brother of the state Republican party chair, LeVander had never held office. He was a popular commencement and occasion speaker, however, and known in political circles for his representation of the state's electric cooperatives. While governor, LeVander continued speech making at a punishing pace. His daughter, Jean LeVander King, then his speech writer, estimates that in his first year in office LeVander gave nearly three hundred talks to groups of all kinds.[17] LeVander seemed to feel that for a governor, requests for speeches were mandates from the people. Besides, he was most comfortable communicating in the speech-making mode, as opposed to through press contacts or television, a medium that did not serve him well.

From all accounts, LeVander had a very definite sense of his responsibility to become governor but not a sense of what particularly he was supposed to do once he had the job. In political terms, he did not have an agenda, or, to put it more grandly as governors from other states have done, he did not have a "magical vision."[18] He did have a ring his Lutheran pastor father had given him, a ring inscribed with the motto "To succeed, serve." The service, he seemed to feel, was in attaining the office of governor and dispatching its duties with honor, and he managed to do both those things.

Despite his lack of a plan, LeVander presided over a flowering of structural innovations in Minnesota governance. Both houses of the legislature were controlled by the conservative caucus, but the conservatives were yielding more and more influence to legislators from the metropolitan area who were openly active in the Republican party, legislators who were oriented toward providing the services of government more efficiently and completely, not in simply maintaining the status quo. These metropolitan legislators were, in turn, strongly influenced by the Citizens League, which provided an innovations blueprint for state government. It is ironic that many of the legislators who participated in this burst of legislative innovation had opposed LeVander during the primary phase of the election. They considered him "old hat" but found in LeVander's chief of staff, David Durenberger, a like-minded reformer. Together, the legislature and Durenberger, with LeVander's amiable acquiescence, were able to craft a remarkable record of achievement.

The LeVander years brought regional governance: the Metropolitan Council for the Twin Cities area and regional development commissions for the rest of the state. He also instituted direct state aid to local governments, both school districts and cities and counties. LeVander created the state's first Department of Human Rights and the Pollution Control Agency. A 1969 "Crystal Waters" program attacked a growing problem in the state—polluted wells, lakes, and rivers. But the increased state commitment to education in the LeVander years clearly had the most impact on the budget and on taxpayers. In late 1969 the Minnesota Republican party distributed to its leadership a comprehensive report on the LeVander administration, preparing itself for an expected reelection campaign the next November. Said the report, "Our educational investment by itself more than equals the state budget for all purposes just four years ago."[19] The report goes on to brag that LeVander had massively increased spending on all forms of education—by 379 percent in the junior colleges, 67 percent at the University of Minnesota, and so on.[20] The congratulatory tone of the Republican party's report when talking about spending increases speaks to the difference between the party of that time and that of later years, which adopted a more conservative, dollar-saving tone.

LeVander and Durenberger were particularly adept at using the lever of federalism, in these years a rapidly growing area. The Metropolitan Council, for example, was created as much to provide planning responses to federal mandates as it was to help Minnesota's population center plan its destiny. LeVander also used his political party to good advantage. Staff from the time say that LeVander, in his first year in office, actually kept a copy of the Republican party's platform on hand since it embodied most of what he thought he ought to be doing. By and large, the party's platform was LeVander's platform, and he was proud of it. There were political and social crises in America during this period, the era of the escalation of the Vietnam War and the continuing battles over civil rights, but LeVander had no real crisis to manage in the state. Minnesota generally disapproved of the Vietnam War and approved of civil rights extensions; hence, there was less tension in the state than in many others. Finally, as head of state, LeVander was able to articulate the state's growing consensus over spending whatever was necessary to achieve clean water in particular and environmental quality in general.

LeVander's single term witnessed one of the most productive periods in Minnesota's governmental history, a productivity fueled by an active, Republican/conservative Minnesota legislature.

Wendell R. Anderson, 4 January 1971 to 29 December 1976

If passing significant legislation is accepted as the hallmark of gubernatorial success, then Wendell Anderson was perhaps the most successful governor in Minnesota's history. In his first term, faced by conservative majorities in both houses of the legislature, Anderson pushed through what came to be called the "Minnesota Miracle," indeed a miraculous commitment to the payment of education costs using statewide sales and income tax revenues instead of local property taxes. The level of education services became much less dependent on the property wealth of the individual school districts.

Besides the Minnesota Miracle, the 1971 legislature passed another law that helped give the state a national reputation for innovation. Called fiscal disparities, this tax-base sharing measure pooled some of the tax benefits that accrued to local governments in the metropolitan area which were successful at attracting businesses and gave those benefits to have-not communities. The idea was to share the wealth and cut down on intergovernmental wars over business location. Both the Minnesota Miracle and fiscal disparities were part of the significant group of legislative enactments that had begun in the Citizens League and came to Minnesota through the conservative/Republican caucus.

In Anderson's third year in office the liberal caucus in both the house and the senate gained the majority—the first time the Minnesota senate had ever been controlled by the liberals/Democrats. Anderson, flanked by his tough and able chief of staff, Tom Kelm, and the DFL-dominated legislature, passed an incredible array of legislation they had favored for years but could never get enacted: money for education and the disabled, an open-meeting law, a prohibition on corporate farming, an anti-strikebreaking law, and the Public Employees Bargaining Act, which guaranteed strong unions among Minnesota's public employees. The Equal Rights Amendment (for women) to the federal Constitution was ratified easily. Party designation for all subsequent legislatures was approved. A new state zoo was authorized. The next year added campaign-finance reform, no-fault auto insurance, the creation of a Housing Finance Agency, and elimination of income taxes for the working poor.

Anderson won reelection in 1974 with 63.8 percent of the vote. For the first time, legislative candidates ran with party designation, and DFL candidates captured a comfortable ten-vote margin in the 67-member senate; in the house the DFL majority was an overwhelming 104 to 30. In 1973 *Time* magazine had a cover picture of Wendell Anderson proclaiming that Minnesota was the state "that works."

Anderson used well all the levers available to a governor. The rapid expansion of federal programs had not been curtailed under the Nixon presidency, and Anderson's administration spent considerable time transferring federal largesse to beneficiaries in the state. His personal executive ability and use of the power of the governorship seemed very well honed. There was no major crisis in Minnesota, but the national constitutional crisis presented by Watergate and the presidential resignation had so tipped the balance in favor of the DFL party that Anderson was given dominant legislative majorities, which he used with great skill. Anderson's approval ratings were in the mid-50s through 1975 and 1976. Here, then, was a governor with high popularity, a tremendous output of legislation, and national recognition for his leadership. Despite all that, few would rate Wendell Anderson as among Minnesota's greatest governors. The reason: his so-called self-appointment to the U.S. Senate.

After Minnesota senator Walter Mondale was elected vice-president in 1976, Anderson resigned as governor. Lieutenant Governor Rudy Perpich assumed the governor's chair and then appointed Anderson to the U.S. Senate. It was the end of Anderson's political career. He failed to win reelection to the Senate and failed to gain party support for another attempt at a Senate campaign in 1984. The public's negative reaction to the "self-appointment" was so thorough and so profound that people have asked Anderson for years, "Why did you do it?" Part of his answer highlights something about the office of governor. A governor is "on" seven days a week and is always being featured by the media, he said. It's a hard job, and one where you can wear out your welcome easily. Anderson figured that his popularity would ride out the temporary upset voters had with his appointment.[21] But he was wrong. It could be that self-appointment is a particularly egregious offense in a state as highly moralistic as Minnesota. After his elected public service Anderson served for twelve years on the Board of Regents of the University of Minnesota, ending in 1997. He continues to practice law in Minnesota and is the honorary consul to Sweden.

Albert H. Quie, 4 January 1979 to 3 January 1983

Al Quie was a popular and influential Republican congressman in 1978 when he decided he wanted to leave Washington and come home to Minnesota. He was elected governor during what Democrats referred to as the "Minnesota Massacre," when Republicans Rudy Boschwitz and David Durenberger were being elected to the U.S. Senate and Quie was beating Rudy Perpich, all in response to the Wendell Anderson "self-appointment."

Quie came to Minnesota's governorship with goals that were contradictory when viewed from a budgetary perspective. On the one hand, he wanted to curb the state's appetite for spending and to make it impossible for the state to reap revenue benefits from inflation. On the other hand, he wanted school class sizes significantly smaller than were the current norm. In his first session Quie passed his major conservative initiative—income tax indexing. The impact was substantial. According to an estimate prepared by the Department of Revenue for Quie's staff, indexing and other adjustments provided $1.4 billion in tax relief for the years 1980–83. In addition, Quie supported and passed $2.9 billion in property tax relief.[22]

Quie also sought to make constitutional changes that would hold down spending, such as initiative and referendum and the requirement of a super-majority to raise taxes. Initiative and referendum were placed on the ballot and received a majority of votes cast on the issue, but not quite sufficient votes to pass a constitutional amendment.

Quie was unable to get the legislature to adopt his dramatic class-size reduction plans. He was proposing a maximum of eight students per class in early grades, one-third the average in many districts. Quie actually testified in front of a legislative committee in an attempt to move the idea along, but the precedent-breaking move didn't work. There was more spending for education, however, so, on the one hand, Quie and the legislature shut off the tax-generating spigot by indexing income taxes and reducing property taxes; on the other hand, they increased future obligations. There undoubtedly would have been a future crunch under any circumstances, but soon after the 1980 session the economic bottom fell out.

In a 1996 interview former governor Quie observed that "the guy who understood the state's budget" had died just before he took office.[23] Whether the state was in fact bereft of people who understood how to make a budget, it certainly looked like no one knew how. By the summer of 1980 it had become clear that the state's July 1979 to July 1981 budget wouldn't balance. Quie "unallocated" $195 million unilaterally. Quie and staff aides maintained later that one of the chief motives for his unilateral budget balancing was protecting legislators from having to make the cuts themselves just before the November election. The gesture was not appreciated, however, and Quie says now it was a mistake. Politically, the budget deficits became Quie's and Quie's alone.

There was more bad news for the 1981 session. The national economic "malaise" had hit Minnesota especially hard. The decline in the second quarter of 1980 was the most serious the state had seen in thirty years. The 1981 budget-setting session was focused almost exclusively on the financial crisis, but the situation was so chaotic that a special session had to be called in June to complete the budget. Except it wasn't finished. From June 1981 through December 1982 Minnesota had one regular and six special sessions to wrestle with the fiscal difficulties. At the time, and later, Quie and his economic advisers were accused of constantly opting for the rosiest forecasts, resulting in shortfalls as the situation proved to be even worse than anticipated.

Al Quie was the only governor of the seven examined here who had a genuine crisis. The economic downturn of the early 1980s was the most severe since the Great Depression. He was unable to use the crisis leverage well, however. In terms of executive ability, Quie came to be portrayed as someone who couldn't manage the budget. But the Quie administration was not without enduring conservative accomplishment. Income tax indexing remains the law in Minnesota, and changing back to a system in which the state's income tax revenues increase because of inflation is politically unthinkable.

Throughout his term as governor, Al Quie gathered every Tuesday morning with a men's Bible-study group. Thus, there was little surprise when, after his gubernatorial service, Quie became increasingly active in the Prison Fellowship, actually managing the organization for a time and becoming, with Charles Colson, one of its principal volunteers and activists, a service he continues to the present.

Rudy Perpich, 29 December 1976 to 4 January 1979 and 3 January 1983 to 7 January 1991

Rudy Perpich would often admit that he sought the office of lieutenant governor because he knew that the state would never elect a "bohunk from the Range" as governor unless that "bohunk" backed into the job.[24] Perpich did back in, becoming the first Catholic and the first Iron Ranger to hold the job. He was also governor longer than any other person in state history, ten years. His parents had emigrated to the United States from Croatia. He had served in the state senate before running for and winning DFL endorsement for lieutenant governor under Wendell Anderson.

In his first, short, two-year term Perpich was primarily a reactor to current events as opposed to the peripatetic idea-generator he would become during his second, eight-year term. The first term began not long after permits had been issued for the construction of a major power line to run diagonally across the state. Farmers and more militant environmentalists strenuously opposed the line, and Perpich received extensive publicity for driving out alone and unannounced to talk to people along the line's route. Staff from the period insist that Perpich's actions were not studied. He was not trying to create the image of a caring populist. Rather, he simply decided he wanted to talk to opponents and then did it before anything could be organized.

Compulsive openness was another first-term Perpich trait. He declared his office open, and reporters and citizens were encouraged to attend whatever meeting was going on. A commissioner from the period observed dryly in an interview for this book that "nothing inhibits the two-way flow of communication like being chewed out by the governor in front of a reporter." Perpich's actions during his first year in office were enormously popular with the public.[25] Soon, however, the novelty of openness began to be replaced with concerns that Perpich was disorganized.[26] Perpich lost to Al Quie 52 percent to 45 percent.

For the next four years, Rudy Perpich lived in Europe, where he represented Minnesota-based Control Data Corporation in international trade. The experience was apparently transforming. When he returned to become governor in 1983, Perpich was a committed, some felt overly committed, internationalist. His next eight years would be focused on ensuring that Minnesota was "world class" so that the state's citizens could compete successfully in the global economy. While in Europe, Perpich also acquired a degree of comfort with business leaders, a highly unusual trait for a politician from the Iron Range. More than any of the seven governors analyzed here, Rudy Perpich attempted to manage the future. His job, he felt, was readying Minnesota for the new day.

One important strain of Perpich's activity focused on education. Chapter 10 describes Minnesota's national firsts in education—open enrollment, charter schools, and postsecondary options—all accomplished by a group of policy entrepreneurs who would have failed without Perpich's energetic support. That support was politically costly, however. Teachers' unions backed Perpich's 1990 opponent because of Perpich's support for education innovation. Perpich also created a state-supported arts high school for talented young Minnesotans.

Another strain of Perpich's activity focused on economic development. He was constantly looking for ideas abroad and products to sell overseas. Some of his unending stream of ideas were clearly not feasible; others were brilliant. One of the unfeasible ideas was his proposal to marry Minnesota's supply of wood with Asia's continuing need for eating utensils by creating a chopsticks factory. Unfortunately, Minnesota had the wrong kind of wood and lacked chopsticks-making expertise. The project failed.

Even Perpich's successful schemes seemed initially bizarre to many Minnesotans. When he first proposed a plan sold to him by a group of Canadian developers, a retail/entertainment complex that would become a major tourist attraction, many openly scoffed, but in 1992 the largest retail mall in the country opened in Bloomington, and in 1996–97 the Mall of America drew 42.5 million visitors, "more annual visits than Disney World, Graceland and the Grand Canyon combined."[27]

Perpich won reelection in 1986 handily but began to develop political barnacles during his next term. Like most political people, he thought press coverage of him very unfair, but unlike most politicians, he complained about it constantly to the media. A series of inconsequential acts eroded public confidence. He decreed that his name should be changed from "Rudy Perpich" to "Rudolph G. Perpich," though no one ever used the new appellation and he eventually dropped the idea. He groused about the condition of the governor's mansion and proposed selling it. For the second period in his public life, Perpich dyed his hair, but the second time, unlike the first, he refused to admit it. Republicans began calling him "Governor Goofy," and the phrase became popular for a time.

Perpich did not have a major crisis and so did not use that lever of power. His relationship to the DFL party was complex, as was the relationship of most DFLers from northeastern Minnesota, who were generally more socially conservative and much closer to labor than party activists from other parts of the state. Perpich defeated the party's endorsed candidate in 1982, though the party endorsed him in 1986 and 1990. Perpich gained enormous political power from his rock-solid home base of pro-Perpich, always-DFL voters on the Iron Range and in Duluth. He used that power to make the party support him and to be the state's longest-serving governor.

Federal programmatic presence in a number of areas was in moderate decline during Perpich's last eight years, making the federalism lever less available than it had been. As for Perpich's use of executive ability, he was always thought to be a mediocre administrator at best. In fact, there were many policy areas he didn't care about; he was perfectly content to let legislative leaders dominate in those areas. But when he wanted something, he was very persuasive and goal-oriented, and in the end, he always seemed to get what he wanted. His executive style was that of a classic Iron Range politician, for whom deal making is the order of the day. But he was also governor, and when he needed to, he could use that lever of power more effectively than any other governor.

Perpich sought reelection in 1990, despite advice from many friends that he not do so. He easily defeated the state's commerce commissioner, his appointee, who challenged him for the DFL endorsement and in the primary. But, in one of the most bizarre elections in Minnesota history, described below, Perpich was defeated by Arne Carlson.

Minnesotans' genuine affection for the peripatetic, folksy internationalist became most apparent in 1995 when he died unexpectedly of a cancer he had kept secret from virtually everyone except his family. His funeral attracted thousands and was broadcast live on Twin Cities television stations.

Arne H. Carlson, 7 January 1991 to 4 January 1999

Arne Carlson did not seek his Republican party's endorsement for governor in 1990. Despite his twelve years as state auditor, Carlson knew he was not well liked by party activists and delegates who dominated the party's selection process and who considered Carlson's positions on the so-called social issues, particularly abortion and gay rights, to be anathema. Carlson's stance on those issues was the same as it had been since he was first elected to the Minneapolis City Council in 1963; he was pro-choice and in favor of gay rights, just like the dominant faction of the state's Republican party of that earlier time.

In the three-way 1990 primary Carlson finished a distant second (49.4 percent to 31.6 percent) to a man who did share the average Republican partisan's view on the social issues. Carlson, then the state auditor, was out of a job, and the man who won the gubernatorial primary, Jon Grunseth, seemed to be on his way to a victory in the general election. Then the *Star Tribune*, based in Minneapolis, published allegations that nine years earlier Grunseth had been swimming in the nude with two teenaged friends of his daughter's. The allegations about Grunseth were first published on 16 October. Carlson began a write-in campaign on 22 October, just twenty days before the general election. Grunseth withdrew from the race on 29 October, continuing to deny the allegations, and the state supreme court decided that Carlson and his running mate, Joanell Dyrstad, as the second-place winners of the Republican primary, could be on the ballot to oppose Rudy Perpich. During the highly confusing and sensational series of events, polls showed that the Grunseth allegations had hurt both Grunseth and Perpich. Some people had a sense that Perpich was somehow behind the lurid publicity, though there was no evidence of that. Perpich's negative ratings had already been relatively high. Carlson had strong name identification but few negatives, and he was able to win despite the short campaign, 50.1 percent to 46.8 percent.

Thus, Arne Carlson began his governorship under most unusual circumstances. In both personal and political terms, he was a loner. Republican party activists distrusted him and had just soundly beaten him in a primary. Many Democrats, remembering Carlson's years of biting criticism, a hallmark of his long political career, were unwilling to work with him. Carlson was elected governor without what every other governor has, a group of political people who want and accept jobs in the new administration. The only people he could and did turn to were Republican party activists from twenty and more years previous, people who, like Carlson, had been left homeless when the party took its rightward lurch in the early to mid-1970s. The lack of a political support base meant that Carlson knew few of the applicants for jobs in his administration. Not surprisingly, executive turnover in the Carlson years was very rapid. There was little political loyalty, and Carlson's acerbic personality generated little personal loyalty.

In his first session Carlson was faced with a billion-dollar structural budget deficit; that is, if the state simply continued present spending and took in projected revenues, there would still be a billion-dollar gap. Because Minnesota is constitutionally forbidden to run a deficit, Carlson had to reduce expenditures, which he did well. At the same time, however, he accepted the advice of aides who wanted him to attempt to reform the property tax system while coping with the deficit. His proposals, though arguably good policy, were politically unpopular because they would have resulted in property tax increases for many Minnesotans, particularly those in rural areas. Carlson was skewered by opposition DFLers and the media for the plan, and his popularity plummeted to a record low for a Minnesota governor.[28] For the next six years of his administration, Carlson seemed loath to propose policy changes. His method of governance was generally through conservative management of the budget process and through the veto, in the use of which, as table 9 demonstrates, he set records. Another outcome of unseasoned staff was that Carlson missed the deadline on vetoing the DFL legislature's redistricting plan in 1991. As a result, the plan designed to favor Democrats became law without Carlson's signature.

Carlson's veto strategy worked very well for his popularity. His approval ratings soared. In 1994 Carlson was blessed with a Republican-endorsed primary opponent whom the public viewed as far too conservative and a DFL general-election opponent whom the public viewed as far too liberal. It was a banner Republican year nationally, and Carlson won reelection with the largest margin of victory for a Republican since the creation of the DFL party in 1944.

Carlson's personality and style were unlike those of any Minnesota governor in memory. He was not a positive or particularly likable person. He much preferred reading by himself to public contact, and he particularly disliked small-group meetings where people pleaded for his support for their cause. As often as not, Carlson lashed out at the pleaders. Carlson did not appear to have a view of the governorship as a bully pulpit from which he could effect change. Rather, he seemed to see his role as the jockey on an un-tamed horse with the whip as the preferred method of persuasion.

The deficit Carlson had to manage when he came to office affected him profoundly. He, and many others, became convinced that government's re-sponse to societal problems was growing faster than the problems them-selves. At the start of his second term Carlson received a much-publicized study he had commissioned which posited a long-term structural deficit. Ironically, the next budget forecast, issued later the same month, stipulated that Minnesota's next biennium would have an $800 million surplus.[29] The Carlson administration had correctly estimated the demand for state dollars and services, but it had missed in its estimate of the supply of those dollars. Minnesota's economy was a much better than average participant in the na-tional economic upturn of the 1990s. Budget surpluses became a constant presence in Carlson's final years in office.

With the income side shining brightly, Carlson's generally negative view about government spending may have been what was needed in those expan-sive times. Despite the surpluses, the rhetoric surrounding fiscal debates changed at the capitol. The Carlson administration had disciplined the bud-geting process. Long-term impacts of policy changes were always consid-ered, and, if those impacts meant more spending, the changes were usually rejected. The normal Minnesota DFL legislative tendency to use surpluses for expansion had been curbed.

In his final budget-year legislative session, 1997, Carlson played out what he felt was a major accomplishment of his administration—moving toward greater freedom of choice in education. As chapter 10 describes, he agreed to tax incentives for educational choice after straight vouchers again proved politically untenable. Carlson received national recognition in conservative and Republican groups for education choice leadership.

As for the levers of power available to Governor Arne Carlson: the le-verage of federalism was declining in importance because federal participa-tion in state activities was decreasing. The accepted perception of Carlson when he began his administration was that he would be extremely competent at the mechanics of the job; thus, he could benefit from the leverage of the very good administrator. Despite early difficulties, the overall sense of the Carlson administration was that of good management. Generally, Carlson controlled costs well, and he changed the nature of the state's budget discus-sion. The deficit that Carlson greeted when he was elected was a serious problem but not a crisis. And Carlson had little relationship with his political party. Like Perpich before him, but in a totally opposite way, Carlson effectively used the leverage of being governor, particularly through the constitutional right he had to veto legislation.

Arne Carlson's overall approach to his job was negative and unpolitical. Nonetheless, it worked. Carlson was able to prevent spending excesses while continuing to provide the high level of services Minnesotans expect. He led Minnesota during a period of national conservative ideological dominance vis-à-vis government activity and spending. Many in the Republican party—certainly his two principal primary election challengers in 1990 and 1994—would have attempted to move Minnesota into much more conservative territory and would have undoubtedly had a gridlocking clash with the DFL legislature. Carlson managed to avoid that gridlock.

At this writing it is too early to assess the performance of Arne Carlson's gubernatorial successor, Jesse Ventura, but it is possible to observe that Ventura came to the office in 1999 with a professional life totally unlike that of any previous Minnesota governor and, for the first time since the Great Depression, with the support of a third party. After high school graduation in Minneapolis, James Janos (Ventura's given name) joined the U.S. Navy's Underwater Demolition (SEALS) unit, where he served four years of active duty, some of it in Vietnam, and two years in the reserves. After military duty and some time in community college Janos moved to California and became a professional wrestler, adopting the name Jesse "The Body" Ventura. He acted in a number of movies toward the end of and after his wrestling career. He returned to Minnesota and in 1990 was elected to a four-year term as mayor of Brooklyn Park, a suburb north of Minneapolis with 56,381 people. Ventura ran because of disagreements with the city administration over the placement of a storm sewer. Brooklyn Park is an example of the weakest mayor–local government system Minnesota has to offer, and Ventura reportedly had relatively little impact on the city's policy direction, though his tenure in the part-time job, particularly in its earlier phases, was highly publicized. After his mayoral term Ventura became a talk show host on a Twin Cities radio station.

Ventura's astonishing gubernatorial election caught many Minnesotans by surprise. He was supported by 37 percent of the 60 percent of eligible voters who exercised their franchise on 3 November 1998. The second-place finisher, St. Paul mayor Norm Coleman, received 35 percent of the votes. Attorney General Hubert H. ("Skip") Humphrey III received 28 percent of the votes. After the election Minnesotans tried to decide just what kind of governor Ventura would be. He had taken few positions during the election, but those he did take were generally opposed to government involvement. His most often quoted and discussed remarks were his view on funding for early childhood education—it's "terrible for children" because it undermines parents—and his opposition to college tuition aid delivered in admonitions to students that "if you're smart enough to go to college, you're smart enough to figure out how to get there."[30] Despite the comments, in his first legislative session as Governor, Ventura would approve significant increases in Minnesota's already large early childhood and student aid budgets. Minnesotans began to appreciate that Ventura's rhetoric and actions were not always consistent. The rhetoric, however, was always entertaining.

Minnesota's governors have available to them a series of levers: (1) the leverage of federalism, (2) the leverage of crisis, (3) the leverage of personal executive ability, (4) the leverage of the political party, and (5) the leverage accruing to the head of state.

Elmer Andersen had too short a time to be a good (or a bad) governor and too little time adequately to test the levers of power. He was, however, Minnesota's outstanding ex-governor, and his continuing contributions to the state's public life made him easily one of the most important figures in Minnesota public affairs in the last half of the twentieth century.

Karl Rolvaag failed to use any of the levers available to a governor, and he left little imprint in terms of formal, governmental accomplishment. Years later, we would learn that there was a reason his administration seemed to have no rhyme or reason, namely, that he was a practicing alcoholic while governor. Rolvaag did eventually make an important public policy contribution. His example helped Minnesota become a national leader in terms of understanding and treating chemical dependency.

Harold LeVander did an outstanding job of using two of the available levers of power, federalism and the political party. His administration localized and rationalized the rapidly growing federal presence. He also captured and used well the practical yet progressive positions of the Republican party of that era. Overall, LeVander has to be seen as one of Minnesota's better governors.

Wendell Anderson may have used the levers of the office of governor better than anyone else in the state's history. The amount and scope of legislation passed in the Anderson years are astounding. He was particularly skilled at using the lever of the office of governor and at using his then-dominant political party. Anderson's self-appointment to the U.S. Senate and his subsequent rejection by Minnesota voters represents one of the tragic miscalculations in Minnesota political history.

Al Quie had twenty-one distinguished years in Congress before facing four awful years as governor of Minnesota, years when he was the only modern governor to be presented with a genuine crisis, the worst economic downturn since the Great Depression. Quie did not use the crisis lever, or any of the other potential levers of gubernatorial power, well. His principal legacy may be the one he would prefer, namely, that a man with his deep religious faith can hold and bear witness to that faith while participating in public affairs.

Rudy Perpich used his status as a governor as well as any other holder of the office. Particularly in his second try at being governor, he seemed to have a vision for where the state should be and how it should get there. Perpich helped move Minnesota to a condition of global awareness and competitiveness which leaves the state with one of the healthiest economies in the United States. He clearly must rank as one of Minnesota's best governors.

Arne Carlson used the negative side of the lever of the governorship to discipline the state's tendency for attempting to do more than is prudent. Carlson vetoed more bills and appropriations than all the other governors in this list combined. But Carlson seemed right for his time, because a very good national economy and an even better state economy provided a tempting pool of resources for establishing new and expensive programs that could have eventually caused financial distress when times were not quite so good.

Jesse Ventura represented a dramatic stylistic change in Minnesota governors. Most of the previous seven governors were either career politicians or close to the political establishment. Ventura was a classic antipolitician, whose populist rhetoric alternately charmed and stirred Minnesotans. Soon after his election Ventura was being compared to Floyd B. Olson and Rudy Perpich because of the strong sense all three conveyed that they were of the people, not one of the tired establishment. If, as Orville Freeman said, governors "make the music," then Minnesotans began the Ventura administration anticipating some of the more exciting and raucous tunes ever heard in the state. But at least in his first legislative session, Ventura policy music proved to be middle-of-the-road and soothing.

CHAPTER 8

Minnesota's Courts

The second floor of Minnesota's capitol building contains, on its east wing, a magnificent supreme court chamber replete with rich woods and four astonishing murals painted by America's master muralist, John LaFarge. Though the chamber is still periodically used for supreme court arguments, it generally serves now as the judiciary's symbolic presence in the capitol, a place that, together with the governor's reception room and the legislative chambers, helps remind tourists that Minnesota has three branches of government. Capitol architect Cass Gilbert apparently believed that his celebrated capitol would house all of Minnesota state government for all time. Indeed, the capitol did house Minnesota's entire appellate court system from its construction in 1905 until 1983, when a court of appeals was authorized and initially housed in a downtown office building.[1] The court of appeals helped provide impetus to a desire already expressed by the judiciary in Minnesota, a need to find a home separate from the capitol building. That home was authorized in 1984 and finally completed in 1995. The beautiful Minnesota Judicial Center, located adjacent to the capitol, now houses the supreme court, the court of appeals, and the two executive branch courts, the workers' compensation court and the tax court. In addition, there are the state law library, administrative services, and the boards that regulate the practice of law.[2]

Occupying a new home is the most visible recent change experienced by Minnesota's courts, but there are many others. Minnesota courts have gone from among the least to one of the most "unified" systems, that is, having a single, rational, hierarchical structure. The cases that courts now deliberate are substantially different than they used to be. Minnesota courts spend less and less time adjudicating disputes among citizens and more and more time processing criminals. The composition of the judiciary has changed as well.

Minnesota was the first state with a majority of women on its supreme court. Though that condition no longer exists, it now has a woman as chief justice, the tenth state to do so in American history. In the midst of these changes Minnesota's courts have established a deserved reputation for efficiency. There are no giant backlogs, no stories of defendants being forgotten or turned loose by mistake. There are more and more defendants, however, most of whom are involved with drugs, as users or purveyors. Minnesota courts are attempting a new, streamlined drug court for the former; for the latter, the penalties for trafficking in drugs grow more serious every year.

Some things have not changed. Minnesota has separated judicial elections and partisan activity for virtually all the twentieth century and will likely do so for the twenty-first, though challenges to the current nonpartisan system for judicial elections were more frequent in the 1998 campaign period than ever before. Minnesota's judicial branch has remained near the top of quality and innovation rankings by court scholars. In terms of judicial federalism—the expansion and protection of individual rights and righting of group wrongs by state courts—Minnesota courts are not usually described as being in the forefront of this movement, though they have participated in it.

A SIMPLIFIED, UNIFIED COURT SYSTEM

During the 1950s and 1960s the American Bar Association and legal and organizational scholars began urging state court reforms such as centralized judicial management and court consolidation and simplification. A 1981 article, using data from the mid-1970s, showed Minnesota with the third lowest score in the country on the factor "court consolidation and simplification."[3] Minnesota's courts were among the least "reformed" in the country. The mid-1970s, however, was about the time that the long struggle for court streamlining began in the state, headed by a band of aggressive and dedicated judicial leaders.

Today's court system has been simplified and unified according to the model proposed by judicial reformers. There is a seven-member supreme court, a sixteen-member court of appeals that decides cases with three-member panels, and 254 district court judges who normally process all types of cases. Gone are the justices of the peace, the municipal courts, the probate and juvenile courts, and (except in a few holdover instances) the magistrates of old. There are two specialized executive-branch courts, one for taxes and one for the state's overly complex workers' compensation system; otherwise, all legal matters flow through one unified court. District court judges are divided among ten judicial districts that range in size from eleven to fifty-eight judges. The state's two largest counties, Hennepin and Ramsey, are districts unto themselves, and the Fourth District, Hennepin County, is by far the largest. Each district elects chief and assistant chief judges and an administrator. In sum, there is now active, centralized management of the court process. Whereas Minnesota courts in the mid-1970s were among the least consolidated and simplified, by 1993 a U.S. Department of Justice survey listed Minnesota as one of the six most consolidated systems.[4]

A STATEWIDE OR LOCAL SYSTEM?

In terms of legal practice, then, Minnesota has a statewide court system. In administrative and financial terms, however, Minnesota's courts are partly statewide and partly local. Whereas twenty years ago more than 80 percent of the total costs of Minnesota's court system were paid from local property taxes, that figure has dropped to about 40 percent.

Minnesota is one of sixteen states with a statewide public defender who has responsibility for coordinating indigent defense. It is one of twenty-three states that pays for this system through state funds (though it was paid locally twenty years ago).[5] About 90 percent of the criminal cases in Minnesota are handled by a mix of full-time and part-time public defenders.[6] Minnesota's budget for public defense was $41.7 million in 1998. In a report prepared for the American Bar Association in 1996 showing public defense spending statistics from twenty-eight states, Minnesota ranked twentieth in terms of its public defense cost per case, $216. It ranked eighth in its public defense cost per capita, $8.23.[7]

THE JUDGE'S JOB HAS CHANGED

The court's organization has changed and so has the funding, but what has changed most of all is the job of judge. A steep decline in the caseload in civil law, combined with skyrocketing increases in criminal and juvenile filings, means that judges are now primarily managers of the criminal justice system. A. M. ("Sandy") Keith, chief justice in Minnesota from 1991 to 1998, estimated in an interview that civil case declines could be attributed to the private sector's recognition that dispute resolution in court often takes too long and is too expensive.[8] Voluntary arbitration and mediation have become additional methods of dispute resolution by the practicing bar.

The decline in the handling of noncriminal cases by general courts is a na-

Figure 8: Minnesota District Judicial Workload (%)

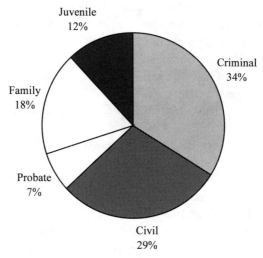

Juvenile
12%

Criminal
34%

Family
18%

Probate
7%

Civil
29%

Source: Minnesota State Court System, 1996 Annual Report.

tional phenomenon, but Minnesota seems to be leading in civil nonlitigious-ness. From 1994 to 1996 tort filings in Minnesota declined 9 percent. Only six of the twenty-seven states reporting tort activity to the National Center for State Courts had tort-filing rates lower than Minnesota's. The story is the same in other noncriminal areas. Minnesota ranks forty-third in the number of civil cases filed per 100,000 people. Contract filings declined 33 percent from 1994 to 1996; only seven of the twenty-one states reporting contract activity to the National Center had rates lower than Minnesota's.[9]

Keith's successor as chief justice, Kathleen Blatz, detailed the growth of the criminal load in Minnesota's courts during her first state-of-the-judiciary speech, delivered in June 1998: "In the last ten years, the number of serious criminal cases increased by 70 percent and the number of juvenile cases doubled. There has been an explosion in drug cases with a 155 percent increase and a remarkable 60 percent increase in dependency/neglect and termination of parental rights cases."[10]

Figure 8 shows the average judicial workload for district court judges in Minnesota. Civil and probate cases account for a little over one-third of a judge's time. The rest of that time is focused on the more heart-wrenching aspects of criminal, juvenile, and family law.

Minnesota's entire court system seems fiercely committed to expeditious processing of its cases. Judges argue that not only is "justice delayed justice denied" but swift criminal prosecution is a far better deterrent to crime than ever-longer sentences.[11] To ensure expeditious processing, Minnesota's courts have had timing goals for case processing since the 1980s. In the 1995 annual report the state court administrator published the entire "trial court case timing objective," together with scores on how the system was doing meeting the objectives. Juvenile and domestic abuse cases were to be processed in no more than two months' time, and in more than 90 percent of the cases, they were.[12]

Minnesota's court system is permeated with concern for rapid but thoughtful justice. There is no sense of cases dropping through the cracks or of plea bargains gone mad as is periodically reported in other jurisdictions. The businesslike yet thorough orientation of Minnesota's courts can best be understood through—and may have been influenced by—the creation of the court of appeals. The basis for the statutes governing the court of appeals is a constitutional amendment passed in 1982, which authorized this intermediate court. The first chief judge of the court of appeals, Peter Popovich, was a stickler for promptness, and he seemed to instill that ethic into the entire Minnesota court system. Popovich, who became supreme court chief justice after serving on the court of appeals, persuaded the legislature to insert in law a provision that the court of appeals has but ninety days to make its initial response to cases.

In its first full year of operation, 1984, the court of appeals handled just over 2,000 cases. That number rose slowly to 2,456 cases in 1996. From its earliest days the court of appeals prided itself on fast turnaround and on being accessible throughout the state. Accessibility was ensured through adopting a "circuit rider" concept. Panels of court-of-appeals judges hear oral arguments at eleven different sites in the state. In its first five years Minnesota's court of appeals handled cases with oral arguments in an average of 188 days, well under the guidelines of 255 days for appellate courts recommended by the American Bar Association. Appeals judges in Minnesota are expected to work fast and hard. The ABA guidelines suggest an appeals court judge should be writing between 70 and 80 opinions a year. In Minnesota that average was 112 per year.[13]

The new court of appeals, the Judicial Center, and court consolidation all were implemented under the remarkable leadership of Douglas K. Amdahl, chief justice from 1981 to 1988. Amdahl was said to be the ultimate Minnesotan: Norwegian, hard worker, practical, with unquestioned integrity. Amdahl liked to work with his hands, and a fellow justice, Lawrence Yetka, called Amdahl the "great carpenter" of court change first put into coherent form by a court planning committee in the 1970s.[14]

THE CHANGING FACE OF THE JUDICIARY

Minnesota's is the only supreme court thus far that has had a majority of women justices. In 1992 there were only fifty-nine women high court judges in the nation, and four of them were in Minnesota. No other high court at that time had more than two women. The situation was made even more striking because, despite its reputation as a progressive state, Minnesota has actually had a fairly pedestrian record in terms of women in public office.

It wasn't until 1974 that the first woman reached the district court bench in Minnesota, though three women served on the lower, municipal bench that existed at that time. Given this record, how is it that Minnesota found itself with a female majority on its highest court? The answer is simple: Governor Rudy Perpich, who served for ten (interrupted) years. He vowed when first elected to "make the judiciary look like Minnesota." Though Minnesota has a nonpartisan judicial election system, in practice the governor appoints most judges, and Perpich took advantage of his ability to determine who should sit on the court. He appointed the first woman to the supreme court in 1977. After Perpich's defeat in 1978, Republican Al Quie appointed the second woman, in 1982. Quie also established what Perpich didn't have, an elaborate judicial appointment committee system for district court appointments throughout the state. Seated judges and representatives of the bar would make recommendations for judicial appointments on a district-by-district basis as positions became available. As in all such systems, however, it was difficult for the committees to recommend women at a pace fast enough to redress past imbalances.

When Perpich returned to govern for eight more years (1983–91) with the first woman lieutenant governor, he changed the judicial appointment system by creating a statewide committee with people he knew would respond to his demands for more diversity on the bench. Critics saw more than feminism on Perpich's mind, however. The statewide judicial selection committee was seen as being made up of too many people with political as opposed to legal or judicial backgrounds. Many of his judicial appointments, the women on the supreme court included, were quietly criticized for being "too political." Perpich didn't seem to mind. He used Minnesota's governor-dominated selection system to create a source of state pride. In 1997 Minnesota became the tenth state with a woman as chief justice: Kathleen Blatz, a former legislator whose father had been a state senator, was appointed to the job by Governor Arne Carlson.

THE POLITICS OF JUDICIAL SELECTION

Minnesota has the nonpartisan electoral system, in which, in theory, potential judges file and run without partisan endorsement against one another for open judicial seats. Or they file and run against sitting judges when their seats are up for reelection. In practice, sitting judges resign before their terms expire so as to allow the governor to appoint a successor, thereby creating an instant incumbent. Since the reelection rate for judicial incumbents exceeds 90 percent, this practice tends to deter challengers in the initial election (and subsequent ones every six years thereafter). Minnesota judges don't like elections, and many of them express distaste at having to participate in them. Most judges would prefer having governors appoint their judicial successors even if the governor is from the opposite political party.

In 1996 there were 121 judicial elections at both the district (general) and appellate levels. Of these, only 3 were "open" seats, that is, the judge served his or her full term, thus denying the governor the opportunity to appoint a successor. The tradition of favoring initial appointment over election is long-standing in Minnesota. A 1970s study showed Minnesota with the highest percentage of elected trial judges originally gaining office by appointment, whether the election system was partisan or, like Minnesota's, nonpartisan. At that time 93 percent of Minnesota's judges had been appointed by the governor.[15] Ninety percent of the judges listed in the 1997–98 *Legislative Manual* were appointed by the governor.[16]

In the 118 district and appellate court elections in 1996 where there were incumbents, thirteen of those incumbents were challenged, close to the 10 percent average that court observers say has been the norm since the courts were consolidated. The 1996 challenges were unusual, however, because nearly all took place in the state's media centers and received extensive publicity. Both candidates for reelection to the supreme court were challenged, and seven of the eleven district court challenges were in the metropolitan area. Serious challenges in the metropolitan area were more rare in the past because, it was felt, the job of judge wasn't financially attractive and it was difficult to achieve enough visibility in the campaign to defeat an incumbent. But the large number of lawyers had made it more and more difficult to make a living practicing law; in addition, the bar association in the state's largest county, Hennepin, with more than half the state's lawyers, had institutionalized the practice of polling lawyers and rating the district's judges on qualities such as judicial temperament and knowledge of the law. Not surprisingly, the judges challenged for reelection were those with the lowest bar poll ratings. The practice of judicial ratings had created an opportunity for challengers to make an issue out of competence.

In 1998, ninety judicial seats were up for election, one on the supreme court, four on the court of appeals, and eighty-five in the district courts. Of these ninety elections, only one seat was open, so eighty-nine judges were seeking reelection. Ten of the eighty-nine were challenged, again close to the historic 10 percent rate. But although the statistics concerning the 1998 judicial elections appeared normal, the year was abnormal because of the raising of a serious challenge to Minnesota's nonpartisan judicial tradition. Judges on the ballot in Minnesota have the designation "Incumbent" next to their names, unlike all the other elected officials in the state. Judges do not carry party designation on the ballot. Minnesota's political parties routinely bestow preprimary endorsements on other nonpartisan offices, such as city, county, and even school board officials, but preprimary endorsements by political parties have not been given to judicial candidates.

The seeds of the 1998 controversy over judicial elections were sewn during the 1996 campaign. In that year the state's most prominent antiabortion interest group, the Minnesota Citizens Concerned for Life (MCCL), distributed a flyer that recommended the defeat of the two state supreme court judges on the ballot. The flyer also recommended the election of three candidates for district court because they were known to be "pro-life." Interest groups generally did not participate in Minnesota judicial elections, except that most of the money raised by judges to seek reelection came from lawyers. The entry of MCCL into the election was seen by many judges as threatening. One of the three district court MCCL recommendees was elected in 1996; both of the supreme court justices targeted for replacement were reelected. Despite the general success of incumbents, the supreme court undertook a rewriting of the canons relative to judicial campaigning. In the new rules judicial candidates were prohibited from personally seeking campaign contributions, announcing their views on issues, declaring political affiliation, seeking party endorsement, and attending political meetings—all understood to be part of the rules previously, though in some cases unwritten. There was, of course, no prohibition against interest groups' endorsement of candidates, but there was prohibition of candidates' attempting to solicit such endorsements.[17]

In 1998 the Republican party of Minnesota joined with a candidate for the state supreme court in challenging the rules concerning judicial elections. The federal district court denied the Republicans an injunction against the rules in February. In a two-to-one ruling issued 2 November 1998, just one day before the general election, a panel of the Eighth U.S. Circuit Court of Appeals supported that position, denying the Republican party its appeal. The candidate who was a party to the original suit had been defeated in the primary. In the general election the victorious incumbent judge, Alan Page, received the most votes ever tallied by a Minnesotan in a contested election, 1,303,920.

THE COURTS IN NATIONAL PERSPECTIVE

In the late 1970s a massive database was assembled which enumerated all the out-of-state citations from all fifty state supreme courts for the years 1870–1970.[18] Scholars using the data made the general assumption that courts cited more frequently had more prestige.[19] Minnesota ranked fourteenth among the fifty states in the frequency in which its decisions were cited by other states.[20]

A composite index of four studies examining state supreme court policy innovation, published in 1999, showed Minnesota's court tied for seventh place nationally. California, New Jersey, New York, Massachusetts, Washington, and Pennsylvania ranked ahead of Minnesota, with Illinois and Minnesota having the same scores. The four studies were published from 1981 to 1992.[21] Minnesota seems, then, to have been considered a very good court system except for the previously mentioned slowness to consolidate and centralize, a job done thoroughly once it was undertaken.

Minnesota and New Judicial Federalism

During the 1990s Minnesota's supreme court has had a relatively activist, relatively liberal tone, at least when compared with the tone of the U.S. Supreme Court. As such, Minnesota could be said to have been participating in the "new judicial federalism," the name given to the practice of state courts "carrying on the cultural revolution started when the U.S. Supreme Court was more liberal."[22] Minnesota was not a leader in judicial federalism, however, at least if leadership requires academic recognition. Most academic recognition went to states that used the new judicial federalism to make very large policy changes, such as New Jersey, which equalized school funding through the courts. There are no modern examples of Minnesota courts ordering reluctant bureaucracies and legislatures to change policy. As chapter 10 demonstrates, Minnesota seems to prefer to change its policy and respond to perceived societal needs through the political rather than the judicial process.

Some examples of new judicial federalism: in 1991 the court ruled six to one that the legislature could not set higher penalties for crack cocaine than for powdered cocaine. Crack was, according to the case, overwhelmingly the choice of African Americans whereas powder users were mostly white, and though that reality did not enter into the decision, it was the principal issue cited in media reports about the case.[23]

In 1993 the court threw out a 1991 state law that pegged welfare benefits for new arrivals to the state at 60 percent of the state's normal payment for a period of six months. The law was intended to discourage what was perceived by many legislators to be considerable in-migration from states with lower welfare benefits. The court's majority said that the provision interfered with the right to travel, which it called a "basic right."[24] The legislature repassed a version of the law in 1997, but a 1999 U.S. Supreme Court decision in a California case cast considerable doubt on the Minnesota law.[25]

In 1994 the court stopped the highway patrol from setting up roadblocks to look for drivers who might be under the influence of alcohol. Drivers, the court ruled, can be stopped in Minnesota only when there is objective reason to suspect a violation.[26]

Also in 1994 the court created a furor when it ruled that the state could not hold two repeat offenders under the state's new sexual predator law because the two did not display "an utter lack of power to control their sexual impulses." The standard of proof for the sexual predator law was changed from "utter inability to control" to "likely to engage" in the prohibited practices. The supreme court eventually accepted the new language.[27]

In 1995 the court ruled that Minnesota could not refuse to pay for the abortions of women on medical assistance, overturning a seventeen-year ban on the practice. The ruling was specifically cited by Minnesota Citizens Concerned for Life in its previously mentioned participation in the 1996 supreme court election.[28]

The Tobacco Case

The state of Minnesota and Blue Cross Blue Shield of Minnesota filed a lawsuit against the tobacco industry in 1994, alleging, for the first time, not simply that tobacco companies were selling a dangerous product but rather that the companies had acted illegally by conspiring to hide the product's danger. The case was the first state case against the tobacco industry to go to trial, in

January 1998, in Ramsey County District Court, and when it was finally settled in June that year, on the day jury deliberations were supposed to begin, it
had become "a brawl that helped shape the debate on one of the most significant public health issues of the twentieth century."[29] The Minnesota tobacco
case was significant because, on a per capita basis, the $6.1 billion settle-
ment for the state was the largest of similar cases settled to that time.[30] The
case also took on national, even international, significance because part of
the settlement required the tobacco industry to make public previously secret
documents that soon began showing up in tort claims in the United States and
England. Besides prohibitions on marketing inside Minnesota, including a
halt to billboard, bus, and transit advertising, under the settlement the industry agreed to shut down the Council for Tobacco Research and to stop providing placement fees for the use of tobacco products in movies. Attorney General Hubert H. ("Skip") Humphrey III, under whom the case was
prosecuted, attempted, after its successful conclusion, to be the first attorney
general in Minnesota history to become governor, an attempt that failed.

THE GROWTH IN CRIME

Minnesota's reputation and reality had always been one of low levels of
crime and incarceration. That reality was demonstrated in a 1998 report from
the U.S. Department of Justice which showed that, for the year 1997, Minnesota had the second lowest incarceration rate in the United States, at 113
per 100,000 people. Neighboring North Dakota had the lowest rate, 112 per
100,000. Minnesota was one of four states (with North Dakota, Maine, and
Vermont) that had incarceration rates smaller than one-third the national average of 410 per 100,000.[31]

Table 12 shows Minnesota's growth in incarceration compared with the
rest of the country from 1987 to 1997 and for three five-year periods inside
that ten-year span, 1990–95, 1991–96, and 1992–97. Generally, Minnesota's rate of incarceration is not only low but growing more slowly than the
rate in the rest of the country. There was a statistical spike in Minnesota's incarceration rate about 1991, however, so that, for the 1990–95 and 1991–96
periods, Minnesota's incarceration rate actually grew faster than that of the
rest of the country. For 1992 to 1997, the situation was back to "normal,"
and Minnesota's growth in incarceration was lower than the national average.

In Minnesota, sentencing guidelines were responsible for part of the increase in incarcerations. Before the establishment of sentencing guidelines,

Table 12: Growth in the Number of Prisoners: Minnesota vs All Other States

Period	Minnesota (%)	All States–Average (%)	Difference (%)
1987–97	108.4	113.5	-5.1
1992–97	38.8	41.5	-3.2
1991–96	48.6	44.1	+4.5
1990–95	53.1	43.3	+9.8

Source: U.S. Department of Justice, Bureau of Justice Statistics Bulletins, "Prisoners in 1997," "Prisoners in 1996," "Prisoners in 1995."

judges had more leeway in meting out punishments, and though there were many examples of judges under the old system giving out stiffer penalties than the guidelines would have allowed, there were many more examples of judges giving out lesser punishments than now required by the guidelines.

Other structural changes increased prison time in Minnesota. By the late 1980s an annual "major crime bill" became a Minnesota legislative tradition, with particular emphasis on longer sentences for drug dealers and the creation of new crimes such as stalking. Figure 9 portrays the outcome of these various crime bills and Minnesota's sentencing guidelines. As can be seen, Minnesota has the second longest prison terms for violent crimes in the American states.

The phenomenon of an incarceration surge in Minnesota about 1991 finds a companion in statistics related to felony filings. From 1991 to 1993 there was a decline nationally and in Minnesota in tort and contract cases. Nationally, there was a decline in felony filings as well, but in this area Minnesota was different from the national trend. Felony filings during this brief time increased over 5 percent in only ten states, one of them Minnesota, where filings grew by 5.7 percent. Though Minnesota experienced stronger growth in felony filings than the average state, the state's rate of felony filings per 100,000 people continued to be quite low compared with the rest of the country. For the year 1993, Minnesota had 388 felony filings per 100,000 people. The median rate for all states was 620 cases per 100,000.[32] In the 1994–96 period Minnesota's surge in felony filings had subsided. The growth in that three-year period was only 2 percent, and the state's rate compared with the rest of the country continued to be low.[33]

Figure 9: Average Minimum Months Served by Violent Offenders, 1994

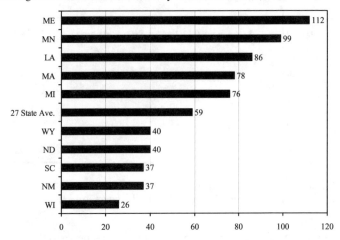

Source: U.S. Department of Justice, as reported in "Paying the Price," 1996 Report from the Minnesota Planning Agency, p. 5.
Note: Figure shows highest five, average of reporting states, and lowest five states.

Despite the brief escalation of criminality and incarceration in the early 1990s, Minnesotans and others continued to think of the state as a relatively crimeless sort of place until 1996, when the *New York Times* published a front-page Sunday story entitled, "Nice City's Nasty Distinction: Murder Soars in Minneapolis." The story noted that a 1995 surge of murders in Minneapolis had left Minnesota's largest city with a murder rate of 27.1 per 100,000, 70 percent higher than the New York City rate of 16 per 100,000.[34] Minnesota's statewide homicide rate was 3 per 100,000 in 1994.[35] New York, like most major cities except Minneapolis, experienced a significant decline in homicides in 1995. Nineteen ninety-five *was* a most unusual year in Minneapolis with regard to homicide. For the previous decade, the number of murders in the city varied between 40 and 60 annually, with 63 being the all-time record. In 1995 there were 95 homicides in Minneapolis, 12 more than had occurred in the entire state in 1985.

Was this a statistical aberration? Or had the denizens of Lake Wobegon traded in their fishing rods for 9mm Berettas? According to the theory developed by police, criminal justice, and media experts and accepted by all sides, in the early 1990s Minneapolis was the victim of gang and drug entrepreneurship. "The lads from Chicago are coming up here to sell their pharmaceutical products," a sergeant in Minneapolis's homicide division told the *New York Times*.[36] Unlike Chicago, for example, where two major gangs were said to control most of the drug and prostitution traffic, police in Minneapolis in 1995 estimated there were thirty to forty local gangs, none with the "clout" to enforce discipline.[37] Minneapolis presented economic opportunity to entrepreneurs unwilling to work through the more rigidly stratified drug-distribution systems in other cities. Besides, crack cocaine sold in Minneapolis during 1995 for about twenty dollars a rock, twice the rate in Chicago.

For 1996, there were 85 homicides in Minneapolis, fewer than the 95 of the previous year but still far above the previous record of 63 and taken as an indication that "Murderapolis" was permanent.[38] For 1997, the FBI reported 58 homicides in Minneapolis, a return to historic levels.[39] The period of "Murderapolis" appears to have been a statistical spike, but its challenge to the Minnesota notion of crimelessness was profound.

MIGRATION AND CRIME

Star Tribune research on the 1995 homicide victims noted that 25 percent of the 95 killed had lived in Minneapolis for less than five years. Thirteen of the 55 suspects arrested in the killings had the same short-term characteristic.[40] Police and community leaders believed those figures low. Through the 1980s African-American community leaders had always bristled at the suggestion that Minnesota's social and criminal problems were a result of the in-migration of African Americans. In 1995, however, Sharon Sayles Belton, the African-American mayor of Minneapolis, said openly and often that the problem was immigrants who came with "liabilities," and African-American community leaders usually agreed with her.[41]

For years—at least twenty years—there had been a belief among many in Minnesota about people coming from other states to seek generous welfare benefits or lenient criminal justice systems. The former had at least rational choice plausibility. Minnesota's benefits for various forms of public assistance have consistently ranked higher than those in most states. Periodic studies revealed, however, that most people migrated to the Twin Cities for economic opportunity or an improved social and educational climate for their children, not for a larger AFDC grant. As for a lenient criminal justice system, we have already noted Minnesota's ranking as second most severe in the country in terms of violent crimes. Whether a perception of leniency in Minnesota sentencing existed in other states is unknown. What is known is that migration became, peripherally, a political issue in Minnesota. Those from the governing establishment, both bureaucrats and elected officials, would deny that in-migration was costing Minnesota taxpayers any appreciable money in welfare payments or that new migrants were presenting extraordinary problems to the criminal justice system. Various studies proved the case, but it really didn't matter. Many people believed that the opposite was true. Until the mid-1990s, however, the issue remained largely unspoken in political debate. Then "Murderapolis" and a rapidly changing migratory picture throughout the state changed the nature of the discussion.

THE DRUG COURT

For the courts, especially in Hennepin and Ramsey counties, the new realities were chilling. Offenders were startlingly younger and more violent. The specter of drugs was a pervading presence. Ironically, court system response to drugs was arguably more effective before the introduction of sentencing guidelines, when judges could and often did offer offenders a choice between treatment and jail. The Minneapolis area returned to those days in January 1997 when Hennepin County district court judge Kevin Burke began a two-year experiment with a drug court. A principal element in the apparent success of drug courts is that judges can require treatment and follow-up as well as punishment and incarceration for drug users. Another factor in drug court success is that cases are handled immediately. In the first year of the Hennepin County drug court experiment the average time required for adjudication and sentencing of drug offenders dropped from four to six months to thirty days. The speed allowed Hennepin County to save more than $250,000 in jail costs for the first year of the program.

All indicators in the Hennepin drug court report were positive. Nearly half the offenders were successfully completing programs or had remained off drugs in the first year. The numbers of offenders who were successfully employed after being in court increased dramatically. Unlike the treatment of offenders before sentencing guidelines, when the offender's choices were treatment or jail, most participants in the modern drug court receive treatment *and* jail. In fact, in the first year of Hennepin's drug court experiment 82 percent of the offenders spent some time behind bars, compared with only 59 percent of drug offenders who served time in the year before the drug court's creation.[42]

According to the National Association of Drug Court professionals, the first drug court opened in 1989, and there were four hundred of them in 1998.[43] Minnesota was clearly not in the vanguard of the movement. But once in, the state performed admirably. The association cited Hennepin's as a model program for the nation.[44]

Of the three branches of government, Minnesota's judicial branch has seen the most change in the past twenty years. The seat of the judiciary moved out of the capitol building to a new Judicial Center. The courts became unified and consolidated according to the recommendation of judicial reformers; indeed, Minnesota's courts went from being among the least to the most "reformed" in the country. The nature of the court's work also changed. Judges spent less and less time deciding civil conflicts and more and more time processing criminals.

In the midst of all the changes, Minnesota's courts have achieved a deserved reputation for efficiency and innovation. Cases are handled with dispatch, at both the original and appellate levels. Minnesota courts regularly better national time guidelines for processing cases and appeals. Minnesota courts also rank near the top of states in judicial innovation.

Minnesota's system of selecting and retaining judges appears to be a contested-election model; in practice, however, 90 percent of the judges are initially appointed by the governor, and when they face the electorate, 90 percent are unopposed for reelection. Judges have been nonpartisan since early in the twentieth century. Political parties have not traditionally become involved in judicial elections, and Minnesota has judicial canons prohibiting judges from speaking to or being supported by political parties, though these rules came under legal challenge in 1998.

Minnesota's supreme court has been participating in the "new judicial federalism" being practiced in other states, whereby extensions of individual rights, once granted only by the U.S. Supreme Court, are being granted by state courts based on state constitutions.

Though there has been a large increase in crime and in criminal cases in Minnesota, the state continues to lag behind national averages and most other states in criminality. Despite having the second most stringent sentences for violent crimes in the nation, Minnesota has the second lowest incarceration rate, following only its neighbor North Dakota. In 1997 Minnesota's largest district court instituted a flexible drug court, oriented toward treatment and punishment, based on models throughout the country. The court and its judge-creator have received national recognition for having one of the best drug courts in the nation.

CHAPTER 9

Minnesota and the Federal System

Both the greatest conflicts of American history and the day-to-day opera-tions of American government are closely intertwined with American feder-alism—the division and sharing of authority and power between the federal government and the states and localities. Throughout American history there has been vigorous, sometimes violent debate about federalism, about which arena of government should govern in certain circumstances.

Generally, Minnesota and its federal officeholders have been supportive of national supremacy, that is, of the view that the federal government has a significant role to play in domestic matters. In many cases Minnesota is al-ready providing the service it wants the federal government to encourage in other states. That was the case, for instance, in the 1997 federal program for encouraging states to provide uninsured poor children with health insurance. Minnesota had addressed the issue in 1987 with the children's health plan and again in 1992 with the adoption of MinnesotaCare. By 1994 Minnesota had one of the lowest percentages of children without health insurance cov-erage in the nation, 6 percent versus the national average of 13 percent.[1]

In addition to supporting national supremacy, Minnesota tends to support cooperative as opposed to dual federalism, in part, again, because it is often providing the service being sought. Part of the motivation for supporting fed-eral encouragement of state programs to provide children's health insurance, for example, was the reality that Minnesota would receive some federal funds for a program it was already offering. This aspect of federalism con-tains a negative element for Minnesota, however. Congress is invariably drawn to providing more money to states that need the most encouragement to provide a service. In the case of children's health insurance Minnesota was deemed to have less of a problem than most states; thus, it received less federal money under the formulas devised to administer the program. Generally, in programs involving human services or environmental concerns, states with the most need (or, in Minnesota terms, the poorest records) receive more money than states such as Minnesota with good records. Those needy states also happen to be predominantly in the sunbelt, where, increasingly, presidential elections are ultimately contested.

Despite these differences, the dominant political and social goals in Minnesota have been quite similar to those dominant in the nation as a whole, so the state has a consistently high record of intergovernmental cooperation and rarely gets into conflicts with the federal government. If anything, Minnesota often is ahead of the federal government as they move down the same road. This has been less true since the Reagan years (1981–88), but the differences have only tended to sharpen Minnesotans' sense of self.

Minnesota's recent legal history vis-à-vis federal-state issues continues to demonstrate the state's commitment to cooperative federalism. Minnesota rarely appeals to states' rights in its disagreements with the federal government. An exception was the National Guard case, filed in 1987 and described later.

Intergovernmental collaboration in Minnesota antedated statehood, yet after 1858 it did not diminish in either extent or intensity. On the contrary, collaboration between governments increased with the expansion of government activities in general as the state matured. In short, as the role of government expanded, so did sharing between governments.[2]

The types of cooperative activities and the means of their administration in Minnesota are familiar. All the land-grant programs, except those designed to aid in the reclamation of arid lands, were in operation in familiar patterns. (Direct federal aids to individuals and groups were subject to state influences, much as described later in this chapter.) Cooperative exchanges of goods and services in Minnesota were recognizable as parts of the national pattern. So were the paraphernalia of administration. An ex officio State Land Board and its agents, the General Land Office and its local land officers, and local school and county officials all played their roles in the sharing process. Indeed, few federal and state offices in Minnesota were exempt from intergovernmental cooperative procedures.

In both the nineteenth- and twentieth-century grant-in-aid programs, federal aid provided a proportionately larger share of the budgets of the smaller states, the newer states, and the poorer states.[3] The proportionate role of federal funds in the Minnesota budget has fluctuated from a high of 40 percent in the early years of statehood to less than 10 percent in the early twentieth cen-

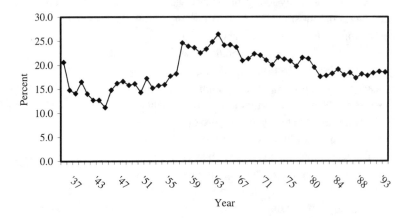

Source: *Statistical Abstract of the United States,* various years.
Note: This graph represents the federal portion of all available general revenue. This includes funds carried over from previous years and funds collected from lower units of government.

tury. Since the mid-1980s it has hovered around 18 percent (see figure 10). The federal government actually provided proportionately less in the last decade than in the 1960s and the 1970s.

The politics of sharing in Minnesota is also familiar. The role of the governor was and is central, not only because of his duties as chief executive but through his role as the political head of state. Still, the governor's influence waxed and waned in relation to his political position. In general, the governor served as the major political broker in the state's relations with the federal government. The office that the state of Minnesota established in Washington in 1986 to maintain a full-time state presence at the nation's capital was created and continued as a subset of the governor's office.

The central fact that emerges from an analysis of state-federal relations is the sheer weight of political time devoted to intergovernmental cooperation. Not only are administrators heavily involved in cooperative activities, but the programs most highly developed as shared programs also preempt a major share of the policymakers' time. Minnesota governors and legislators together are much occupied with intergovernmental cooperative programs.

A look at the extent and scope of intergovernmental programs indicates why this is so. By the end of the second decade of statehood the regulatory functions of government were also being shared, partly because the activities being regulated were tied to already cooperative programs (as in the case of railroad regulation) and partly because it was just more convenient to cooperate (as in the case of regulating state and national banking institutions). A survey of the governors' messages, the legislative journals, the statute books, and the opinions of the attorneys general reveals the extent of this concern with cooperative programs, which was not over the processes of collaboration but over other aspects of the program. Indeed, collaboration itself seems to have been taken for granted. Federal-state cooperation was a fact of life; hence, the policymakers rarely refer to it directly in their public messages, except to attack "Washington" when they believe they have reason to do so. The system of sharing is all the more impressive because of its implicit acceptance as part of the process of government.

MINNESOTA IN NATIONAL POLITICS

Minnesota stands out in national politics in several ways. In its earliest years of statehood, immediately before and during the Civil War, Minnesota was something of a national bellwether because active competition between Republicans and Democrats reflected the same burning issues that stirred the nation. After the Civil War Minnesota joined the solidly Republican North that had been settled by New Englanders and was dominated by their politics. When issues of a better deal for farmers and social reform in the towns and cities came to the fore, Minnesotans preferred to establish state and local third parties rather than either maintain or end their national political allegiance to the GOP. As a small state, Minnesota had relatively little influence in national GOP circles until the twentieth century.

In the late nineteenth and early twentieth centuries the Democratic party was essentially confined to the area along the Mississippi River from the state's southern border to St. Paul. It was known to be the strongest party in the Mississippi River towns mostly because it represented the "wet" element of the population, namely, those who opposed prohibition of alcoholic beverages, principally voters of German and Irish background. In the decade before World War I Minnesotans acquired some prominence in national Democratic circles, and Governor John A. Johnson was even touted for the Democratic presidential nomination before his untimely death in 1909.

Nationally as well as within the state, Minnesota's appearance on the political stage was as one of the radical prairie states whose congressional delegation pushed for radical, almost "socialistic" reforms on behalf of farmers and workers, while its voters, who supported third-party candidates of that stripe in other elections, continued to vote faithfully Republican for president. In the 1920s the Farmer-Labor party dominated Minnesota's congressional delegation, and in the elections of the 1930s it took control of state government, thereby weakening Minnesotans' Republican loyalties. When the Great Depression brought the Democrats and Franklin Delano Roosevelt to the fore nationally, Minnesotans supported FDR, breaking with tradition for almost the first time since the Civil War. This time the break was not only personal but also institutional. The Farmer-Labor leadership backed FDR, who, in turn, did not support the state Democratic party but threw his support to the Farmer-Laborites.

The national Democratic leadership ultimately urged the two parties to get together, which they did under the new leadership of Hubert H. Humphrey and his group in the early 1940s. Over the next decade the resultant Democratic-Farmer-Labor party became the majority party within the state. Humphrey became a U.S. senator and presidential candidate. Although he never won the presidency, for three decades he was one of the nation's most visible political leaders who slowly brought his close supporters into national prominence and national office. From the 1950s through the 1980s two Minnesotans, Humphrey and his protégé, Walter Mondale, were Democratic presidential candidates. Both also were elected vice-president. Former governor Orville Freeman served in the Kennedy cabinet, former congressman Bob Bergland was Jimmy Carter's secretary of agriculture, and Senator Eugene McCarthy became a presidential contender as the darling of the progressive wing of the Democratic party in 1968. Not only that, but even among the Republicans, Minnesotans became prominent. Warren Burger became chief justice of the United States in 1969. He and his colleague, Harry Blackmun, were appointed to the U.S. Supreme Court at about the same time and were known as the "Minnesota Twins."

The Republican party, faced in the 1950s with this rising DFL tide, began to rebuild itself. Both state parties recognized their uniqueness even within the national party fold. Suggestions to drop the Farmer-Labor appellation of the DFL were consistently rejected, especially after DFLers went to the Democratic party's national convention in 1960 and discovered how different Minnesota's Democrats were from most other Democrats. Not only that, but the Republicans decided that they had to mark their difference from the national party symbolically as well. Hence, they adopted the name "Independent Republican" in the 1970s and kept it until the 1990s.

These symbolic differences were very telling because they reflect a reality that Minnesotans of any political affiliation have been loath to relinquish. Indeed, as time went on, Minnesota politics became even more different, and its national role has reflected that. Since the 1960s Minnesota has voted Republican only once, in 1972, remaining in the Democratic column even during the Reagan sweeps.

One way states gain national political influence in America is through their impact on the nomination and election of presidential candidates. On this measure, when Minnesota candidates are not in contention, the state may have the least influence of all but the smallest states. Both Republicans and Democrats take it for granted that Minnesota will vote for the Democratic presidential candidate and the most liberal one at that, so they see little reason to campaign within the state. In addition, the state does not provide for a presidential primary, so there is no publicity or political mileage to be gained from a presence in the state before the November election.

Those members of Minnesota's congressional delegation who attain Washington influence generally do so in a typically Minnesota fashion. They are known for being policy wonks, not political operatives. Without presidential campaign clout, Minnesota congressmen and senators have little to offer a current or prospective president. Thus their influence tends to hinge on relationships with other members of Congress and on the strength of their ideas. During the past twenty-five years Minnesota congressmen with more than average influence have included Rep. Tim Penny, who was the most prominent of the neoconservative "new Democrats" before his 1994 voluntary retirement; Rep. Vin Weber, an early supporter and confidant of eventual Speaker Newt Gingrich; Rep. Bill Frenzel, who became a leading fiscal expert and ranking Republican on the Ways and Means Committee before his 1988 departure and who now provides fiscal analysis and commentary at the Brookings Institution; Sen. David Durenberger, universally acknowledged as the Senate's leading expert in healthcare policy, now a healthcare policy analyst; Rep. Martin Sabo, chair of the House Budget Committee before the Republicans won control of the House in 1994; and Rep. James Oberstar, ranking Democrat on the House Transportation Committee.

MINNESOTA AND NATIONAL PROGRAMS

The exact number of federal grant-in-aid programs for the states and localities depends on how and what one counts, but one can say that there were about 633 different programs in 1995, a kind of smorgasbord of choices. No state can choose all of them. Not all are relevant to every state, and all, or virtually all, programs require the states and localities to put in matching funds either directly or through supplementary services. Over the last quarter century there have been regular efforts to consolidate programs into block

Table 13: Federal Grants to Minnesota Government by Agency and Selected Programs, 1996 (in thousands of dollars)

Medicaid	1,579,616
Support Payments (AFDC)	254,650
Highway Trust Fund	241,577
Child Nutrition	141,950
Section 8 Housing Assistance grants	100,733
Children and Family Services	92,703
Education for the Disadvantaged	79,827
Public Housing Grants	76,032
State Unemployment Insurance and Services	54,584
Special Supplemental Food Program (WIC)	47,399
Low-Income Home Energy Assistance	46,135
FAA-Airport Trust Fund	45,864
Food Stamps	45,428
Education for the Handicapped	37,246
Job Training Partnership Act	33,561
Office of Justice Assistance–Justice Programs	25,899
Construction of Wastewater Treatment Facilities	24,379
Federal Transit Administration	24,375
Substance Abuse and Mental Health	22,822
Vocational and Adult Education	18,598
School Improvement Programs	13,211
Corporation for Public Broadcasting	12,814
Economic Development Administration	9,399
Centers for Disease Control	7,826
FEMA-Disaster Relief	7,618
National Guard Centers Construction	3,915
SSI	1,103
State and Private Forestry	637
State Justice Institute Grants	13

Source: Adapted from the Council of State Governments, *The Book of the States,* 1998–99, Vol. 32, pp. 288–91.

grants, some of which have partially succeeded, but with every consolidation, new programs proliferate or new ways of requiring state and local allocations of funds within the block grants themselves are introduced by Congress.

Despite this large number, the federal grant programs that provide the major share of federal assistance to the states are just four: Medicaid, welfare, environmental protection, and highways (see table 13). At one time, federal grants were designed to help the states provide a few basic services deemed desirable nationwide. Since the mid-1960s they have become means to try to press the states to move in national policy–driven directions. Originally, the provisions attached to the grants were designed to make certain that they would be used effectively for their intended purposes, but beginning in the mid-1960s Congress began to add cross-cutting conditions, that is, provisions designed to establish new federally enforced standards attached to all programs, particularly in the field of civil rights.

There has also been an effort to add "crossover" provisions only loosely connected with the purposes of a grant. Thus, for example, states accepting federal highway grants have to ban billboards within a certain distance from interstate highways or lose a share of the funds. Later the states were threatened with loss of a greater share of highway funds if they did not raise the drinking age to 21. This led to the kind of paradox that sometimes occurs in such complex situations. Minnesota originally lowered the voting age from 21 to 18 as a result of the passage of a federal amendment that Congress initiated and sent to the states. Then the state was forced to raise the drinking age back to 21, from 19 in Minnesota, by another congressional action that put them in a different untenable position.

Vis-à-vis other states, Minnesota often ranks near the bottom in terms of the "benefits" it receives from the federal system. For example, Minnesota ranked forty-seventh in terms of per capita expenditures for federal government direct payments to individuals in 1995. Direct payments include Social Security, Medicare, federal retirement, veterans' benefits, food stamps, student loans, farm-subsidy payments, and miscellaneous items. Minnesota's 1995 average was $2,315, nearly 15 percent lower than the $2,714 national average,[4] despite the fact that Minnesota had the fifth highest amount of government farm payments in 1995.[5]

Likewise, a frequent focus of state discontent is the ratio of federal grants received to tax burden; poor states are winners in this redistribution, whereas states such as Minnesota are losers. In FY 1995 Minnesota had the fifth largest deficit in per capita terms. Only Delaware, Illinois, New Jersey, and

Connecticut were bigger losers.[6] Between 1981 and 1995 the state's rank on this deficit ratio measure has varied from a high of fortieth to a low of forty-seventh.

Another way the federal government affects states is through the direct provision of services and concomitant employment of federal employees in the state. Thus, there are U.S. Postal Service employees in Minnesota, employees of the various federal departments in their regional offices, employees of the Veterans Administration hospitals, as well as full-time military personnel. The state ranked very low, forty-sixth, in per capita expenditure for federal government salaries and wages in 1995 and forty-fifth in terms of the numbers of federal civilian employees.[7] As indicated in chapter 1, Minnesota might be the actual center of the variously named Upper Midwest or Northwest, a region coincident with the Ninth Federal Reserve District, but the federal government has rarely treated Minnesota as a regional center. Minnesota has few federal regional facilities.

Another reason Minnesota ranks low in terms of per capita expenditures for federal government salaries and wages is the state's traditionally small full-time military presence. Minnesota ranks forty-sixth in the number of active-duty military personnel stationed there[8] and forty-third in per capita U.S. Department of Defense expenditures. Minnesota does a little better in another key defense statistic, ranking twenty-seventh in the per capita dollar value of U.S. Department of Defense contracts in 1995, not far below its population ranking as the twentieth largest state.[9]

In one "military" category the state ranked quite high, eighteenth in total U.S. Department of Defense contracts for civil functions, 18 percent above the rate its population would have "earned." This is the result of the fact that all navigable waters, which means all the rivers and some of the lakes in the state, can benefit from the navigation improvements provided directly by the U.S. Army Corps of Engineers. The principal beneficiaries in the state have been the Mississippi River and Lake Superior. In both, the Corps of Engineers was active since before statehood, improving river navigation and improving Minnesota's Lake Superior ports. Although this program is nominally a unilateral direct federal program, in fact the state and the cities benefiting from it must do their share to cooperate in acquiring rights-of-way and in providing certain ancillary improvements for the federal program to work at all. Most of Minnesota's benefits in this area come from the Upper Mississippi River Program, an enormous project stretching 854 miles from Rock Island, Illinois, to the head of navigation in Minnesota. The corps has built twenty-nine locks to enable river traffic to move up and down this waterway. Tens of millions of tons of shipping are moved along the river every year, and the tonnage is constantly rising. Obviously, these are not military expenditures but civil ones carried out by the Corps of Engineers for historic reasons.

Without large military institutions, very little federal activity takes the form of direct services or payments for services. Federal transfer payments play a more important role, and most important of all are federal-state-local cooperative programs, whereby the federal government funds states and localities to provide services the federal government wants to encourage but which are constitutionally outside its powers to provide directly.

In recent years many have complained that what was once a program of federal aid to the states has become a form of federal intervention, manifested either through regulation or through mandates. The first federal regulatory program, established in 1794, was aimed at the production of bourbon whiskey. In the nineteenth-century federal regulation and licensing of steamboats and railroads became a part of American life. Since all these were engaged in interstate commerce, there was little if any conflict over the federal role per se, only over the level of effectiveness of the programs. Regulation expanded tremendously in the twentieth century, with rules on civil rights and the environment leading the way.

The second form of extensive federal intervention is through federal mandates on states and their local subdivisions, whereby Congress requires state and local governments to undertake and pay for certain activities deemed to be in the national interest without providing any significant federal assistance to meet the costs. Civil rights mandates were among the earliest. In general, Minnesota has accepted federal regulation and mandates with little criticism or disagreement because Minnesotans have shared the federal policy goals they are designed to advance, but the radical extension of federal mandates in the 1980s and early 1990s led some Minnesota officials to join in the rising chorus to limit such federal intervention.

STATE-LOCAL RELATIONS

State-local relations are quite different from federal-local relations. Whereas the relations between the federal government and the states are relations between two formally sovereign civil societies that are linked, indeed intermeshed, through constitutional agreement, the state-local relationship is between a civil society and its civil communities, which are creatures of the state. Under U.S. constitutional law, as interpreted by the U.S. Supreme

Court, all political subdivisions of the states are creatures established by the states and dependent on them. The states are considered unitary rather than federal systems, and their internal governmental relations are therefore different from the state-federal relationship.

In some states, Minnesota among them, the prevailing state doctrine differs historically from that view, holding that local political subdivisions have a certain inherent right of home rule. Minnesota, like most states, has incorporated that view into its state constitutions as constitutional home rule. Residents of cities and sometimes counties have the right to adopt home-rule charters for their political subdivisions, determining their structure and, to a limited extent, their functions. In almost every case, however, the constitution gives the legislature the power to declare a state interest and to override the functional provisions to some degree.

More than that, as a state settled initially by New Englanders, Minnesota has a strong tradition of local self-government. Only in recent times have state programmatic actions and financial aid become dominant. Because of that tradition, Minnesota's municipalities have always been relatively strong. Nevertheless, state law mandates, defines, limits, or regulates local actions in almost every imaginable sphere because of the state's preeminent authority. Today Minnesota's fiscal system is almost completely interdependent. As discussed in chapter 11, about 87 percent of the state's $18 billion budget is redistributed to cities and other local taxing jurisdictions or directly to taxpayers in the form of "tax relief."

MINNESOTA AND THE NATIVE AMERICANS

A difficult aspect of federalism is found in the relationship of the state to Minnesota's indigenous people, who were here when the whites arrived— the Native Americans. Under the U.S. Constitution, the federal government has primary jurisdiction over relations with the Indians. Congress at one point made the Indian tribes federal wards. Under constitutional and international law, however, the Indian tribes retain a residual sovereignty. Constitutionally, they have been defined as "domestic dependent nations" since 1831; hence, the territories they control are within Minnesota but also independent of it for certain important purposes.[10] Those territories are known as reservations—lands reserved for the Indians as a result of their treaties with the United States.

There are eleven Indian reservations in Minnesota, each established by treaty between the Indians and the federal government. Seven are Ojibwe, and four are Dakota. Both nations spread over large regions of the northern United States and northwestern Canada. Since Congress passed the Indian Reorganization Act in 1934, each reservation has been governed according to a tribal constitution adopted by its Native American residents and approved by the Bureau of Indian Affairs. Each reservation elects its own local government, called the "reservation business committee," and the tribal government consists of a twelve-member executive committee.

Immediately on adoption of the 1934 act, six of the Minnesota Ojibwe reservations federated to form the Minnesota Chippewa Tribe. Red Lake, the seventh Ojibwe reservation, never ceded its land by treaty to the United States, so it has retained its independence to the point of writing its own constitution in 1918, long before the Indian Reorganization Act. The Red Lake Ojibwes refuse to cede their sovereignty to the federal, state, or other tribal governments. Strictly speaking, their territory is not even unambiguously part of the United States, a point they are quick to make. Of the eleven Indian reservations, only the Upper Sioux community has constitutional ties across state lines to other Dakota reservations in South Dakota.

The Minnesota Indian Affairs Council (MIAC) was established in 1963 as the official liaison between the state of Minnesota and the eleven tribal governments within the state. Its responsibilities cover the range of liaison and programmatic activities on behalf of Native Americans in Minnesota. The council includes representatives of the state government, the Indian tribes, and the public interest groups concerned with Indian affairs. MIAC is not only a liaison body; it also makes recommendations to the legislature for action. All the state departments dealing with Indian affairs are represented on MIAC, which also has a subcommittee named the Urban Indian Advisory Council to deal with the special problems of tens of thousands of urban Indians living in Minnesota, particularly in the Twin Cities.

Indian affairs in Minnesota, as in other states, formally remain a federal responsibility, but Minnesota has made its own efforts to improve the lives of the Native Americans at least since 1946. At first the state initiated efforts to eliminate racial discrimination against Native Americans by non-Indian Minnesotans. Then it undertook attempts to provide social services and economic development activities. The latter had less success than the state's efforts in human rights, and state activities in the social and economic fields continue to wax and wane.

Minnesota has the twelfth largest Native American population in the country. According to the 1990 census, there were just under fifty thousand Native Americans in Minnesota, a 37 percent increase since 1980, a much faster increase than the U.S. average. Approximately one-third lived in Minneapolis and St. Paul, and 15 percent more lived elsewhere in the metropolitan area. According to the 1990 census, approximately a quarter lived on the reservations, although that number is rising because of job opportunities in the casinos. According to the Minnesota State Planning Commission, in 1993 some 6.3 percent of the state's total population were people of color, of which the Native American population was the smallest proportion. Although the smallest group overall, Indians rank lowest in almost all the quality-of-life measures used in the state.

The real transformation in the Native American situation came from the development of gambling casinos on Indian reservations. Nationally, Indian gaming began to develop after the 1987 U.S. Supreme Court decision in *California v. Cabazon Band of Mission Indians* and the passage of the Indian Gaming Regulatory Act in 1988, itself a response to the Court's decision.[11] Tribes are allowed to negotiate compacts with the states in which they are located, compacts that specify the location and types of gambling to be permitted. In essence, the compacts are licenses to erect and operate casinos. Minnesota tribes were especially aggressive in negotiating these compacts. As indicated, the state had supported Indians through civil rights and economic development activities for some time. There was a long history of relationships between the state's bureaucrats and Indian administrators. In addition, the states' two political parties openly vied for the support of prominent Indian leaders. And Minnesota tribes had began erecting and operating bingo parlors in the early 1980s. Indeed, the 1988 regulatory act was at first opposed by tribal leaders in Minnesota because they feared they would lose the bingo business.

Thus, when the opportunity for local tribes to make deals with the states over gambling arrived, Minnesota's tribal leaders had sufficient political sophistication to consummate the deals rapidly. In addition, Minnesota governor Rudy Perpich moved quickly to establish a small commission to represent the state in negotiating the compact. Of the first thirteen Indian gaming compacts negotiated in the United States, eleven were in Minnesota.

Minnesota's tribes got the best deals in the nation; unlike other states' compacts, Minnesota's are in perpetuity. This means Minnesota's tribes are free to operate casinos indefinitely without sharing revenues with the state.[12] Minnesota reached eighteen casinos through its twenty-two compacts by 1997. No new ones are planned, though there are expansions at the existing sites. Two of Minnesota's compacts are among the eight largest Indian gambling operations in the United States.[13] The largest in Minnesota are the Mystic Lake Casino, located in the Twin Cities metropolitan area in Prior

Lake and the second largest Indian casino in the nation, owned by the tiny Mdewakanton Sioux band; and the Grand Casinos at Hinkley and on Lake Mille Lacs, owned by the much larger Mille Lacs band of Ojibwes.

How much Native Americans profit from gambling was a question that had both legal and political implications in the successful suit by the Mille Lacs and Fond du Lac bands and others against the state of Minnesota concerning hunting and fishing rights. The suit began in federal court in 1990. The Mille Lacs band asserted that the 1837 treaty signed between the Chippewa tribes and the United States was still in effect in the east-central part of Minnesota where their reservations were located and that the abrogation of those rights in 1850 by then president Zachary Taylor was improper.

Similar lawsuits in other parts of the country had been decided in favor of the tribes, so Minnesota's Department of Natural Resources negotiated a settlement that it presented to the legislature in 1993. The settlement was narrowly rejected by the legislature, in part because gill netting and spearing were to be allowed—both practices abhorred by sport-fishing groups—and in part because Indian gaming had become successful. Many legislators thought the public believed that Indians no longer needed game- and fish-harvesting rights for survival. Lawyers representing sports groups and local governments made the same economic argument to the three-judge Eighth Circuit appeals court panel that heard the case in 1997. The court ruled in favor of the Indians, however, and in March 1999 the U.S. Supreme Court, in a 5–4 decision, agreed.[14]

MINNESOTA AND GLOBALIZATION

Changing world realities are adding a global dimension to intergovernmental relations in Minnesota. Under the U.S. Constitution, foreign affairs are the virtually exclusive province of the federal government. Defense affairs, though formally cooperative, have become overwhelmingly a federal responsibility. Nevertheless, post–World War II globalization has inserted Minnesota more extensively into world affairs than ever. At present, the state's relations to the rest of the world have no separate constitutional dimension but unquestionably are affected by U.S. agreements with other countries.

For example, Minnesota has had to bear costs of refugee absorption stemming from American foreign policy activities. The collapse of South Vietnam in 1975 led to a flow of refugees from Indochina to the United States. Various church groups with ties to Minnesota began sponsoring the resettlement of the Hmong people to St. Paul. Among those resettled first were clan and military leaders, who soon sent for their extended families. Eventually, St. Paul came to have the largest concentration of Hmong in the United States. The Hmong not only introduced a new cultural dimension into the region but also produced special problems of assimilation because they traditionally lived as nonliterate farmers.[15] More recently, other refugee groups have come into Minnesota. In the five counties in the state's southwestern corner the proportion of minority residents grew enormously, from, in one county's case, 1.18 percent in 1980 to an estimated 14.19 percent in 2000, with increases of at least 400 percent in the other four counties. The newcomers are Lao, Vietnamese, Somali, Mexican, and other Hispanic.[16]

American military policy increasingly has involved the Minnesota National Guard in an active capacity as the U.S. military establishment has integrated the various state National Guard units more fully into the total force structure. In a highly publicized conflict between Minnesota and the federal government in the later 1980s, Governor Rudy Perpich challenged the federal government's authority to send Minnesota National Guard units to Honduras, ostensibly for training missions but actually to assist the American forces there in helping the Honduran government suppress an insurgency. Perpich claimed that the federal government had no such right in peacetime when the Guard was under state jurisdiction. The case went to the U.S. Supreme Court, which ruled in favor of the federal government on the grounds that these were just training missions and the federal government could train National Guard units when and where it saw fit.[17]

In a still uncharted area, Minnesota's regulatory powers, like those of the rest of the states, could be seriously affected by the North American Free Trade Agreement (NAFTA) with Canada and Mexico. NAFTA has provisions for overriding state regulatory powers in a number of cases to enable goods and services to flow more freely throughout North America. The matter has not yet been tested, so the scope of its impact on Minnesota has yet to be determined.

In sum, it is accurate to say that government in Minnesota heavily involves intergovernmental relations: federal-state, state-local, relations with Native Americans, and a growing field of intergovernmental relations extending beyond the borders of the United States in an era of globalization, and all the various combinations thereof. As a state, Minnesota is both limited and gains greater autonomy through its handling of these intergovernmental relations. In a world of growing interdependence we may assume that intergovernmental relations will expand in all directions in the future.

CHAPTER 10

Public Policy

Consistent with its moralistic political culture, Minnesota is the epitome of a "high taxing/high spending" state. For example, in 1994 Minnesota ranked seventh in state and local tax burden and sixth in state and local general expenditures, both expressed in per capita terms.[1] But Minnesota does not just spread money around; it innovates in a number of policy areas. Minnesota was the first to ban smoking in restaurants; it was the first to allow schoolchildren choice among public schools; it was the first to enact pay equity based on comparable worth for male and female state employees. The state was a leader in the reform of criminal-sentencing guidelines in the 1970s; in reorienting welfare to work and in recycling waste in the 1980s; in guaranteeing healthcare, in fostering charter schools, and in suing tobacco companies in the 1990s. And citizens are generally very positive about their state government: in a 1995 poll 75 percent said they got their money's worth from their state and local taxes.[2]

REVENUE POLICY

Minnesota is a high-tax state in part because it is relatively affluent and in part because its citizens believe in public services. In 1997 Minnesota's per capita personal income was $26,797, which placed it tenth among the states, meaning that its wealth is well above average.[3] But Minnesota is not in the affluence league of Connecticut or New Jersey. A more precise measure of resources to be taxed is the tax capacity index of the former U.S. Advisory Commission on Intergovernmental Relations (ACIR), which includes a variety of sources besides personal income. On this measure in 1994 Minnesota ranked fifteenth.[4] So aside from comfortable personal wealth, Minnesota does not have unusually deep pockets.

Where Minnesota stands out is in its historic willingness to tax: on the ACIR's measure of tax effort Minnesota ranked sixth among the states in 1994.[5] This score measures a state's tax collection efforts relative to its overall tax capacity; thus, Minnesota puts forth a greater tax effort than forty-four of the states. It is also worthy of note that Minnesota did not adopt a tax or expenditure limit during the tax revolt of the 1970s. Minnesotans, by and large, expect to pay for their public services.

Minnesota's tax system also stands out in its progressiveness: it was first in progressivity in 1995.[6] Actually, it is more accurate to say that Minnesota ranks last in regressivity. A recent analysis shows that Minnesota's overall tax system is proportional in its incidence except for the lowest income class; however, other states' tax systems are so regressive that Minnesota's proportionality appears progressive in comparison.[7] At any rate, Minnesota's tax system is noteworthy in the extent to which it does not unduly burden the poor.

The primary reason for its progressivity is a decision to rely heavily on the individual income tax as a generator of revenue. But the rates are not steeply progressive. As of July 1999, the rate of taxation per income level ranges from 5.5 percent to 8 percent; an earned income tax credit took effect in 1991 and has been increased twice since then, further helping the working poor.

State revenue breakdown for 1997 is shown in figure 11 (local government finances are discussed in chapter 11). The individual income tax yielded more than a quarter of total revenue, followed by the sales tax at less than a quarter. Minnesota has also sought to make the sales tax less regressive in its incidence. The 6.5 percent sales tax excludes food, clothing, and prescription drugs, thus mitigating its impact on the poor. The sales tax has gradually been extended to a variety of services, as has happened in many states, thereby broadening its base and increasing its yield. Minnesota also gets about 4 percent of its revenues from a corporate income tax, which, with a marginal rate of 9.8 percent, is among the higher rates imposed by the fifty states. Unlike the case in some states, Minnesota's rate is not graduated for corporations of different sizes.

Local governments rely on the property tax, but the state controls those property taxes to a greater extent than in most states, setting rates for twelve classes of property.[8] Some state mechanisms make the property tax's impact less regressive, for example, the rate structure, the circuit breaker (whereby a property tax bill exceeding a certain percentage of income is partially re-

Figure 11: Total State Revenues for Fiscal Year 1997 ($15,419 in Millions)

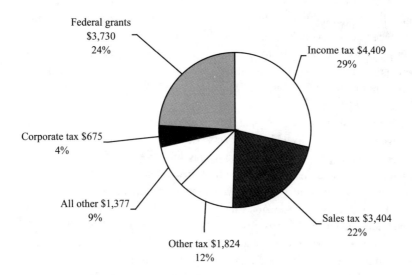

Source: Minnesota Data Book for Legislators, 2d ed. (St. Paul: Research Department, Minnesota House of Representatives, 1997), p. 27.

funded), the homestead credit (whereby people living in their own homes get a tax break), and the renters' credit. All these mechanisms contribute to a less regressive tax structure than in any other state.

In addition to the major taxes, Minnesota has a variety of smaller taxes included in the 12 percent total, such as taxes on gasoline (20 cents a gallon), automobiles, cigarettes (48 cents a pack), alcoholic beverages, mining, and licenses for various activities, such as fishing, hunting, and cross-country skiing. In recent years Minnesota has derived money from its lottery, amounting to less than 1 percent of own-source general revenue in 1994.[9] The lottery totals are included in the 9 percent "all other" revenues in the figure. Forty percent of the lottery proceeds are earmarked for the Environment and Natural Resources Trust Fund, and 60 percent goes to the general fund. Charitable gambling and horse racing contribute smaller amounts to the revenue coffers; casino gambling is especially popular, but casinos are located on Indian reservations so they do not contribute direct tax revenue, according to treaty laws.

The only other major revenue source is the federal government. The state got about a quarter of its budget from the federal government in 1997, a percentage that has been declining for a while. Minnesota is a state that always supplies more in taxes paid to the federal government than is returned in federal grants to the state, reflecting its relative affluence. But still, federal revenues are much sought after, and Minnesota's bureaucratic grantsmanship is vigorous.

In recent years the Minnesota revenue stream has become more balanced between the income tax and the sales tax. After bitter experience in the 1980s the state has also kept a sufficient "rainy day" reserve (now $622 million) on hand to avoid sudden, damaging shortfalls in revenues. The state operates on a biennial budget cycle with a four-year planning horizon, so that, for example, the 1997 legislative session (the "long session") generated the FY 1998 and 1999 budgets and the planning estimates for 2000 and 2001. The 1998 session (the "short session") then was used for any midcourse corrections needed to keep the budget on target plus passing the capital budget. Whenever a legislative committee considers a policy change, the finance department provides a fiscal note that details the four-year implications of that change, including the implications for other departments and local governments. Minnesota, like forty-eight other states, has a balanced-budget requirement, which is taken seriously.

EXPENDITURE POLICY

As might be expected from a high-taxing state, Minnesota is also a big spender. Figure 12 shows the proportionate distribution of the generous amounts of money spent by the state government. As in most states, Minnesota's largest chunk of money goes to education; in 1997 27 percent went to support elementary and secondary education and 9 percent went toward higher education. This represents an increase in the share for K–12 education and a diminution for higher education. A lesser proportion, 22 percent, goes to health and human services, where Medicaid was the fastest growing program. The other large sector is transportation, which received 14 percent of the total funding. Minnesota covers a large geographic area, ranking twelfth among the states in square miles, and the cold weather takes its toll on road surfaces. Historically, more roads were built between farms because Minne-

Figure 12: Total State Spending for Fiscal Year 1997 ($12,113 in Millions), Excluding Federal Funds

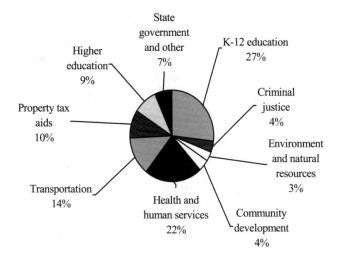

State government and other 7%

Higher education 9%

K-12 education 27%

Property tax aids 10%

Criminal justice 4%

Environment and natural resources 3%

Transportation 14%

Health and human services 22%

Community development 4%

Source: Minnesota Data Book for Legislators, 2d ed. (St. Paul: Research Department, Minnesota House of Representatives, 1997), p. 27.

sota's homestead plots were smaller than in other states. Finally, the other significant recipient was property tax aids, with 10 percent of the pie. We explain this expenditure more fully in chapter 11. Other programs receive less than a 10 percent share; of these, corrections was the fastest growing area in the 1990s, as was true in many states.

POLICY INNOVATION IN MINNESOTA

By a variety of measures, Minnesota stands out as an innovative state. For example, in the best-known ranking of policy innovation in the fifty states, Minnesota was twelfth.[10] In the Ford Foundation's annual awards program for Innovations in American Government, Minnesota has won five times since 1986. Minnesota's bureaucracy is very professional, and its lawmakers are often interested in taking bold steps to solve public problems, both characteristics typical of a moralistic political culture. Its citizens are accustomed to public services at a very high level. But Minnesota's innovations are not as liberal as reputation would have it; rather, they are often pragmatic as well as innovative, combining public sector with private sector responses.

Table 14: Postwar Minnesota Reorganization and Reform Efforts

Study	Dates	Type
Constitution Commission of Minnesota	1947–48	Constitutional reforms, constitutional office changes
Efficiency in Government Commission	1949–50	Reorganization, administrative reforms, strengthening the legislative branch, increased control for the executive
The Minnesota Self-Survey	1955–58	Executive reorganization
Governor's Council of Executive Reorganization	1968	Executive reorganization
Loaned Executive Action Program (LEAP)	1972–73	Executive reorganization, management reforms
Minnesota Constitutional Study Commission	1973	Reforms in all three branches, constitutional office changes
Governor's Task Force on Waste and Mismanagement	1977–78	Managerial reforms, some executive reorganization
Governor's Task Force on Constitutional Officers	1984	Constitutional office changes
Strive for Excellence in Performance (STEP)	1985–90	Managerial and programmatic reforms
Commission on Reform and Efficiency (CORE)	1991–92	Executive reorganization, managerial and programmatic reforms

Source: State of Minnesota Commission on Reform and Efficiency, *A Minnesota Model: Recommendations for Reorganizing the Executive Branch*, Summary Report (St. Paul: State of Minnesota, 1993), p. 25.

We have chosen a few policy areas that exemplify Minnesota's approach to public problems. We begin with state government itself.

Innovations in the Bureaucracy

The STEP Program Among Minnesota's award-winning innovations is the STEP program. As table 14 illustrates, the Minnesota bureaucracy has endured several rounds of efficiency and productivity enhancements, including Governor Rudy Perpich's ban in the mid-1970s on office coffeepots as wasteful of energy, both human and electrical. After being defeated and sitting out four years in Austria working for Control Data, in 1982 Perpich returned a new man. He had seen how angry Austrian office workers got when their wine was banned from their office coolers and at lunch, and he finally understood Minnesota's workers' ire, which he believed cost him the 1978 election.[11]

At the beginning of his second term Perpich appointed William Andres, chairman of Dayton-Hudson, the retailing giant, to chair another management-improvement group. Andres teamed up in 1984 with Sandra Hale, the new commissioner of administration, to design a new kind of management-improvement program. Perpich gave them the mandate "to help make Minnesota the best managed state in the nation."[12] Hale and Andres changed the STEP program's name from "Strive Toward Efficiency and Productivity" to "Strive Toward Excellence in Performance."

Their political strategy was inclusive. For the steering committee, they recruited top business leaders and the major public sector unions and enlisted the governor as cochair. The committee worked closely with the Minnesota Business Partnership (a group of the top CEOs in the state), which initiated an annual award for the best STEP manager. State employees submitted to the committee proposals to improve productivity, each of which had to have a private sector partner. The aims were to foster innovation among bureaucrats and to change the bureaucratic culture, sort of a forerunner of Total Quality Management.

Three hundred proposals came in from twenty-three agencies; thirty-seven were chosen in the first round in 1985.[13] Illustrative projects included streamlining the processing of workers' compensation claims, sentencing prisoners to community service as an alternative to incarceration, accepting credit cards from those buying seasonal parks permits, reducing backlogs in various agencies, and preparing an *Economic Report to the Governor*. None of the STEP projects was a major innovation, but collectively they signaled a change in bureaucratic culture, an orientation toward excellence and high performance.

Enterprise Management The STEP program set in motion a number of other changes in the bureaucracy, such as the introduction of "enterprise management" in 1986 wherein functions of the Department of Administration were classified either as monopolies or as marketplace activities.[14] Monopolies were managed as public utilities, and their rates were set through negotiation with their customers. Marketplace bureaus were opened up to competition, from either the public or the private sector: examples include data entry, central stores, copying services, and management consulting. Competition was thought to be the force that would spur innovation in these agencies. There was also an effort to match up funding with agency type so that monopolies had general fund appropriations and marketplace activities had revolving fund financing so that earnings could be retained.[15] After initial skepticism legislators went along with the idea. This initiative was an early example of the "reinventing government movement" later popularized by David Osborne and Ted Gaebler.

Pay Equity In the early 1980s Minnesota became the first state to adopt and implement a comparable worth policy for government employees. The legislature passed the State Employees Pay Equity Act in 1982. Two years later the state extended the policy to Minnesota localities.

For advocates in Minnesota and elsewhere, the issue behind comparable worth was the income gap between men and women and, to a lesser extent, between minorities and nonminorities. During the 1970s women as a group earned two-thirds of what men did. Receiving equal pay for equal work was not the only issue in the debate, however. Women often found themselves segregated into low-paying jobs. This job segregation was evident in Minnesota: 97.8 percent of clerk-typists were female, and 99.9 percent of senior highway maintenance workers were male.[16] No female-dominated job class was paid at or above the average wage for male-dominated jobs with the same job rating.

In order to equalize men's and women's pay scales, Minnesota used a job evaluation system developed earlier by Hay Associates to rank state employee jobs. Unlike most other states, Minnesota used the salary levels of male-dominated jobs as a standard with which to compare the salary levels of female-dominated jobs. It then raised females' salaries to the level of the males', rather than lowering males'.

The politics of the bill's passage were relatively noncontroversial. Prodded by the American Federation of State, County, and Municipal Employees (AFSCME, the major public sector union) and the Council on the Economic Status of Women, the legislature passed the bill easily, despite the fact that the state was in a recession. Expecting that funding would be delayed a year, Republican governor Al Quie signed the bill; there was no opposition from the business community, and the media took little note. When Governor Perpich entered office in 1983, however, he decided to begin implementation immediately.

By 1987 more than eighty-five hundred employees had received pay-equity raises. The impact on the state budget was significant because the cost was $22 million, or 3.7 percent of the 1983 salary baseline budget.

Education Reform

The story of Minnesota's educational policy in modern times has three important landmarks. The first came to be called the "Minnesota Miracle."

The "Minnesota Miracle" Passed at the insistence of Governor Wendell Anderson in 1971, during the longest special session in the state's history, the funding plan boosted the state's share of educational expenditures, as compared with local's share, from 43 percent to 70 percent.[17] The concept of the "Minnesota Miracle" was hatched by the Citizens League and was sold to the public and the legislature as a matter of equity. It was argued that students in the poorest districts should have the same opportunity as those in the wealthiest, a premise that resonates well in a moralistic political culture. The "miracle" essentially left the state in control of school finances. Interestingly, Minnesota was the only state at the time to equalize intrastate school-financing inequities through the political process rather than through the courts.

The "miracle" has not fully erased intrastate inequities, however. It has reduced discrepancies in per pupil operating expenditures significantly, but capital spending remains substantially dependent on the local property tax. Hence, suburban school buildings normally look better than those located in the inner cities of Minneapolis and St. Paul or most rural districts. Reformers continue to dream of the day when education is completely removed from the local property tax and loaded onto a statewide tax.

School Choice The second major period of education reform was during the 1980s. In 1982 the Citizens League issued a report favoring school vouchers, and two years later the Minnesota Business Partnership followed up with its own eighteen-month, $250,000 study, *The Minnesota Plan*. The reports cautioned that Minnesota's reputation for excellence in education created a feeling of complacency and a false sense of confidence.[18] The Citizens League's impact has been singled out as particularly influential: one scholar commented, "No other organization matches its staying power or sustained influence as an agenda-setter on educational reform issues."[19]

Most important, in 1984 a group of nine individuals emerged who were very important in the reform effort. These "policy entrepreneurs," who were mostly outside government and outside education, caucused frequently to discuss their own ideas of "deep reform," centering on empowering students and parents to make choices among schools and empowering teachers as professionals. Some had been active in the Citizens League, some in the Business Partnership; others were scholars or policy analysts. They included people such as Joe Nathan, a nationally known education expert, and John Brandl, a state senator and public policy professor. They promoted the idea of school choice before it surfaced nationally; the best-known book on choice, *Politics, Markets, and America's Schools*, was not published until 1990.[20] (This book coincidentally was written by two political scientists with University of Minnesota Ph.D.'s.) No one in Minnesota thought it odd that nine people with no particular constituencies and no ax to grind other than making a better education system contributed the most important ideas to the policy debate.

Of course, it was critical that these policy entrepreneurs were able to get the ear of Governor Perpich, who championed their policy initiatives. Perpich was in the market for an education program as part of his strategy to make Minnesota the "brainpower state." He had also been a dissatisfied parent who wanted to send his daughter to a school outside her district of residence.[21] In January 1985 he issued his *Access to Excellence* proposal, which featured open enrollment or choice for students and parents.

Perpich was very active on the issue, forming bipartisan alliances with legislative leaders, personally lobbying lawmakers, making media appeals, and mobilizing grassroots constituencies. But victory was not immediate. In the 1985 legislative session all the reformers managed was the Postsecondary Enrollment Options Act (PSEOA), in which high school juniors and seniors of ability could go to college on either a full-time or a part-time basis and get credit toward high school graduation. Because school aid follows the student, high schools lose money when students exercise this option. This program has proved to be popular with high school juniors and seniors wanting to take more challenging courses and get a free head start on college.

By the 1987 session school choice was a more accepted idea, but it was not until the 1988 session that the K–12 Enrollment Options Program was enacted; this was the first mandatory school-choice program in the country. A student could choose to go to any public school in the state, unless to do so would adversely affect racial balance. State school aid follows the students, thereby placing financial pressure on the schools to compete for students.

School choice has been popular, especially with star athletes trying to find a potential state-championship team, but it affects a relatively limited number of students, 17,500 in 1995–96.[22] It has had greater impact on schools in rural Minnesota than in the cities. The overcrowding of schools in the metro area, the unavailability of transportation, and racial imbalance are factors constraining the exercise of choice. Moreover, reformers have argued that unless students can choose among competing "brands" of schools, the choice is meaningless. So in 1991 Minnesota lawmakers were the first in the country to enact charter schools (public schools free of many state mandates, organized by teachers and parents around unique philosophies). They have been a slow but unqualified success. By the fall of 1997 twenty-seven charter schools had been opened. In the fall of 1998 forty-one were expected, and an association of charter schools was formed in the summer of 1998.

Vouchers The third period of education reform occurred during the mid-1990s under Governor Arne Carlson. Carlson strongly believed that choice should apply to private schools as well as public. He pushed for this idea in the 1996 and 1997 regular legislative sessions but failed to interest lawmakers, even members of his own party. Then he called a special session in June 1997 and got a compromise plan adopted. The new legislation allows for a significant increase in allowable education deductions plus new tax credits for parents who spend personal funds on their children's education. The compromise was sufficiently muddled that both opponents and supporters of vouchers claimed victory, but everyone agrees that the teachers' unions lost. The trend toward individual student empowerment is clear.

Another critical development during the Carlson years signaled a loss of status for the education establishment. In 1995 Governor Carlson initiated a change in the name and mission of the Department of Education. The new name is the Department of Children, Families, and Learning; the new mission is "lifelong learning," encompassing everything from subsidized day care for those on public assistance to senior citizen education programming. In the 1997 session the legislature realigned its committee structure along similar lines. One result of this restructuring was a substantial funding increase for "baby ed," including a 61 percent increase in Head Start.[23]

Minnesota made news for its experiment in privatization of public education. In 1993 the Minneapolis School Board hired a private management firm, Public Strategies Group, Inc., to run its schools. The firm's president, Peter Hutchinson, a former state finance commissioner with no teaching credentials, became the de facto superintendent of schools. His consulting firm includes several of the individuals involved in the "enterprise government" and the STEP program described earlier, and it is linked to Osborne and Gaebler's network. PSG had a pay-for-performance contract with the Minneapolis School Board. Although relations with the board were sometimes rocky, on the whole the experiment worked until mid-1997, when the school board decided to return to a traditional superintendent.

The story of school reform in Minnesota is the story of policy entrepreneurs, the Citizens League, governors of both parties, and legislators of both parties. Absent from the list are local school boards, school superintendents, and teachers' unions, which vigorously opposed most of the reforms. Although teachers' unions have been generous financial supporters of the DFL party and, to a lesser extent, of the Republican party, they have been unable to stem the reform tide. In September 1998 the Minnesota Education Association (MEA) and the Minnesota Federation of Teachers (MFT) merged into one organization. Whether the larger union—Education Minnesota—will be able to block a full-fledged voucher system is unclear.

Healthcare Reform

A handful of states have enacted formal commitments to universal health coverage; of those, Hawaii in the 1970s and Minnesota, Florida, and Washington in the early 1990s had the most comprehensive programs in that they attempted to control costs and to ensure access to healthcare. Washington and Florida repealed their laws in part, however; Minnesota has chipped away at its law, but key parts of it remain intact. Hawaii remains the only state to have truly universal coverage.

Minnesota's journey to healthcare reform is aptly described by Howard Leichter as "the trip from Acrimony to Accommodation," referring to the fact that in 1991 Republican governor Carlson vetoed one health-reform bill; ten months later he signed another bill into law.[24] The ten-month trip was an interesting saga. To understand it, we have to set the stage.

The structure of Minnesota's healthcare industry is unusual because the Twin Cities' market is among the most HMO-penetrated markets in the country, exceeded only by California markets. By law, Minnesota hospitals and

HMOs must be nonprofits. The problems identified in Minnesota in 1991 were familiar ones—access, cost, and quality, though quality was not much of an issue. Yet, by national standards, Minnesota was in good shape on all dimensions. But as Senator Linda Berglin, chair of the Health and Human Services Committee, said, "Being a little better than the mess in the rest of the country isn't good enough."[25]

As in education, major healthcare reform built on previous legislation, in this case the Children's Health Plan (CHP), enacted in 1987. In the same year, a major study of financial access to healthcare was conducted by the Department of Health. Subsequently, the Health Care Access Commission was created to further study and review the access problem. The commission was to play a major role in the next reform period.

The commission's recommendation resulted in a 1991 bill sponsored by two of its members—Rep. Paul Ogren, DFL, chair of the House Health and Human Services Committee, and DFL senator Linda Berglin, who had spearheaded the pay-equity issue. This bill passed comfortably, though on a party-line vote. It was then vetoed by Republican governor Carlson, previously a supporter of healthcare access, because it was "budget busting."

The reformers' fate changed in 1992, partly owing to luck and partly owing to political skill. The luck was that Ogren, a liberal DFLer, happened to speak at a luncheon where Republican state representative Dave Gruenes was also speaking. They found they had much in common; after lunch Gruenes suggested that they work together. They assembled the "Gang of Seven," a bipartisan group of experienced legislators, all of whom were committed to a strategy of accommodation. In an important step all the members agreed that once the group had reached consensus on a bill, they would stand together in defending all of it.[26] This group was as important to healthcare reform as the nine policy entrepreneurs were to school-choice reform.

The Gang of Seven met weekly and in secret to craft a bill; eventually, the group produced a working document that was then reconciled with what the governor wanted in terms of cost control. It focused first on cost containment, setting up a regulatory commission to impose global budgets on providers. Sixty pages later in the bill was access, which was accomplished by offering subsidized insurance, with copayments, to the uninsured in the lower income brackets. There was no employer mandate to provide coverage, and hence no guarantee of universal coverage. The insurance subsidies were to be funded by a 2 percent tax on healthcare providers and by a cigarette tax. The final HealthRight law closely resembled this original bill.

The Gang was faced with a severe time crunch because it had only five working days to move the bill through six policy committees in order to meet legislative deadlines. The bill managed to clear the necessary deadlines; at this point, however, the blitzkrieg tactics ceased to work as opposition mounted, primarily from the Minnesota Medical Association, the Minnesota Hospital Association, insurance agents, and rural interests. They opposed the financing mechanism—a 2 percent provider tax—and instead urged an income tax surcharge. The latter was adamantly opposed by the governor. Over a quarter million faxes and letters were received in opposition to the bill. More liberal provider groups, however, such as the HMO Council, supported the legislation, along with social-welfare, religious, and labor organizations. During the conference-committee process the bill was "watered down" in order to accommodate the opponents, though the hated provider tax remained.

The HealthRight bill was adopted easily in the senate but passed on the house floor only after a dramatic vote when the clock was stopped and the voting board was held open an hour to allow the DFL Speaker and the Republican governor time to round up the necessary votes. This time the governor signed the bill. However, the secrecy of the Gang of Seven contained the seeds of its own destruction. Healthcare providers were very bitter about the process and came back in subsequent sessions to chip away at the law.

After the session it was determined that the HealthRight name was copyrighted, so the program is now called MinnesotaCare (MnCare). MnCare has been modified in every subsequent legislative session. The full expansion of the insurance subsidy to all poor adults was halted, and a goal of fewer than 4 percent uninsured was settled for; a key element of cost control—regulation of doctors' rates in the fee-for-service sector—was eliminated. By 1997 close to one hundred thousand people were enrolled in MnCare; its provider tax had generated such an embarrassingly large surplus that the rate was reduced and its permanence threatened. So healthcare reform is alive in Minnesota, although neither universal nor comprehensive in coverage. Still, Minnesota has gone further than almost any state, and a hundred thousand people are better off as a result.

This example of reform shares some elements with previous examples. One is that Minnesotans are great tinkerers; the legislation does not emerge in one fell swoop but is produced in fits and starts over several years and then gets refined again and again. A second commonality is the bipartisan effort; healthcare reform did not happen until the two political parties got together. A third is that Minnesotans don't rest on their laurels: most states would be pleased to have Minnesota's health statistics, but Minnesota leaders said they weren't good enough. A fourth point of commonality is the emphasis on the private sector. A significant part of the DFL party (including U.S. senator Paul Wellstone) embraces the single-payer solution wholeheartedly, and one might expect liberal lawmakers in this battle to propose it. But instead, they proposed a market-oriented solution, very much like what President Clinton advocated nationally in 1993.

One unusual aspect of the healthcare example is that a strategy of inclusiveness was not followed; rather, the HealthRight bill's contents were a surprise to affected interests. This tactic ultimately backfired, as the bill's opponents were able to mount a significant assault on the law in subsequent years, curtailing several of its provisions. A price was paid for not getting the providers on board.

Economic Development Policy

The fourth area we select for demonstrating Minnesota's proclivity for policy innovation is economic development policy. Like most states, Minnesota has been active in economic development for many years, but more than most states it has made a transition from the old style of locational incentives to the new style of entrepreneurial policies. Locational incentives refer to direct grants, loans, and tax breaks to companies, whereas entrepreneurial orientation refers to more active government interventions such as venture capital programs, high-technology development, and the fostering of new market opportunities, as well as innovative public-private partnerships. In a 1994 national study Minnesota ranked near the bottom in its emphasis on locational incentives and third from the top in its reliance on entrepreneurial ventures.[27] Minnesota has been at the forefront of efforts to reinvigorate economies through entrepreneurship. But somewhat like healthcare reform, these efforts have proceeded in fits and starts, and not always successfully.

Foreign Trade and Investment One entrepreneurial emphasis has been in foreign trade and development. Minnesota has a historic interest in international affairs and in international business. In 1983 the state launched a series of initiatives aimed at taking maximum advantage of the international economy. In that year the Minnesota Trade Office was created, given a substantial budget, and told to create jobs by increasing the number of Minnesota companies that export and by attracting foreign investment.[28] The MTO is designed to assist small business in identifying and taking advantage of business opportunities in western Europe and Asia and to encourage foreign direct investment from those areas. Minnesota focuses its export-promotion efforts on several key industries: high technology, computer software, medical technology, electronics, agricultural processing, and wood products. Initially, the state established two overseas trade representatives, in Oslo and Stockholm, but later expanded to eleven locations, including Taiwan, Japan, and Hungary, consonant with evolving trade opportunities.

Economic Development in Greater Minnesota Minnesota has been particularly active in economic development efforts outside the Twin Cities, including the development of indigenous industries and the targeting of particular regions and sectors in an industrial policy vein. One example is the work of the Iron Range Resources and Rehabilitation Board (IRRRB). The IRRRB was established in 1941, but its purview has been expanded several times, especially when 1982 legislation made available funds from a tax on taconite, totaling $47 million in that year.[29] The 1982 legislation set priorities for the economic protection fund and established a governing board on which a majority of legislative members must represent the "taconite tax relief area."

The IRRRB offers loans at below-market rates for new and existing businesses in the targeted area. Low-cost financing is available to improve resort properties, and industrial revenue bonds are available for manufacturing projects. Also available is research assistance for new product development and marketing. Finally, the board offers community development grants to local governments for infrastructure purposes.

Unfortunately, according to economic analysis of the early years of the IRRRB's funding allocations, little economic analysis was used in determining which economic sectors to target. Rather, political considerations prevailed. This meant that many promising projects were ignored.

A later rural economic development agency suffered a worse fate. The Greater Minnesota Corporation ("greater Minnesota" refers to rural or outstate Minnesota), or GMC, was established in the 1987 legislative session. Patterned after the Edison Program in Ohio and the Ben Franklin Partnership in Pennsylvania, this private, nonprofit corporation received $12 million initially in state aid (remember Minnesota's fondness for public/private partnerships). Later it captured half the lottery proceeds, amounting to at least $50 million annually. The GMC was supposed to promote research in higher education institutions and invest in companies producing jobs in depressed areas, including the Iron Range. A particular emphasis was on developing new uses for farm products; four regional research institutes were set up for this purpose.

Instead, the GMC became embroiled in various peccadilloes of its leaders.

Its CEO had to resign amid sexual harassment charges; the board chairman resigned because of involvement in a financial scandal in his own business; and the legislative auditor criticized GMC for its lack of control over expenses.[30] By the end of the 1980s the GMC had lost its political credibility and was reorganized into two separate development agencies.

A Bonanza for Northwest Airlines Despite its 1994 ranking near the bottom in locational incentives, Minnesota has engaged in the most expensive bidding war in history, the contest to locate two Northwest Airlines facilities. In early 1991 the Twin Cities–based airline announced its intention to build two maintenance bases in northern Minnesota, slated to employ fifteen hundred people; the state responded with an offer of about $740 million.[31] But when some of the financing fell through, Northwest opened up the bidding to forty other cities, and that's when the stakes got raised. By late 1991 the state of Minnesota had put together an $838 million package of financial incentives, including a loan of $270 million, as well as tax credits, bonds, and grants. The financing partners were the state, the city of Duluth where the facility would be located, the IRRRB, and the Metropolitan Airports Commission in the Twin Cities.

The deal was both complex and highly controversial. Again, it was a bipartisan effort, involving Republican governor Carlson; Democratic congressman James Oberstar, in whose district the facilities would be located and the ranking Democrat on the U.S. House's Transportation Committee; and the DFL-controlled legislature. The pros and cons of the deal were hotly debated in the media and in the legislature, and Northwest Airlines aggressively lobbied for its cause. The major issue was the size of the financing package and the shaky financial position of Northwest Airlines. There was a distinct possibility that Northwest would go out of business and leave the state with a big debt. Ultimately, interest in saving the state's only airline from bankruptcy produced a deal.[32] A lawsuit then delayed issuance of the bonds for a few months.

Northwest Airlines promptly used the $270 million cash in the deal to prop up its operations. Eventually, the airline became profitable again, and two facilities were finally opened in 1996, but not the ones intended because Northwest had not bought as many planes as anticipated. Instead, Northwest opened one maintenance facility, where salaries average about $50,000, and one reservation center, where salaries are about half that of maintenance workers. The total number of jobs came to only 950, not 1,500. If we assume repayment of the $270 million loan, this means that Minnesota offered an incentive package of $597,894 per job; the previous high bid a state had made was $166,000 per job for the Mercedes Benz plant in Alabama. This is a staggering amount of money, even if one assumes that part of it went to bail out a significant local company rather than just to lure new jobs. Apparently, Minnesota learned a lesson from this experience, as state leaders had a year-long debate on public financing of a new sports stadium and then said no in 1998.

In summary, it is fair to say that Minnesota has been generous, even lavish, in its support of economic development. Although generally it has avoided locational incentives, when necessary it has paid top dollar to retain key businesses. More often the state has engaged in entrepreneurial efforts, particularly in international trade and high-technology development. The state has especially focused on rescuing the economically depressed Iron Range. The passage of economic development policy has almost always been a united bipartisan effort, usually led by the governor.

Minnesota economic development policy seemed to be shifting significantly in 1999, driven by yet another Citizens League report, *Help Wanted: More Opportunities than People*.[33] The report emphasized that the economic development problem of the present and future for Minnesota was not developing jobs for people but finding people to fill the jobs that were developing. In the ensuing policy debate, locational incentives became passé while job training and retraining moved to the fore.

The general patterns of taxing and spending in Minnesota are clear: the state likes to spend and is willing to tax. Perhaps because of this proclivity, Minnesota also innovates in a number of different policy areas. In its bureaucracy the state encouraged quality management before TQM became the rage, it tried enterprise government before "reinventing government" was invented, and it realigned the pay scales of men and women before any other state government did so. In education Minnesota was the first to enact school choice and charter schools. In healthcare the state has gone a long way toward providing health insurance for all citizens, further than any state except Hawaii. In economic development policy Minnesota has the dubious distinction of having paid more per job than any state in its effort to keep Northwest Airlines' facilities in the state. In general, Minnesota has defied the competitive pressures of the "race to the bottom" in taxing and welfare spending and has been proud to be at the top on many policy dimensions.

Several characteristic features of Minnesota public policymaking emerge. One is the prevailing view of public officials in this moralistic culture that "pretty good" is not good enough. Many states would be glad to be in Minnesota's position on education or healthcare rankings. But Minnesotans have not been complacent; they want to stay ahead of the problems that might emerge.

A second feature is the inclusivity: the most successful policies are ones for which all interests are brought to the table and a consensus is hammered out. This happens quite often; the bipartisan nature of most enactments is especially noteworthy. When all interests have not been brought on board, as in healthcare reform, the process is less successful.

The third characteristic is the harmonious relationship between the public and the private sector: most successful policies involve some kind of partnership between the two. There is a heavy reliance on the private sector which belies Minnesota's "big government" liberal image. Many policies, such as open enrollment, enterprise management, and healthcare reform, are based on business concepts and analogies or on operations of the private market.

The fourth characteristic is that Minnesota has an unusual number of policy entrepreneurs, from private individuals, to public affairs organizations such as the Citizens League, to public officials who devote themselves to improving policy in their area of expertise. These policy entrepreneurs typically proceed by analyzing a problem within a coherent intellectual framework, gathering data, and coming up with a creative solution. They often write about their experiences and share their ideas to an unusual extent with other states.

Fifth, as is true elsewhere, Minnesota's innovations are often attained incrementally. Most of the major innovations, such as open enrollment and healthcare reform, were preceded by earlier trials and followed by more tinkering with the legislative product. They rarely spring up overnight, and they rarely are perfect the first time. But slowly and surely, Minnesota policymakers make progress.

Finally, it is important to note that both the governor and the legislature are strong policymakers. Sometimes the impetus comes from one and sometimes from the other, but neither has dominated historically. Minnesotans do not have the constitutional option of making policy through the initiative process, so public sentiment and interest-group desires are channeled into the two institutions. The absence of the initiative has led to thoughtful and sustained policy deliberation in representative institutions rather than hyperresponsiveness at the ballot box.

CHAPTER 11

Local Governments and Other Partners of the State

Chapter 10 described Minnesota's high-taxing, high-spending status vis-à-vis other states. This chapter looks at those entities that spend most of the money: local school districts, cities, counties, townships, regional planning commissions, and the state's two higher education organizations, the University of Minnesota and MNSCU, pronounced "Minskew," standing for Minnesota State Colleges and Universities. We examine Minnesota's complex local government financing system. And we look briefly at Minnesota's excellent private colleges and at a community and political phenomenon, the Minnesota State Fair.

THE GOVERNMENTS OF MINNESOTA

Not only does Minnesota have a lot of government, it has a lot of governments. The census of governments conducted every fifth year by the U.S. Department of Commerce's Bureau of the Census showed that Minnesota had 18,870 elected officials in 1992, 43.3 elected officials per 10,000 population, more than twice the national average of 20.8 elected officials per 10,000 population, good for twelfth place among the states in the number of elected officials per capita. The eleven other states preceding Minnesota were considerably smaller, however. Of the larger states—three million people or more—Minnesota has the nation's highest number of elected officials per capita.[1]

All those elected officials serve a very large number of local units of government. Minnesota has 87 counties, 855 cities, 1,796 townships, 481 education districts of various kinds, 142 housing and redevelopment authorities, 22 port authorities, 91 soil and water conservation districts, and approximately 150 special districts.[2] Overall, Minnesota ranks sixth among the states in number of different government bodies. Unlike most states, where education-related districts make up more than half the governmental units, education accounts for less than a third of Minnesota's local governments, and the number of education districts is falling. Minnesota ranks first among the states in the number of townships within its borders, seventh in the number of cities, eleventh in the number of counties, thirteenth in the number of school districts, and twenty-first in population. It is only in the number of special districts that Minnesota ranks lower (twenty-fifth) than it ranks in population. Special districts are typically created when local governments lack the muscle and flexibility to provide needed services; Minnesota's local governments usually have powers broad enough to accomplish their objectives.

EDUCATION

The largest public expenditure in Minnesota is made for education. On a per capita basis, spending for education in Minnesota is higher than it is in most states. A 1998 calculation showed Minnesota in eighth place in terms of per capita spending for elementary and secondary education, 20 percent higher than the national average.[3] But in terms of spending per pupil, Minnesota is about average. Per pupil expenditures in elementary and secondary schools in 1997 were $5,877, very close to the national average of $5,885.[4] The high per capita spending is caused by a larger proportion of school-age children in Minnesota than is the national norm, coupled with the second highest public high school graduation rate, meaning more students remaining in school longer.[5]

Most of the money spent in K–12 education in Minnesota is spent by the independent school districts that cover the state. The number of school districts has been declining rapidly in the 1990s. There were 433 districts in 1989 and 350 at the beginning of the 1997–98 school year, a decline of 19 percent.[6] Many of these consolidations were the result of a program begun in 1978 and substantially enriched in 1989 to provide incentives for declining-in-population school districts to begin edging toward what was viewed as the inevitability of consolidation. Incentives were deemed necessary because, although consolidation may have seemed programmatically inevitable, it has been a most difficult concept for many small school districts to accept. Minnesotans universally don't like combining units of government and systematically resist rationalization of structures. School consolidation was especially difficult because it often meant closing schools in one town and busing students to a larger community nearby. Convenience, pride in sports teams, and nostalgic belief in the superiority of the small schools in which they were educated all made consolidation the hottest issue during the 1980s for many nonmetro Minnesotans.

School boards in Minnesota consist of either six or seven members who serve for four years after their election. The timing of school board elections has been a subject of controversy for many years. School board elections used to be held by themselves, in May. Now they are held in November of odd- or even-numbered years, at the discretion of the district. Municipal elections are also now relegated to November of odd-numbered years. The controversy over the timing of school board elections was often fueled by beliefs about what kind of candidates would win in low-turnout elections. Teachers' organizations at times felt they could dominate with their candidates, but from the mid-1980s on, there was a growing belief (and evidence) that very conservative candidates won most readily with low turnout. School elections were finally moved to November, but despite the wishes of those wanting the maximum turnout possible, districts continued to have the option of holding the elections in "off" years, that is, when voters are not choosing legislators, constitutional officers, and members of Congress.

COUNTIES

Minnesota's eighty-seven counties are administrative arms of the state. According to a booklet published by the Association of Minnesota Counties for new commissioners, the following are "some powers and responsibilities" of Minnesota counties:

provide for the protection of the general health and welfare of county residents;
promote economic and industrial development;
administer and provide human services and income maintenance programs;
undertake comprehensive planning, zoning, and development controls;
provide emergency management;
provide for law enforcement and correctional facilities in the county;
plan and provide for parks, playgrounds, and other recreational facilities;
build and maintain storm water collection systems and drainage ditches;
provide for solid waste collection and disposal;
store, purify, and distribute water.[7]

It is counties that calculate and collect property taxes, sharing the revenues with cities, towns, and townships according to state law and rules.

Counties administer motor vehicle registration; keep land records; manage the human services, medical assistance, and welfare programs; provide emergency services; prosecute crimes; provide probation supervision; offer short-term incarceration and help administer the court system; manage the solid-waste program, which used to be simply landfills and now involves elaborate recycling pickup and processing; run the state's election system; provide public health services; offer parks and libraries (and, in a few cases, golf courses and hockey rinks); and manage their own roads.

The scope of the services provided by counties can vary widely, as can the size of counties, though size is not necessarily a determinant of a county's willingness to provide "extra" services. Cook County, at the northeastern tip of the state, is the state's smallest in terms of population, with 4,166 people. At the opposite extreme is Hennepin County, which has 1,063,631, 25 percent of the state's population.[8] Hennepin provides a vast array of services, including Hennepin County Medical Center, a solid-waste incinerator, plus hundreds of programs for violence prevention, chemical dependency, and many other pathologies. Little Cook County obviously doesn't have as many services as Hennepin, but it has some Hennepin doesn't have. Cook is one of two Minnesota counties with a combined county hospital and nursing home. Eleven other counties (including Hennepin) have hospitals, and twelve others have nursing homes. Hennepin County reported 10,563 full- and part-time employees in 1996; Cook County had 96. (Traverse County, the next smallest in terms of population, had only 74 employees.)[9]

Figure 13 shows the total expenditures for Minnesota counties in 1996. The biggest percentage change in the past three decades has been a shift from highways to human services as the most important part of a county's service package. As late as the 1960s and early 1970s, county boards in many rural counties administered their welfare programs by discussing the names of proposed recipients and deciding on a case-by-case basis whether to grant benefits. During that time most money—and interest—was focused on transportation. Public assistance spending grew very rapidly in the 1970s, but since the early 1990s county spending on human services has stabilized and even declined slightly, while the most significant increases have come in public safety spending.

Figure 14 shows where Minnesota counties get their money. The largest source is the local property tax, but as in education, one of the main policy debates concerning counties in Minnesota revolves around substituting state income and sales tax funds for local property taxes, at least for those services deemed to be statewide in nature. As indicated in chapter 8, some beginnings have been made toward having the state take over criminal justice

Figure 13: Total Expenditures for Minnesota Counties in 1996, $3,317,323,779

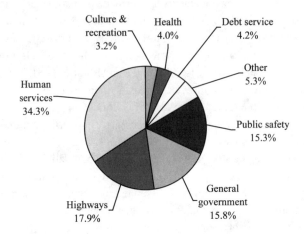

Source: Minnesota Office of the State Auditor, *Revenues, Expenditures, and Debt of Minnesota Counties*, December 31, 1996, p. 7.
Note: Other includes Conservation (1.7%), Sanitation (1.6%), Economic development (1.0%) and Other (.6%) expenditures.

funding, specifically the cost of public defense and a portion of court costs. Also, the state assumed the cost of income-maintenance programs in the late 1980s. Many involved in county intergovernmental relations agree that, in a perfect world, the entire cost of human services and criminal justice would be borne by the state, not by local property tax payers. But the world is not perfect. Welfare costs, particularly, are in flux at this writing. Welfare reform, both federal and state, should theoretically result in lower costs for counties. Some county officials, however, feel that welfare reform may eventually bring an increased burden to property tax payers. If significant numbers of public assistance recipients fail to find work and are dropped from programs, per the "work or no benefits" federal mandate, they may increase their use of those services the counties pay for more completely, such as homeless shelters and general cash assistance in emergencies.

COUNTY GOVERNANCE

Eighty-one of Minnesota's counties are governed by five-member boards.

Figure 14: Total Revenues for Minnesota Counties in 1996, $3,287,486,961

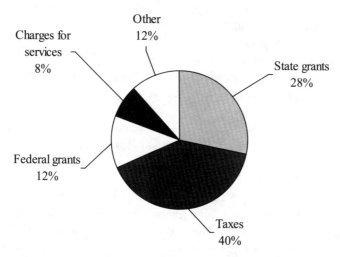

Source: Minnesota Office of the State Auditor, *Revenues, Expenditures, and Debt of Minnesota Counties,* December 31, 1996, p. 4.
Note: Total revenue excludes borrowing. "Other" includes Interest earnings (3.8%), Local units (.7%), Fines and forfeits (.6%), Special assessments (.7%), Licenses and permits (.4%), and Other revenues (4.9%).

Six larger counties have seven members. Board members serve for four years. The pay ranges from $5,645 annually on the low end (in frugal Traverse County, on the state's western border) to $70,327 for the seven Hennepin commissioners. A county commissioner's job is considered part-time in all counties except Hennepin. Pay in the other large metro counties besides Hennepin ranges from the low thirty thousands to the mid-forty thousands. Most of the rest of the counties pay between ten and twenty thousand.

At one time there were eleven elected county officers in each county in addition to the five board members. Counties elected the assessor, the surveyor, the court administrator, the coroner, the highway engineer, even the agricultural inspector (universally called the weed inspector). Currently, four counties, including the state's two largest—Hennepin, which encompasses the city of Minneapolis, and Ramsey, which has St. Paul—elect only the sheriff, county attorney, and board members. Most of the rest of the state's counties elect a treasurer, a recorder, and an auditor along with the sheriff and county attorney, though twenty-nine counties have combined the treasurer and auditor positions.

Minnesota has four different administrative arrangements for its counties. Eighteen counties (including all the largest ones) have professional county administrators; thirty-one counties have what are called county coordinators. The difference: all the county departments usually report to the administrator whereas departments normally report to the board in coordinator counties. Nine counties specify that the elected auditor will be the administrator, and twenty-nine appoint one or the other department head to administer the county's activities.[10]

Counties were organized as needed throughout the late 1800s. The widely believed "fact" about their organization is that counties were geographically set up so that no resident was more than one day's buggy ride from the county seat. Whether that is true or not, Minnesota counties are roughly the same size, but population varies considerably. Periodically, there are proposals to make counties more efficient by consolidating many of them. One proposal offered a number of times in the legislature would have Minnesota's eighty-seven counties become just ten. Like all governmental consolidation proposals in Minnesota, this one receives very little support.

Hennepin County has had a long tradition of activity in the National Association of Counties (NACO). In 1997–98 the president of NACO was Hennepin County commissioner Randy Johnson.

CITIES

Minnesota has 184 "big" cities (population over 2,500) and 671 small cities. Whether big or small, Minnesota cities have a very activist tradition. They respond to what their citizens want or need. The city of Worthington (population 10,260), for example, in the southwestern quadrant of the state, has eleven different "public service enterprises" it offers its citizens. The phrase "public service enterprise" comes from the state auditor, who tracks the financial performance of cities as the main component of her job. Worthington has the usual sewer and water responsibility but also offers city-owned liquor stores, a city-owned hospital and nursing home, electricity, plus an airport, a housing and redevelopment authority, an industrial wastewater treatment facility, a parking system (that is, the city makes money on parking lots and meters), an auditorium, and a golf course.[11] In a sense Worthington, like many Minnesota cities, is a small holding company with a number of different businesses from which it attempts to make money. Of course, Worthington also has parks, police, and fire protection and maintains city streets and buildings.

Thirty-four Minnesota cities own golf courses, including the most heavily used course in the state, Braemar Golf Course, in Edina, just southwest of Minneapolis. But the city of Climax, in the northwestern quadrant of the state, also has a golf course. Its 1990 population was 261. Two hundred fifty-two cities have municipal liquor stores or bars. Thirty-nine own their own nursing homes. In all, ninety-two cities of all sizes in Minnesota own and manage at least one "culture and recreation" enterprise—swimming pools, boat docks, ice rinks, community centers, cable television, and so on.[12]

Some of the entrepreneurial activity of Minnesota cities is aimed more at economic development than at responding to citizens' desire for amenities. Duluth has used aggressive city entrepreneurship and a great deal of state and some federal money to establish itself as a year-round tourist destination, despite what can be forbidding winter weather. Duluth owns and manages a civic and convention center, a zoo, a ski hill, and a golf course. Even farther north, close to the northeastern corner of the state, the city of Grand Rapids (population 1,226) has a marina, swimming pool, golf course, and recreation area, all municipally owned, all designed to attract tourists. The city of Clontarf (population 169), in northwestern Minnesota, owns its own restaurant because it felt the community would wither without one.

All these enterprise activities bring in money to Minnesota cities. For 1996, the net positive transfer of funds from these various businesses to city coffers was $44.3 million, not inconsequential but only a small fraction of the $3.5 billion Minnesota cities expended that year.[13] Most of the various city-owned and managed enterprises were designed to provide citizens and/or visitors with urban amenities the private sector wasn't willing to provide. Minnesota's moralistic culture, in which communal provision of services is accepted and applauded, paves the way for cities aggressively to improve the quality of life of their citizens.

Municipal liquor stores in Minnesota were originally created to improve the community's quality of life through allowing city control of the sale of alcohol, but in modern times municipal liquor's reason for existence is usually to make money for the city. That has proved to be increasingly difficult, especially for smaller communities. The number of city-owned liquor stores and bars declined from 315 in 1988 to 278 in 1996, or 12 percent. Liquor made $14.4 million for cities in 1996, $10.8 million of which was transferred to city budgets.[14] One-third of the city-owned liquor profitability can be traced to the twenty-one facilities located in Twin City suburbs.

The largest single source of revenues for small cities in Minnesota is the state. Thirty-two percent of small cities' revenue comes from the state, and 26 percent comes from taxes.[15] For larger cities, taxes make up 37.7 percent of the total, and state grants, 25.5 percent.[16] It was a Republican governor, Harold LeVander, who instituted the practice of direct state aid to cities, aid that cities could use as they saw fit. The practice was greatly expanded as a result of the 1971 passage of the "Minnesota Miracle," a scheme to equalize education funding throughout the state. The egalitarian thrust of the "Minnesota Miracle" spread to funding for cities and counties, too. Just as no student should be hampered by residing in a property-poor area, it has been argued, no citizen should be denied basic municipal services for that reason. Property taxes make up the overwhelming majority of the taxes cities collect, but a rapidly growing revenue source is hotel/motel/entertainment taxes. These require legislative approval and are usually instituted for economic development reasons.

Economic Development by the Cities

As would be expected, Minnesota's large cities spend the most money on debt service, public safety, and streets and highways. Each of these categories accounts for about 20 percent of total expenditures. Interestingly, the next highest expenditure is for economic development, which claims 10.8 percent of total expenditures, even more than is spent on administration and general government.[17] Minnesota cities compete aggressively for businesses and jobs. The principal tools in this economic development contest are development and port authorities and tax increment financing.

Not surprisingly, Minneapolis has the state's largest development agency, the Minneapolis Community Development Agency, or MCDA. MCDA is governed by a board composed of the members of the Minneapolis City Council. It does industrial development, community development, and housing redevelopment in the city, functions usually separated in other venues. St. Paul, for example, does industrial development through the St. Paul Port Authority, community development through the Planning and Economic Development Department of the city, and housing redevelopment through the St. Paul Housing and Redevelopment Authority. The MCDA staff of 160 people currently administers some fifty programs in the areas of home ownership, home improvement, rental housing development, commercial and industrial development, and small business assistance. The array of programs offered is impressive. There are loans available at below-market rates for home buyers with incomes up to $100,000. People with lower incomes can be urban homesteaders, claiming houses for as low as $750 down. There are equity participation loans for families with children, and closing cost loans, and purchase and rehab loans. And there is the ongoing "primary focus" of MCDA, creating living-wage jobs.[18]

Both Minneapolis and St. Paul have traditions of active neighborhood organizations that have become institutionalized participants in community life. In Minneapolis MCDA sends about $20 million each year to eleven neighborhood groups to spend on a program called the Neighborhood Revitalization Program. In St. Paul it was the neighborhood groups that first organized and now run the city's recycling program, which picks up paper, bottles, and cans at every dwelling in the city every two weeks.

Two of the tools used by industrial and economic development agencies in Minnesota are revenue bonds and tax increment financing (TIF), though the latter device is much less popular than it was in the 1980s. Under TIF a city borrows money for redevelopment expenses and pays off the debt with the "increment," that is, the difference between the property's original taxable value and its new, redeveloped value. Cities so aggressively used tax increment financing to lure business that an overly large proportion of some cities' tax values soon became dedicated to paying off debt, leaving insufficient taxes to pay for services. A series of legislative actions in the late 1980s and early 1990s reined in more aggressive users of TIF, but cities still use the device where they can.

City Governance

Three forms of governance are used by cities in Minnesota: strong mayor-council, weak mayor-council, and council-manager. By far the most common organization is weak mayor-council, in which the mayor is essentially just another council member who presides at the meetings. Only four cities have the strong mayor-council arrangements, including the two largest cities, Minneapolis and St. Paul. The defining characteristic of a "strong" mayor-council city is a separation of powers, meaning that the mayor is not a member of the council. Strength in strong mayor-council cities is quite relative. In St. Paul, for example, the mayor is indeed structurally strong with the power and responsibility to prepare budgets, to hire and fire staff, and to negotiate with the city council, which is made up of seven officially part-time members. In Minneapolis the mayor has much less power. The budget is prepared by a city coordinator, who is appointed by the mayor and council together. The three most significant sources of power for a Minneapolis mayor are the power of the veto, the power to appoint a police chief, and the power of the bully pulpit. For persons trying to influence St. Paul's public policy, by changing an ordinance, for example, the first job is to gain the mayor's support. In Minneapolis most people start with the city council's majority leader, whose support is thought to be more crucial than that of the mayor in garnering the votes of a majority of the thirteen-member, full-time city council.

Another striking example of the difference between the two cities lies in economic development. In St. Paul the Planning and Economic Development Department reports directly to the mayor. With that staff resource, the mayor often participates directly in economic development planning and decision making—particularly as they relate to incentives for new business. In Minneapolis all economic development activity is headquartered at the Minneapolis Community Development Agency, which is governed by the city council. Mayors can provide encouragement but little else to those wishing to locate in the city.

In a council-manager system the city council hires a professional city manager to execute council policy and run the city. Since the early 1990s the most consistent trend in governance has been for cities using the council-manager system to shift to a variation called the council-administrator system. Administrators have less authority than managers; the format is chosen to permit councils to exercise maximum direct control over policy.

TOWNSHIPS

Alexis de Tocqueville said, "The township is the only association so well rooted in nature that whenever men assemble it forms itself."[19] In Minnesota more townships have formed themselves than in any other state. The legislature describes the township as the form of local government that most efficiently provides governmental services in areas used or developed for agricultural, open-space, and rural residential purposes.[20] Townships and cities are mutually exclusive; 5 percent of the state's landmass and about 80 percent of its people exist inside the borders of a city. But not all the remaining land or people are governed by townships. When there is no township or city, the land is called unincorporated and the county provides the necessary municipal services.

One characteristic of the township that Tocqueville particularly prized—

the town meeting with its face-to-face democracy—survives to this day among Minnesota townships, even urban townships with populations in the thousands. Every township has an annual meeting in which either three or five supervisors are elected to carry on the township's business and the annual budget is approved and policies discussed. Every voter in the township is eligible to come to the annual meeting and vote on the township's business. In rural areas townships generally focus on the maintenance and upkeep of township roads. In areas where development from nearby cities is beginning to occur, zoning often becomes the township's dominant issue.

REGIONAL GOVERNANCE

The Twin Cities Metropolitan Council was created in 1967. In short order, it became a much ballyhooed innovation. An article in *Harper's* in 1969 referred to the council as "an invention which will prove as significant to American cities as the Wright brothers' first plane was to aviation."[21] Few people in Minnesota today would agree with that hyperbole.

The seeds of the council's difficulties were sown at its inception. Two separate regional governance plans were debated at the capitol in 1967. One plan featured elected Met Council representatives with considerable authority to set policy. This robust configuration actually won support in the house but lost on a tie vote in the senate. What emerged was an appointed council "that would be a coordinating body with no authority to provide service or set policy."[22] The issue of authority has plagued the council ever since.

During its first ten years the council achieved a number of victories. It vetoed a proposal by the Metropolitan Airports Commission to build a second airport, and it vetoed the plan of the Metropolitan Transit Commission to build light-rail transit (whether or not these were the right decisions, they demonstrated that the council indeed had some clout). The council also made some things happen instead of preventing them from happening. Its first job was solving the area's sewer problems, which it did very well by creating the Waste Control Commission. Another positive creation was the planning and development of a regional park system that is managed by the counties.[23] But generally, the council's role came to be preventing what some regarded as bad things. That's what it did in healthcare, preventing the building of expensive hospitals through its Metropolitan Health Board. The council's role in healthcare, like its role in many other areas, was significantly enhanced by its responsibility as the federal government's "A95" review agency, a traffic cop sitting at the intersection of federal largesse and local need.

Eventually, however, federal funds sent directly to cities began to dwindle, and Twin Cities developers and major project planners began to bypass the Metropolitan Council. The country's largest entertainment and shopping complex, Mall of America, located in Bloomington, just south of Minneapolis, was built without significant Met Council participation. The same was true of the Metrodome, in downtown Minneapolis, which houses the football Vikings and the baseball Twins, and the Target Center, also in downtown Minneapolis, which houses the basketball Timberwolves. (All major-league sports teams in Minnesota are called the Minnesota whatevers, as is the principal orchestra. It's part of the culture.) The council also did not participate in the location of the Canterbury Downs racetrack or in the state's decision to build the World Trade Center office building in downtown St. Paul. As one scholar with a longtime interest in the Met Council noted, "The more important the project was to big development interests, the less the Council seemed to affect the decisions."[24]

More fundamental than its lack of a role in siting projects, however, was the council's ultimate failure to deliver on the expectations that surrounded its founding and first ten years. At that time Minnesota was thought to be different. Its large cities did not have extensive, poverty-plagued ghettos. The metropolitan region had not sprawled wastefully. The bus system actually served a fair percentage of people, and visionaries were attempting to install new transit options. Disturbing trends were evident, but this unique Minnesota organization, it was felt, would help Minnesota plan its way out of the problems.

Unfortunately, it didn't work, and the person who helped Minnesota understand that it didn't work was a south Minneapolis legislator, Rep. Myron Orfield, whose dogged pursuit of antisprawl and urban-core rebuilding legislation has made him a lightning rod in urban-suburban discussions. Although there is passionate (by Minnesota standards) debate about Orfield's proposed solutions, there is little room to argue with his characterization of the problem. He noted that from 1980 to 1990 the number of census tracts in Minneapolis and St. Paul with more than 40 percent of the population under the federal poverty line jumped from eleven to thirty-one: "To put this in perspective, taken together the ghetto populations of Minneapolis (61,054) and Saint Paul (17,834) were one-twelfth as large as the massive New York City ghetto (952,484), one-fifth the size of Detroit's (375,548), and almost half the size of Milwaukee's (140,831). On the other hand, they were not quite twice as large as Newark's ghetto (49,189); three times the size of Boston's (28,738), Kansas City's (24,049), and Indianapolis's (23,279) ghettos; and five times as large as the ghettos of San Francisco (12,127) and Portland, Oregon (15,764)."[25]

As the first chapter of Orfield's book, *Metro Politics*, is titled, most Minnesotans believed "It Couldn't Happen Here." Not everyone accepts Orfield's analysis of what caused the concentration of poverty and of what should be done about it. He maintains that developing wealthy suburbs sucked all the infrastructure money out of the region and that they need to give it back by sharing their tax base with the inner city. One does not need to accept that cause-effect proposition to agree that somehow the concentration of poverty did happen and Minneapolis and St. Paul were not saved by the unique Metropolitan Council from sinking at least partway into urban decline.

Another area in which much more was expected out of the Metropolitan Council is transportation. For more than a decade, the council and the Metropolitan Transit Commission fought over whether there ought to be light-rail transit, with the council agreeing with the Citizens League and local editorial writers that the Twin Cities area had insufficient density for light rail.[26] The metropolitan counties eventually took over light-rail planning and development through a joint-powers agreement, bypassing the Metropolitan Council, and the first leg of a light-rail system was approved for federal and state funds in 1999.

Despite anti-Metropolitan Council campaign rhetoric, which he apparently learned as a suburban mayor, Governor Ventura appointed former state senator Ted Mondale as Met Council chairman. Mondale, seemingly with the governor's blessing, espoused an activist agenda for the council, particularly in the rapid development of a light rail system.

REGIONAL DEVELOPMENT COMMISSIONS

When the Metropolitan Council was created, regional development commissions (RDCs) were also being set up around the state to coordinate regional planning and encourage economic development. Soon a firestorm developed as local government officials in some parts of the state objected to the imposition of "another layer of government." Two of the ten proposed regions dropped their RDCs altogether. Regional development commissions survive in the balance of the state, where their roles vary. Some administer aging programs because federal money for that purpose was funneled through them years ago and now the state does the same thing. All the RDCs contract annually with the Department of Transportation to perform some of their required planning. Some RDCs are quite active in attempting to facilitate regional economic development, and others are less active. The original controversy surrounding the RDCs left a legacy of timidity and structural inability to impose disciplined regional planning and coordination.

PROPERTY TAXES: THE HEART OF THE LOCAL/LEGISLATIVE SYSTEM

Cities, counties, schools, and regional governments all receive revenue from property taxes. The percentage of total state and local revenues raised from property taxes in Minnesota (13.9) is not dramatically less than the national average (14.8),[27] but Minnesota's property tax system is different from others, in part because Minnesota's is one of the few property tax systems in the country that attempts to incorporate economic progressivity. Lower-valued homes owned by, theoretically, lower-income people pay a lower percentage of value than higher-valued homes. Economic progressivity is enhanced even further by the reality that only 39 percent of property taxes raised in Minnesota comes from homeowners.[28] Some relief was passed for business in 1996, 1997, and 1998, but business still pays the majority of property taxes in the state. The net effect of this system: low-valued homes in Minnesota pay very low property taxes compared with other states. Defenders of the current system argue that it has worked well. Minnesota has the highest home ownership rate in the nation (75.4 percent),[29] and home ownership encourages community stability, they say.

Detractors maintain that Minnesota's local government financing and property tax system is blatantly political, passed by a succession of DFL-dominated legislatures that kept property taxes unrealistically low on their voters, the people who live in low-valued homes. Regardless of the motivation, it is politically difficult for local board and council members to raise property taxes significantly. They are faced, however, with a citizenry that generally believes it ought to have a wide range of high-quality, government-provided services. The classic Minnesota local government response to this problem is to convince the legislature to appropriate the funds needed for those services and leave the property tax alone. Some observers argue that this system permits government without accountability; the state, it is said, bails out spendthrift local governments. Others say that the statewide revenues should be used to pay more of the local government costs not related to property.

All local governments in Minnesota are more and more dependent on state legislative decisions for their revenue. City managers and school superintendents who come to Minnesota from other states marvel at the depth and intensity of the relationship between local governments and their legislators. If Minnesota's local governments can be seen as a vast business enterprise, then the tax committees of the two houses of the legislature can be thought of as the board of directors.

HIGHER EDUCATION

The University of Minnesota

Often referred to as "the most important institution in the state," the University of Minnesota clearly demands treatment in any comprehensive look at Minnesota politics and government; yet it does not fit comfortably within this chapter because, unlike local governments, it is not a "creature of the state." The university was incorporated by an 1851 act of the Territorial Assembly. In 1858, when Minnesota became a state, the new constitution recognized the university's original charter and granted it constitutional autonomy. That autonomy has had some importance in promoting academic freedom and protecting the university from political influence, but practically speaking, the university depends on the legislature for its appropriations, like any other state agency, and therefore accommodates legislative wishes.

The University of Minnesota is among the largest universities in the country, with 48,690 students in 1996 on its four campuses. The campuses include the Twin Cities campus, with facilities in both St. Paul and Minneapolis, and smaller campuses in Duluth, Morris, and Crookston. The university is unusual in that it is both a land-grant university with a strong tradition of education and public service and a major research institution with scholars of national and international reputation. Unlike many flagship state universities, the main campus is located in the state's major metropolitan area, allowing unusual synergy with businesses and cultural institutions. Finally, the U of M is among the country's most comprehensive universities: it has medicine, agriculture, engineering, the liberal arts, and numerous professional schools. All this in a state of 4.5 million people.

The university is one of the state's largest employers, with about thirty-five thousand workers. Its faculty brings in substantial research grants and contracts from outside the state, $323 million in FY 1996. The university routinely ranks among the top universities in patents issued. Among the notable inventions of its faculty are the black-box flight recorder, the heart pacemaker, the retractable seatbelt, isolation of uranium 235, the Minnesota Multiphasic Personality Inventory (MMPI), the CAT scanner, the Gopher search engine for computers, and the taconite process that saved the iron-ore industry. Much of the state's success in agriculture, computing, biomedical engineering, and other industries can be attributed to research done at the university.

The ten thousand graduates per year are also important "products" of the university, enhancing the skilled labor force. The impact of the university is huge and widespread. People throughout the state talk simply about "the U," and everybody knows what they are referring to. Every citizen has an opinion about what the university should be doing; its business is always featured in the news. With the state capitol located just a few miles from the main campus, its internal machinations and squabbles are readily apparent to the 201 lawmakers; in fact, the *Minnesota Daily*, the student newspaper, is delivered to the capitol every day, thus making sure warts and blemishes are seen and thoroughly enjoyed by the legislators. The university, for its part, was scandal-prone through the 1990s, increasing the media's scrutiny.

Minnesota State Colleges and Universities

In its first year of statehood Minnesota began the creation of what would become a massive higher education system separate from the university. The Winona Normal School began operation in 1858 with a mission of preparing teachers. It was followed by similar schools in Mankato, St. Cloud, Moorhead, and Bemidji in 1911. Eventually, the normal schools became teachers' colleges, then state colleges, and finally, state universities. In 1967 Southwest State University was added to the system in Marshall. And in 1971 the State University System finally established a metropolitan presence with Metropolitan State University in St. Paul. Currently, there are seven state universities in Minnesota; the system also has a campus in Akita, Japan, where Japanese students can prepare before attending school in Minnesota and where Minnesota students can repair for cultural enrichment. In 1998 Mankato State University changed its name to Minnesota State University at Mankato. It is expected that the other schools in the system will follow suit.

After World War II Minnesota began rapidly building a two-year community college system with locations all around the state. At the same time, many school districts had or were setting up vocational-technical institutes designed to make high school graduates job-ready.

State-financed higher education had become a very big business in Minnesota. It was, however, a largely uncoordinated business. Some sort of state-funded higher education institution became a necessity for a town with any size at all, and some with very little size. Legislators from those towns fought hard for their new economic development tool.

Longtime senate majority leader Roger Moe decided, in the late 1980s, that the system had to be rationalized in some way. He determinedly overcame Minnesota's normal resistance to consolidation and restructuring and created and passed the bill that established Minnesota State Colleges and Universities, MNSCU, bringing together all the state's public higher education institutions except the university. When MNSCU finally began, in 1995, it had sixty-three campuses, more than in forty-eight other states. Since 1995 MNSCU has shrunk to fifty-four campuses and thirty-six institutions. Much of the shrinkage was accomplished by combining technical and community colleges. The state universities had an enrollment of 52,888 in the fall of 1997; there were 91,992 persons enrolled in the two-year institutions.

Private Colleges

Besides the public institutions, Minnesota has an exceptionally strong network of sixteen private colleges that collectively enroll 35,500 undergraduates and 16,200 graduate students. Private college students receive 3 percent of the state's higher education spending, about $47 million annually, through state loan and grant programs for low- and middle-income students. Private colleges enroll 30 percent of the state's four-year undergraduates and award 33 percent of the baccalaureate degrees but have higher percentages in some critical areas, including 46 percent of all the science degrees and 48 percent of the mathematics degrees. Seventy-two percent of the private college students are Minnesotans, half from the metropolitan area, half from the rest of the state.[30]

THE GREAT MINNESOTA GET-TOGETHER

The annual Minnesota State Fair is a political and economic phenomenon deserving of mention in a chapter about creatures and partners of the state. In 1998 1.7 million people went to the fair, nearly 40 percent of the state's population. The nation's largest fair is in Texas, with 3.5 million visitors, 18 percent of the population. Minnesota's fair is considered a phenomenon in the fair industry because it is the only one in the nation with absolutely no complimentary tickets. Everyone, from the governor to the fair's general manager, must pay six dollars to enter during the eleven-day exhibition.

The fair is managed by the Minnesota Agricultural Society, made up of representatives from county fairs and exhibitions throughout the state. The fair is located on 360 acres in a suburb of St. Paul, adjacent to the St. Paul campus of the University of Minnesota, which houses the agriculture school. Though the fair continues its agricultural tradition, with huge barns filled with farm animals seeking blue ribbons, the focus has been shrewdly altered over the years so that there are as many attractions for the consumers of farm products as for the producers. This change, together with the fair's location in the Twin Cities region, ensures that the vast majority of the fair's visitors are from the metropolitan area. Especially during election years, the fair is a traditional mecca for politicians, who rent booths or work out of their political party's booth, shaking hands with and talking to Minnesota voters. Indeed, it is said during election years that Minnesota voters don't really start paying attention to the election until after the fair ends on Labor Day. During the 1998 election some Minnesota political observers began to take the campaign of Jesse Ventura seriously when his booth at the fair was constantly surrounded by long lines while the booths of the other candidates were usually empty.

Minnesota has a much higher than average number of government units and elected officials, as befits the state most culturally moralistic. Despite the large number, all these units project a sense of being competently managed. Scandal in local government administration is rare.

Locally elected school boards manage the state's school districts. By far the largest proportion of state spending goes to K–12 education. Education is the only area where Minnesotans have permitted local government consolidation and system rationalization. The struggle to consolidate was a difficult one, however, and succeeded only because proponents promised it would help the children in the schools.

Minnesota counties are in transition as they respond to federal and state welfare reform. Human services, which was the most rapidly growing county function in the 1970s and in part of the 1980s, has given way to criminal justice as the largest growth area.

Minnesota cities are like mini-conglomerates that offer their voters a bewildering array of government-provided services. One of the most important functions of cities is economic development, and cities aggressively use whatever tools they can to lure business and jobs to their cities.

Townships are rural Minnesota's means of governance. The annual meetings, in which township officers are elected and the year's budget approved, hark back to the direct democracy of the earliest town meetings in this country.

Despite very low property taxes on lower-value homes, it is difficult to raise the property tax in Minnesota. This reality, coupled with the people's insistence on a broad array of services, tends to force local government officials to the legislature, where they attempt to pay for increasing portions of their budget by lobbying for more money.

Minnesota has three large higher education components, the University of Minnesota, Minnesota State Colleges and Universities, and the state's private colleges. All three are thought of as being in a leadership class relative to systems in other states.

Finally, the Minnesota state fair has become a gigantic community celebration where politicians from all parties wander the streets talking and listening to voters.

CHAPTER 12

Continuing Traditions and Emerging Issues

Throughout this book we have highlighted four characteristics of Minnesota: (1) a healthy, growing economy, (2) a clean and active government of which its citizens are generally proud, (3) a moralistic culture, and (4) a position as a national policy leader and innovator in many fields. Minnesotans have grown accustomed to being the envy of outside observers, from John Gunther's 1947 characterization of Minnesota as "spectacularly varied, proud, handsome, and progressive," to the glowing 1973 *Time* magazine cover story, to the *Economist*'s 1997 appellation of America's "promised land."[1] General-interest publications weren't the only ones touting Minnesota. Perhaps the best-read writer on state and local governance issues, Neal Peirce, has frequently written about the state. Publications devoted to education, healthcare, and general governance often contain references to Minnesota leadership.

We have developed certain explanations for Minnesota's status, particularly its being an exemplar of the moralistic political culture. Here we reconsider some of these themes and the likelihood that Minnesota will be able to sustain its status among the states.

THEMES

Our overarching theme is Minnesota's survival as an almost ideal example of the moralistic political culture. In the moralistic culture there is a commitment to using community power to intervene in private activities for the good or well-being of the polity. Government is considered a positive instrument with a responsibility to promote the general welfare. Private philanthropic activity is also consistent with the communitarian bent. The conduct of politics is different from that in other political cultures in that issues have an important place in debates. Political parties, consequently, are of somewhat lesser importance than in individualistic political cultures. In the moralistic political culture citizens have a duty to participate in politics and to be concerned about it. Government service is service to the community, and politicians are not expected to profit from such service. Corruption, therefore, is not tolerated, and the merit system is rigidly maintained within government administration.

Newcomers to Minnesota note the vigor with which they are recruited to political party precinct caucuses, a time-consuming activity in today's time-starved world. Newcomers are also astounded that the numerous bodies of water in Minneapolis, "The City of Lakes," are considered public, not private property. There are only a handful of lots with private lakefront in the entire city. Lakes are for everyone's enjoyment.

The political party system is certainly nonregular: the Democratic party still goes by the Democratic-Farmer-Labor, or DFL, label, signifying its historic union of factions. The Republican party for twenty years was the Independent-Republican party, though it has now reverted to the traditional nomenclature. Voters do not stick to party labels: Minnesotans are more likely than other Americans to say that they are independents rather than partisans of either stripe.

Minnesota's political debate is definitely issue-oriented and was recognized as such as early as the 1960s when John Fenton so labeled it.[2] The use of the caucus system, particularly Minnesota's version of it, reinforces the issue orientation in political debate. From time to time the political parties seem more concerned about picking candidates with the "right" stand on the issues than with selecting electable candidates. In the 1994 gubernatorial party endorsements, for instance, both parties weighed issue purity over candidate acceptability. Eventually, in 1998, Minnesotans had an opportunity to punish the two parties for their extremism, choosing Reform party candidate Jesse Ventura in large part because he did not represent either the DFL or the Republican party. Minnesota's tradition of nonpartisanship is in keeping with moralistic political values. Until 1973 the Minnesota legislature was officially nonpartisan, although liberal and conservative caucuses emerged within it. Today many elected offices are nonpartisan; in fact, all but 218 of the 18,870 elected officials are elected without party designation.

The clean government image is another way in which Minnesota embodies the values of a moralistic political culture. With some minor exceptions in the early 1900s, party bosses did not exist in Minnesota in the usual sense because the endorsement process was so open that party-boss control was impossible. Precinct caucuses, for example, are open to anyone willing to say they belong to the party. Special interests do not control electoral financing, owing to strict limits on what PACs and big givers can contribute as well as to the availability of significant amounts of public financing for campaigns. Election fraud is not an issue: same-day registration has existed since 1973, and no serious incidents have been reported concerning voter fraud and abuse. Even when Minnesota courts spent five months deciding what appears to be the closest gubernatorial election in American history, the Rolvaag-Andersen contest of 1962, serious vote fraud was not at issue. The only question about the outcome—determined by a margin of ninety-one votes—concerned voter intention, not political chicanery. The rules governing the relationship between legislators and lobbyists are very stringent: legislators may accept nothing of value from lobbyists or their employers—no meals, gifts, not even coffee and cookies unless offered to the general public at the same time.

In line with its moralistic political culture, politics in Minnesota is unusually open and participatory. The easiest form of participation is voting: Minnesotans' voter turnout is about 20 percent above the national average. The state as a whole ranked fifth in voter turnout in recent years. Same-day registration makes it easy for citizens to participate. On other forms of political participation, such as joining community groups, Minnesotans are more active than most Americans. There are many different groups to join: Minnesota ranked eighth in the number of organized interests that lobby in the legislature, and thus its citizens are afforded many different opportunities to work with others in various political causes.

Minnesota's openness does not extend to electing women and minorities in proportionate numbers, however. Minnesota is one of the few states that has not elected a female governor or sent a woman to Congress in the modern era except by appointment. No minority candidate has been elected to major office, and only occasionally do minorities serve in the legislature. At the highest levels politics is still a white-male activity.

The moralistic political culture's emphasis on the commonwealth is also evident in the wide scope of government in Minnesota and in the many policy arenas where the state has been a national leader. Minnesota is among the nation's highest taxing and spending states. It is fifth among the states in tax effort; it is sixth in the spending of its state and local governments on a per capita basis. These rankings indicate extensive government involvement in society and in the economy. Government is thought to be a positive instrument working for the common good; large majorities report they are getting their money's worth from their state and local taxes.

Besides spending more than the average on government, Minnesotans have more governments on which to spend. Minnesota ranks first in the number of townships, seventh in the number of cities, eleventh in the number of counties, and thirteenth in the number of school districts. This gives Minnesota twice as many elected officials per capita as the average state.

In addition, Minnesota often takes a leadership role in policy innovation, such as comparable worth wages for government employees, school choice and open enrollment, charter schools, and entrepreneurial efforts in economic development. Many other "firsts" could be listed. In other policy areas Minnesota, although not first, is a national leader. For example, Minnesota is among the few states to have enacted comprehensive health-care reform and nearly universal access. Minnesota's government innovations are not necessarily expansions of "big government"; for instance, enterprise management, "reinventing government," and other bureaucratic innovations were efforts to privatize and streamline the state bureaucracy. Moralism, in the political culture sense, implies a commitment to the public good, whether achieved through government or through communitarian or private means.

On all these dimensions Minnesota stands out as an example of a moralistic political culture. Why has Minnesota retained its political culture in a relatively pure form while many other states have amalgams of several cultures? One factor has been the demographic homogeneity of the state's population, coupled with steady population growth. Newcomers, therefore, are absorbed into the culture. A recent study by Rodney Hero and Caroline Tolbert showed that Minnesota, compared with other states, has a very small minority population (blacks and Latinos) and relatively few white ethnics (non-northern and nonwestern European whites).[3] This pattern typifies moralistic states, they say. In Hero's update, which used 1990 census data, Minnesota ranked in the lowest quadrant on both measures of diversity. Hero and Tolbert argue that core values are more widely shared in such homogeneous environments; this value consensus is a luxury created by the absence of significant racial and ethnic cleavages. The consensus means that political debate is often about means rather than ends.

Moreover, Minnesota's rate of population growth has been steady. The sudden influx of immigrants that abruptly altered Florida's traditionalistic political culture, for instance, has not occurred in the North Star State, nor is it likely to occur. In the decade of the 1960s Minnesota's rate of population growth was 11.4 percent; in the 1970s it was 7.1 percent; in the 1980s, 7.4 percent; in the first half of the 1990s, 5.3 percent, all below the national average for the comparable period but, significantly, above the average for the Midwest. The modest rate of population increase means that the dominant culture has a good chance of absorbing newcomers.

Also helping maintain the culture is Minnesota's relative physical isolation. The nearest big cities to the east are Milwaukee, 340 miles away, and Chicago, 400 miles away. To the west, the closest big cities are Denver, 920 miles away, and Seattle, 1,600 miles away. Minneapolis/St. Paul is the big city for many miles around; it is the banking headquarters, the sports mecca, and the culturally dominant center. It is unlikely that migrants of more diverse ethnicity will spill over from any other urban area into Minnesota. Compounding the geographic isolation is the weather; the extremely cold temperatures do not attract idle visitors who may decide to stay, as happens in Arizona and California. Thus, newcomers to Minnesota tend to be purposeful.

Minnesota also stands out in certain critical economic respects. Though not rich, Minnesota has been blessed with a strong economy. Between 1983 and 1992 its economic growth, as measured by inflation-adjusted gross state product, outpaced the national average: 35.2 percent in Minnesota as compared with 29.6 percent in the United States.[4] Minnesota's economy has been particularly robust in employment growth; in the period 1985 to 1994, employment grew in Minnesota by 24.1 percent as compared with only 16.9 percent nationwide. In late 1998 Minnesota's unemployment rate was an unusually low 2.4 percent compared with 4.4 percent nationally.[5] Minnesota's economy has consistently outperformed the economies of other midwestern states.

This impressive performance means that Minnesota has been able to afford its taste in government. It has been able to fund generous welfare benefits, good schools, a cleaner environment, and so on. Minnesota does not have to cope with the poverty problems of a Mississippi or a Louisiana. Nor does it have the problem of rapid growth fueled by immigration, as do Florida and California, or the problem of rebuilding a declining and downsized industrial base, like some other midwestern states. Minnesota's economy allows it some luxuries not available to other states.

Both Minnesota's private and public sectors are healthy. A firm that compiles rankings of states on hundreds of different criteria ranked Minnesota "most livable" in 1996 and 1997.[6] The firm used forty-two different positive and negative factors, from "births of low birthweight as a percent of all births" to "normal daily mean temperature." Most Minnesotans would not be surprised at their leadership in a ranking like this one, but they would argue vociferously about the source of their leadership. Some would postulate that a creative private sector overrode the too heavy hand of government; others would argue that an active government sector provided the forward thrust needed by business. We're not sure which chicken preceded which egg. We are certain that a healthy economy and Minnesota's moralistic political system have created one of America's best states, recognized as such by residents and outside observers.

A more practical answer as to why Minnesota pushes for the top is provided by policy entrepreneur extraordinaire Ted Kolderie:

> The answer, I've always felt, is that Minnesota doesn't—can't—make its living by being simply not-worse than other states. We live in a cold, remote location a long ways from markets and sources of raw materials, trying to run a high-tech/high-service economy in competition with places around the country and around the world where the sun is warm and the water is blue and there are mountains with snow for skiing and where income taxes are low or nonexistent on business. The only way we can run this kind of an economy successfully is to make this the kind of place people want to come to (or, once here, to stay in). Our quality of life is largely "made," and made significantly by public policy; by government. So government *has* to work here.[7]

TRENDS

What are the odds that the moralistic political culture and the strong economy will continue? What trends might affect these characteristics? The most important trend is demographic. Minnesota's population growth is expected to continue to be stronger than in the rest of the Midwest but less than the national average. As already pointed out, Minnesota is very white as compared with the rest of the country: 93 percent white in 1995 compared with 82.9 percent in the United States as a whole. But Minnesota's minority population is growing at a much faster rate than is the white population. In the first half of the 1990s the minority population increased 42 percent, compared with 3 percent for the white non-Hispanic population.[8] Asians were Minnesota's fastest growing and largest minority group. This growth was fueled in part by significant immigration from Laos and Vietnam. The Hmong from Laos have been especially attracted to Minnesota and contribute to the state's relatively high proportion of refugees among its legal immigrants. Many of the refugees have located here because of the resettlement efforts of local church groups. By 1998 the secondary migration of Hmong from California had raised their numbers in the Twin Cities to an estimated sixty thousand.[9]

From 1995 to 2010 Asian population growth in Minnesota is expected to continue to be strong (a predicted 58.9 percent increase) but will be outpaced by black growth at 67.4 percent and overwhelmed by Hispanic growth at 144 percent.[10] The white population is expected to grow by only 6.1 percent. Thus, Minnesota's population will become more diverse in the near future. Given the homogeneity Minnesota starts with, however, the diversification will be gradual. By 2010 the white population percentage is still predicted to be 90.2 percent, well above the national average. Thus, demographically Minnesota is becoming more like the rest of the country, but very gradually. Population growth is strong enough to provide economic stimulus, yet not so strong that the mores of the moralistic culture are destroyed.

One aspect of Minnesota's immigration makes the assimilation process easier than it might be in some other states. Nearly all immigrants come to Minnesota because they have relatives who have found opportunity here. These purposeful migrants expect to work hard; with that attitude their introduction into Minnesota's political culture should be greatly enhanced.

The public schools are feeling the challenge of immigration. The number of students in Minneapolis for whom English is not a native language tripled between 1990 and 1997.[11] Hmong and Spanish are the two most commonly used foreign languages in Minnesota's schools, but some seventy languages are heard. Some unexpected pockets of refugees crop up: of the twenty-five thousand Somali refugees in the United States, a little more than half have settled in Minnesota.[12] Somalian refugees make up one-quarter of the student body at one Minneapolis school. The enrollment of English-as-a-second-language students is heavily concentrated in the Twin Cities, where 21.9 percent of St. Paul's students are enrolled in ESL classes.[13] But even in outstate Minnesota some school districts have more than 10 percent ESL students: Worthington, for example, has 12.8 percent. Worthington's agricultural processing plants attract migrant workers and their families, as do plants in Owatonna, Marshall, and Pelican Rapids. Thus, adapting the education system to recent immigrants is a statewide issue. The mid-1990s saw vigorous debates over the quality of public schools, and the use of private school vouchers was advocated by Governor Arne Carlson.

The second trend that might affect Minnesota's future is the performance of the economy. It is harder to predict the economy's performance far into the future than it is to predict population growth. Nevertheless, above-average growth seems to be continuing. The major sectors of Minnesota's economy are manufacturing, followed by finance, services, and government, each of which constitutes at least 10 percent of the gross state product. Unlike the case in many other states, Minnesota's manufacturing employment growth is still quite impressive, about 15 percent above the national average in recent years. Thus, the largest sector's performance seems safe. Of particular note for the immigration challenge discussed above, Minnesota's number of unskilled job openings is quite impressive. Plenty of openings are expected in jobs requiring a high school diploma or less. The Somalis, in particular, are taking advantage of these job opportunities; less than 4 percent are on welfare.[14]

Despite its strong growth, Minnesota's economy has not lifted all racial and ethnic groups equally. Whereas in 1973 *Time* could say, "The place lacks the fire, urgency and self-accusation of states with massive urban centers and problems,"[15] that statement is no longer accurate. Many disturbing trends affect minorities. During the 1980s the median income of every Minnesota minority group declined while that of whites increased.[16] American Indians continued to be the poorest of the minority groups, though some amelioration has occurred recently with the introduction of casino gambling owned and controlled by the various tribes in the state. The poverty rate for African-American and Native American children is five times that for white children.

Also, in the 1980s the poverty population became more concentrated in certain neighborhoods of Minneapolis and St. Paul; at the same time, such neighborhoods became far more populated by blacks. One author asserted that the Twin Cities was the fourth fastest ghettoizing region in the nation.[17] The violent crime rate in these neighborhoods increased dramatically, as did many other social problems, leading to the embarrassing statistic that Minneapolis's murder rate exceeded that of New York City in 1995. The public schools in the Twin Cities showed the effects of the concentration of poverty and racial segregation as the minority enrollment went above 50 percent in both cities (68 percent in Minneapolis in 1997), as did the percentage of students getting free lunches.[18] The dropout rate for minorities exceeds that of whites; this problem worsened in the 1980s. Thus, the urban areas of Minnesota are no longer immune to big-city problems. Nor are the rural areas. Such problems have taken Minnesotans somewhat by surprise, and thus far, policy remedies have been few and far between.

The third trend in question in the mid-1990s was whether Minnesota would be able to continue its record of clean government. In the early 1990s the legislature was embarrassed by a series of mini-scandals, beginning with

"Phonegate" and continuing with minor peccadilloes committed by various members in their private lives. The misuse of a telephone credit card led to the resignation of the house majority leader, and the Speaker resigned because of failure to manage the house's affairs properly. Other members got in trouble for unauthorized phone calls, drunk driving, shoplifting, and spousal abuse. By early 1997 the legislature was the subject of an unflattering story in a national magazine, entitled "The Sick Legislature Syndrome and How to Avoid It."[19] Minnesota's reputation for clean government was definitely in jeopardy, and most Minnesotans were embarrassed about that.

Yet by mid-1999 we can say that Minnesota politics has withstood its time of sickness. The peccadilloes described above have been dealt with, various policies have been changed to avoid a repetition of "Phonegate," and there have been no new incidents of member misbehavior. New leadership was in place in the house, and many new members had been elected. The 1997 freshman class was rated the "best since the '70s."[20] Good people did run for office after the scandals had died down. We firmly believe that good government will continue to flourish in Minnesota.

It is too soon to tell how the Minnesota two-party system will withstand the shock of a third-party gubernatorial victory in 1998, however. Many Ventura voters seemed to rail against politics as usual: the specific candidates produced by the two major parties in 1998, their financial backers, their pollsters and media consultants, and their previous political experience. DFL and Republican party leaders are desperately trying to "get the message"—if they could only figure out what the message is. One possibility is to drop the informal party endorsement system altogether and rely on the primaries to select nominees. But this reform will increase the role of money in politics, which Ventura voters and most Minnesotans surely don't want. Another possibility is that Minnesota will evolve into a multiparty European system now that four parties have qualified for major-party status on the ballot. The strength of the historical and structural forces surrounding the two-party system argues against that development, however. Rather, we expect that Ventura's legacy will be more as an individual than as a party builder; he will be remembered as one of the quirky outsider governors who have made Minnesota politics so interesting.

Finally, what are the prospects that Minnesota's record of policy innovation will continue? Reasonably good, we think. Minnesota's economy should be strong enough to provide a fiscal basis for generous social services. Like other states, Minnesota might suffer federal budget cutbacks that may threaten some government programs. But to take one significant example, when the federal government ended the AFDC program in 1997 and forced the states to reform their own programs drastically, Minnesota lawmakers rolled up their sleeves and went to work in bipartisan fashion. Minnesota had a head start on welfare reform because for two years it had tested a work program for welfare recipients. It already had a strong child-care subsidy program, which it enhanced in 1997, and a healthcare program for low-income people. Minnesota lawmakers adopted the federal direction for AFDC, "work or else," but they were able to do so with some common sense, greatly increasing day-care and welfare-to-work transportation programs, thus addressing some of the major barriers in putting AFDC recipients into jobs. Moreover, state assistance will replace some but not all federal benefits lost to legal immigrants.

Besides government programs, Minnesota's poorer citizens will rely for assistance on its large and active nonprofit community, which has more than thirty-five hundred charities. A special fund for Minnesota's nonprofit organizations was created in 1997 to help them adjust to federal devolution and to changing patterns in service delivery for those in need. The fund grew to more than $2 million, with a $750,000 contribution from the state and the balance from local foundations.

Minnesota's record of policy innovation continued in the 1997–98 legislative session. In chapter 10 we talk about the continuing policy innovations in education. Of particular interest was the state's massive increase in what is referred to in education circles as "baby ed." With state coffers bulging in 1997, lawmakers acted on the belief that the only way ultimately to improve Minnesota's education product was to intervene earlier with many more children. Despite early protestations from Governor Ventura that government had no responsibility to raise children, the 1999 legislative session continued to increase early childhood spending, and he approved it.

If the past is the best predictor of the future, one has to believe that the North Star State has a bright future. It has a history of rising to the occasion time and again. The negative social trends cited above are small enough and developing slowly enough that solutions are still possible. We expect that Minnesota leaders will find those solutions.

CHAPTER 13

Suggested Sources for Further Study

Compared with the situation in most states, government and politics are well documented in Minnesota. Its historical society was chartered by the territorial legislature in 1849; recently, the society moved into a magnificent new building with extensive archival capacity. State government publishes prolifically; two major metropolitan newspapers conduct public opinion polls, report on politics regularly, and are archived. Yet many gaps remain to be filled by future researchers. For example, the University of Minnesota Press publishes relatively little on Minnesota government and politics compared with the presses of most flagship state universities. The Minnesota Political Science Association meets annually but does not regularly produce a series of papers for publication. So the coverage of the government and politics of the North Star State is uneven.

Of particular note are the extensive electronic sites maintained by state government and especially by the historical society and the Minnesota legislature. These promise to be more important to future researchers than the printed sources listed herein.

GENERAL REFERENCE WORKS

Almanacs, Directories, Atlases, Manuals

Minnesota's "blue book" is the most important single book in this category, and it is actually blue. Its official title is *Minnesota Legislative Manual* (though its title has varied over the years), and it is published biennially by the secretary of state. It contains historical information such as the state constitution, information on all three branches of government, recent election returns, and sections on local and federal government.

A new biennial publication is *Politics in Minnesota: The Directory* (St. Paul: Minnesota Political Press), which began in 1995. The directory contains listings of legislative members (with extensive biographies and complete election histories), leaders, staff, journalists, and lobbyists as well as some information on the judicial and executive branches.

The most important geographical books are those by John R. Borchert: *America's Northern Heartland* (Minneapolis: University of Minnesota Press, 1987), covering the economic and historical geography of the upper Midwest, and *Minnesota's Changing Geography* (Minneapolis: University of Minnesota Press, 1959), an introduction to the state's geography.

Bibliographies and Listings

Among the most useful bibliographical aids is the Legislative Reference Library's listing of state agency periodicals, available on its web page. The Minnesota Historical Society offers many useful aids on its World Wide Web page as well (<http://www.mnhs.org> [September 1998]), including an online catalog of its holdings.

STATE DOCUMENTS BY SOURCE

Increasingly, the most important sites are electronic. Minnesota's North Star site is one of the most comprehensive state-sponsored sites in the United States. It is located at <http://www.state.mn.us/mainmenu.html> [September 1998].

Print versions of most state publications can be purchased at Minnesota's Bookstore, located at 117 University Avenue, St. Paul, near the capitol.

Legislature

The *Official Directory of the Minnesota Legislature* is a small booklet published biennially. It contains listings of members of both houses, brief biographies, and pictures. Also, it lists committee membership, officers of each body, and staff.

The legislature's web page has everything: senate and house bills, bill tracking (also available from Phillips Legislative Service), Minnesota statutes, daily and weekly schedules of committee activity, house and senate journals, staff directories, and information about legislators. One can receive daily and weekly committee schedules by e-mail. The site is located at

<http://www.leg.state.mn.us/> [September 1998] and can be accessed through the state's North Star website.

Each body also publishes a weekly magazine containing highlights of the previous week's activities and a schedule of committee meetings the following week: *Senate Briefly* and, for the house, *Session Weekly*. Committee schedules can also be accessed by calling the twenty-four-hour committee hotline or by picking up the daily schedule at the reception desk in the capitol or House Office Building.

The Legislative Reference Library, located on the sixth floor of the State Office Building, contains an impressive collection of information on Minnesota, some thirty-two thousand items. The library maintains the legislature's web page and archives considerable material on the legislature, its members, and policy issues. The reference service has maintained newspaper clippings since 1970, organized by legislative subject, by personality, and by district. It also has vertical files on policy issues, containing selected journal articles and pamphlets.

Also located here are various official records, including the *Journal of the House* and the *Journal of the Senate* since 1909, both of which are indexed. In addition, one can find the *Minnesota Legislative Manuals* ("blue books") since 1871; Minnesota Statutes since 1941; Minnesota Session Laws since 1871; the governors' proposed budgets; minutes of state boards, commissions, and agencies; and interest-group ratings of legislators. Tapes of committee hearings and floor sessions since 1973 can be obtained from the Legislative History Department of the Legislative Reference Library, located in Room G71, State Office Building. Tapes of earlier hearings are found at the Minnesota Historical Society.

House Research Information Brief is an occasional series on current topics published by the Research Department, House of Representatives. These reports can be obtained from the Research Department, located on the sixth floor of the State Office Building. The Program Evaluation Division, Office of the Legislative Auditor, also publishes periodic reports from its studies.

Extensive legislative information for citizens is contained in *People and the Process: A Legislative Study Guide*, which is published by the House Public Information Office and is available on the Web.

Executive

The *Guidebook to State Agencies* is a good place to start, supplying information on 1,650 state agencies. It is now available on CD-ROM. Nearly every state agency has a publication program, whose entries may be found by consulting the home page of each agency found at the North Star website. Many agencies have their own libraries where materials may be picked up.

Judiciary

The *Annual Report, Minnesota State Court System* contains brief reports and some statistical information on caseloads and other matters. The opinions of the supreme court and the court of appeals are available on-line on the home page of the Minnesota Supreme Court.

SECONDARY SOURCE MATERIAL

Newspapers, Journals, Newsletters

The Minneapolis *Star Tribune*, the state's largest circulation newspaper, is indexed since 1891; copies since 1882 are on microfilm at the University of Minnesota Library. Note that before 1982 the *Star Tribune* was two separate newspapers, the *Minneapolis Star* and the *Minneapolis Tribune*. Its website is <http://www.startribune.com/> [September 1998].

The *St. Paul Pioneer Press*, the state's second largest circulation newspaper, is indexed since 1967; copies since 1849 are on microfilm at the University of Minnesota Library. Note that before 1985 it was two newspapers, the *St. Paul Dispatch* and the *St. Paul Pioneer Press*. Its website, located at <http://www.pioneerplanet.com/> [September 1998], contains much useful information, including the ability to look up the representative and senator for any given address.

The websites for other newspapers in the state as well as television and radio stations can be accessed through the Minnesota Media website at <http://deckernet.com/minn/mnmedia.htm> [September 1998].

One privately circulated newsletter of particular interest to political junkies is *Politics in Minnesota*, which has been published since 1981. It is archived at the Minnesota Historical Society. In addition, all back issues are available and searchable on the publication's website, <http://www.politicsinminnesota.com> [May 1999]. Two newer electronic newsletters are located at <http://www.checksandbalances.com> and <http://www.mn-politics.com>[May 1999]; they are bipartisan journals for cyber political junkies. In addition, the E-Democracy organization offers citizens a variety of opportunities for cyber involvement on its website at <http://www.e-

democracy.org> [September 1998], including e-mail discussion forums, debates, and access to election information.

Finally, the Minnesota Historical Society publishes a quarterly journal, *Minnesota History*.

Books

Notable books include the following:

William Anderson and Edward Widenor, *Intergovernmental Relations in the United States* (Minneapolis: University of Minnesota Press, 1950), is a classic text coauthored by a University of Minnesota expert on federalism.

Laura K. Auerbach, *Worthy to Be Remembered: A Political History of the Minnesota Democratic-Farmer-Labor Party, 1944–1984* (Minneapolis: DFL Party of Minnesota, 1984), is a detailed account of the party's early years.

Theodore E. Blegen, *Minnesota: A History of the State* (Minneapolis: University of Minnesota Press, 1963), is an authoritative history of the state.

Sara M. Evans and Barbara J. Nelson, *Wage Justice: Comparable Worth and the Paradox of Technocratic Reform* (Chicago: University of Chicago Press, 1989), is the definitive account of the adoption and implementation of Minnesota's comparable worth law.

Federal Writers' Project, *Minnesota: A State Guide*, rev. ed. (New York: Hastings House, 1954), is an important historical account.

William Watts Folwell, *A History of Minnesota* (St. Paul: Minnesota Historical Society, 1969), is the classic four-volume history of the state.

Fred W. Friendly, *Minnesota Rag* (New York: Random House, 1981), is the story of *Near v. Minnesota* (1934), a landmark First Amendment case heard before the U.S. Supreme Court.

Royce Hanson, *Tribune of the People: The Minnesota Legislature and Its Leadership* (Minneapolis: University of Minnesota Press, 1989), is a comprehensive study of the Minnesota legislature.

John J. Harrigan and William C. Johnson, *Governing the Twin Cities Region* (Minneapolis: University of Minnesota Press, 1978), describes the creation and operation of the Metropolitan Council in its early years.

John Earl Haynes, *Dubious Alliance: The Making of Minnesota's DFL Party* (Minneapolis: University of Minnesota Press, 1984), is an account of the origins of the DFL party.

Steve Hoffman, Donald Ostrom, Homer Williamson, and Kay Wolsborn, eds., *Perspectives on Minnesota Government and Politics*, 4th ed. (Edina MN: Burgess Publishing, 1998), is sponsored by the Minnesota Political Science Association. Scholars around the state contribute to this collection.

Amy Klobuchar, *Uncovering the Dome* (Minneapolis: Bolger Publications, 1982), documents the ten-year political battle over building the Metrodome.

Jim Klobuchar, *Minstrel: My Adventure in Newspapering* (Minneapolis: University of Minnesota Press, 1997), contains a longtime newspaper columnist's observations on Minnesota politics.

William Lass, *Minnesota: A History*, 2d ed. (New York: Norton, 1998), is a recent informative history of the state.

David Lebedoff, *The Twenty-First Ballot: A Political Party Struggle in Minnesota* (Minneapolis: University of Minnesota Press, 1969), is an account of a serious split in the 1966 DFL state convention, when the party took twenty-one ballots to endorse.

Jonathon Lebedoff, *Ward Number Six* (New York: Scribner's, 1972), is an interesting account of local politics in Minneapolis.

Dennis J. McGrath and Dane Smith, *Professor Wellstone Goes to Washington: The Inside Story of a Grassroots U.S. Senate Campaign* (Minneapolis: University of Minnesota Press, 1995), is a reporters' account of the unique grassroots style of Wellstone's successful 1990 campaign.

G. Theodore Mitau, *Politics in Minnesota* (Minneapolis: University of Minnesota Press, 1960), is the definitive account of Minnesota's politics at midcentury.

Robert L. Morlan, *Political Prairie Fire: The Non-Partisan League, 1915–1922* (Minneapolis: University of Minnesota Press, 1955), is an account of the founding and operation of the Non-Partisan League.

Nancy C. Roberts and Paula J. King, *Transforming Public Policy: Dynamics of Policy Entrepreneurship and Innovation* (San Francisco: Jossey-Bass, 1996), is the definitive account of adoption of school-choice legislation.

Theodore Rueter, *The Minnesota House of Representatives and the Professionalization of Politics* (Lanham MD: University Press of America, 1994), is an academic account of the Minnesota House of Representatives, centering on the concept of institutionalization.

Rod Searle, *Minnesota Standoff: The Politics of Deadlock* (Waseca MN: Alton Press, 1990), portrays the political battle that ensued when the house of representatives was evenly split between Democrats and Republicans.

Ronald F. Stinnett and Charles H. Backstrom, *Recount* (Washington DC: National Document Publishers, 1964), is the authoritative account of the contested gubernatorial election of 1962.

Research Bureaus and Foundations

The Center for Urban and Regional Affairs at the University of Minnesota has published the CURA *Reporter* for twenty-five years. It contains brief reports on research sponsored by CURA and can be subscribed to free of charge. Its Web address is <http://www.umn.edu/cura/> [September 1998].

The Citizens League publishes *Citizen Journal* monthly; it contains a roundup of editorial opinion on various subjects and articles by staff on current topics. The league also publishes periodic reports on current issues. Its Web address is <http://www.freenet.msp.mn.us/ip/pol/citizen/> [September 1998].

The Center of the American Experiment, a conservative think tank, in 1998 began its own journal, *American Experiment Quarterly*.

The League of Women Voters periodically publishes *How to Make a Difference: A Citizens Guide to State Government*. Its website is <http://freenet.msp.mn.us/ip/pol/lwvmn/> [September 1998].

Historical Societies and Special Collections

The Minnesota Historical Society has one of the best-equipped research libraries in the country. It consists of several distinct collections, beginning with the state archives, that is, the official records of state and local governments in Minnesota. It also houses a newspaper collection, totaling three million issues of five thousand newspapers, starting in 1849. Its manuscript collection includes the papers of many individuals as well as records of organizations and businesses. This is supplemented by an oral-history collection, which has audiotapes and printed transcripts. The society owns a vast amount of published material on Minnesota, more than five hundred thousand books, pamphlets, periodicals, and government publications.

Among its more unusual collections is the sound and visual section, totaling five hundred thousand photographs relating to the state as well as recordings documenting life and events in the state. Its map collection contains thirty-eight thousand individual maps plus eighteen hundred atlases. The society also holds many museum items such as Minnesota products and handicrafts and has an art collection of some six thousand paintings, drawings, and sculptures.

STATISTICAL INFORMATION

Economic and Fiscal

The state agency Minnesota Planning publishes an extensive array of documents and reports, typically containing population estimates and forecasts of trends in various policy areas. Also, it has its own website at <http://www.mnplan.state.mn.us> [September 1998], offering databases on city, county, and township populations, population projections, and maps. It furnishes information on government spending, crime and justice, children, state demographics, environment, and development.

Minnesota's Council of Economic Advisers provides biennially an *Economic Report to the Governor*, modeled after the national counterpart. It contains statistical information as well as brief articles on economic topics of interest at the moment.

The website of the Minneapolis Federal Reserve Bank is a useful source for economic data on the state and the region. It offers data on current economic conditions by sector, economic forecasts, plus an archive of the research papers and news briefings by research staff. It is located at <http://woodrow.mpls.frb.fed.us:80/index.html> [September 1998].

Voting Returns

Election results by county can be obtained from the secretary of state's office and are available since 1984. Results from elections before that time are housed at the historical society. Current election returns are available on the secretary of state's home page on the Web. The *Minnesota Legislative Manual* ("blue book") also publishes the most recent election returns by county in each issue.

The Minnesota Historical Society publishes various compilations such as *Minnesota Votes* (St. Paul: Minnesota Historical Society, 1977), which covers 1857 to 1977.

Campaign Contributions and Public Opinion Surveys

The Minnesota Campaign Finance and Public Disclosure Board (formerly the Ethical Practices Board) receives information from political candidates about their receipts and expenditures. This information is aggregated and reported annually in *Principal Campaign Committees, Political Committees, and Political Funds*. The board also registers lobbyists and receives reports on their expenditures. These reports are aggregated and published annually in *Lobbying Disbursement Summary* and *Registered Lobbyists and Associations Represented*. The most current listings are available on the board's home page on the Web.

The *Star Tribune* has conducted the Minnesota Poll, a statewide public opinion poll, since the 1940s; currently, KMSP TV is the cosponsor of the poll. The *Star Tribune* maintains a keyword index to the stories in which the polls are reported. The *St. Paul Pioneer Press*, in conjunction with Minnesota Public Radio and KARE TV, conducts a statewide poll, focusing on electoral campaigns. The Center for Urban and Regional Affairs at the University of Minnesota also conducts a statewide poll annually, as does St. Cloud State University.

Persons Interviewed for
Minnesota Politics and Government

Name	Position	Interview Date	Location
Elmer L. Andersen	Governor, 1961–63	25 Nov. 1996	Arden Hills
Lynn Anderson	Executive assistant and chief of staff for Governor Perpich	19 Dec. 1996	St. Paul
Morrie Anderson	Chief of staff for Governor Carlson; former commissioner of revenue	13 Dec. 1996	St. Paul
Wendell Anderson	Governor, 1973–77	16 Jan. 1997; 20 Jan. 1997	St. Paul; Minneapolis
John Boland	Former legislator; chair of metropolitan council under Governor Anderson	17 Jan. 1997	St. Paul
Arne Carlson	Governor, 1991–99	11 Feb. 1997	St. Paul
David Durenberger	Chief of staff for Governor LeVander; former U.S. senator	3 Dec. 1996	Washington DC (telephone)
George Farr	Former DFL party chair	27 Dec. 1996	St. Paul
Keith Ford	Minneapolis Community Development Agency	Apr. 1997	Minneapolis
Sandra Gardebring	Head of pollution control agency, metropolitan council, and department of human services under Governor Perpich; former member, Minnesota Court of Appeals and Supreme Court	9 Dec. 1996	St. Paul
Curtis Johnson	Chief of staff for Governor Carlson; chairman, metropolitan council; former director, Citizens League	10 Dec. 1996	St. Paul
A. M. ("Sandy") Keith	Former chief justice, Minnesota Supreme Court	19 Aug. 1995	St. Paul
Thomas Kelly and Charles Weed	Staff, DFL party	Apr. 1997	St. Paul
Jean LeVander King	Speech writer for Governor LeVander; chief of staff, Governor Quie	4 Dec. 1996	St. Paul

Joseph R. Kingman	Assistant with personnel responsibilities for Governor Carlson	18 Dec. 1996	St. Paul
David Krogseng	Former chair, Minnesota Republican party	26 Dec. 1995	Minneapolis
James Miller	Executive director, League of Minnesota Cities	Apr. 1997	St. Paul
Roger Moe	Senate majority leader	14 Feb. 1997; 10 Mar. 1997	St. Paul
Terry Montgomery	Chief of staff for Governor Perpich; former president, Greater Minnesota Corporation	10 Jan. 1997	Northern California (telephone)
James Mulder	Executive director, Association of Minnesota Counties	Apr. 1997	St. Paul
Arthur Naftalin	Commissioner, Dept. of Administration, under Governor Freeman; produced eight documentaries on governors; former mayor of Minneapolis	9 Dec. 1996	Minneapolis
James Pedersen	Minnesota Historical Society; formerly executive director, DFL party; staff for Governor Freeman	8 Dec. 1995; 22 Dec. 1995	St. Paul
Albert Quie	Governor, 1979–83	9 Dec. 1996	St. Louis Park
Robert Renner Jr.	Counsel for Governor Quie	20 Dec. 1996	St. Paul
Bill Riemerman	Former reporter, *St. Paul Dispatch*; former senate counsel staff	10 Feb. 1997	St. Paul
Lyall Schwarzkopf	Chief of staff, Governor Carlson; former Minneapolis city coordinator	19 Dec. 1996	Minneapolis
Peter Wattson	Chief senate counsel	4 Feb. 1997	St. Paul
Bruce Willis	Minnesota Court of Appeals	23 Oct. 1996	St. Paul

Notes

SERIES INTRODUCTION

1 In 1998 the Civil War continued, as the Minnesota History Center displayed the First Regiment's tattered flag over the protests of Civil War reenacters in Virginia who wanted the flag back. A legal dispute ensued, as yet unresolved.

2 William Anderson, *Intergovernmental Relations in Review* (Minneapolis: University of Minnesota Press, 1960), and Edward Weidener, *Intergovernmental Relations as Seen by Public Officials* (Westport CT: Greenwood Press, 1974).

3 Donald S. Lutz, *The Origins of American Constitutionalism* (Baton Rouge: Louisiana State University Press, 1988), and Daniel J. Elazar, *The American Constitutional Tradition* (Lincoln: University of Nebraska Press, 1987).

4 Frederick Jackson Turner, *The Frontier in American History* (New York: Dover, 1996), and Daniel J. Elazar, *Cities of the Prairie: The Metropolitan Frontier and American Politics* (New York: Basic Books, 1970), part 1.

5 Theodore Blegen, *Minnesota: A History of the State* (Minneapolis: University of Minnesota Press, 1975), especially chap. 11.

6 See Daniel J. Elazar, "The Metropolitan Frontier," chap. 1 in *Cities of the Prairie*, pp. 23–65, and Daniel J. Elazar, "The Frontier as Chain Reaction," in *Frontier in Regional Development*, ed. Yehuda Gradus and Harvey Lithwick (Lanham MD: Rowman and Littlefield, 1996).

7 Daniel J. Elazar, *American Federalism: A View from the States*, 3d ed. (New York: Harper and Row, 1984), pp. 161–69.

8 Elazar, *American Federalism*, chaps. 5 and 6.

9 Elazar, *Cities of the Prairie*, chap. 8.

CHAPTER 1

1 For a definition of civil society and polity, see Daniel J. Elazar, *American Federalism: A View from the States* (New York: Thomas Y. Crowell, 1966), pp. 2–3.

2 John Gunther, *Inside U.S.A.* (Philadelphia: Curtis Publishing, 1947), p. 296.

3 "Minnesota: A State That Works," *Time*, 13 August 1973, p. 24; "Minnesota: The Land of Good Examples," *The Economist*, 5 July 1997, p. 28.

4 Neal Peirce, "Minnesota: The Successful Society," in *The Great Plains States of America: People, Politics, and Power in the Nine Great Plains States* (New York: W. W. Norton, 1972, 1973), p. 110.

5 Charles Mahtesian, "The Sick Legislature Syndrome and How to Avoid It," *Governing* (February 1997): 16–20.

6 Dirk Johnson, "Nice City's Nasty Distinction: Murder Soars in Minneapolis," *New York Times*, 30 June 1996, p. 1A.

7 John Borchert, *Minnesota's Changing Geography* (Minneapolis: University of Minnesota Press, 1959), chap. 3.

8 Throughout the book we use "Ojibwe," the term preferred by today's Native Americans, rather than the spelling "Ojibway." This group of Natives also uses the term "Anishinabe" to describe themselves; the term "Chippewa" was used by government officials. The Dakota Indians today prefer to go by the term "Dakota" rather than "Sioux," which is what government officials called them. See William E. Lass, *Minnesota: A History*, 2d ed. (New York: W. W. Norton, 1998), pp. 40–42.

9 See Elazar, "Metropolitan Frontier," and Elazar, "Frontier as Chain Reaction."

10 Blegen, *Minnesota: A History of the State.*

11 In 1998 this remote area was the focus of a border dispute when Ontario required those fishing in Canadian waters to stay overnight in Canadian resorts. Some Angle residents threatened to secede if the United States did not protect their right to fish.

12 Elazar, "Frontier as Chain Reaction."

13 See, for example, "Minnesota Memory Upgrade," *St. Paul Pioneer Press*, 9 September 1996, sec. D.

14 Based on the Twin Cities Metropolitan Commission.

15 See Paul W. Gates, *Fifty Million Acres: Conflicts over Kansas Law Policy, 1854–1890* (Ithaca: Cornell University Press, 1954); Thomas Simpson, *The Early Government Land Survey in Minnesota West of the Mississippi River* (St. Paul: Minnesota Historical Society, 1905); John Simpson Dodds, *Original Instruction on Governing Public Land Survey, 1815–1855: A Guide to Their Use in Resurveys of Public Lands* (Ames 1A: Powers Press, 1944).

16 Jack Nordby, *The State Constitution: An Overview* (St. Paul: N.p., 1992); Julius Haycraft, *A Legal and Historical Treatise on the Territorial Existence and Constitutional Statehood of Minnesota* (St. Paul: West, 1950); William Anderson and Albert J. Lobb, *A History of the Constitution of Minnesota*, Studies in the Social Sciences, no. 15 (Minneapolis: University of Minnesota Press, 1921); Millard L. Gieske, "Ideal and Practice in a State Constitution: The Case of Minnesota," *Minnesota Academy of Science Journal* 32 (1964): 51–59.

17 Elazar, *Cities of the Prairie*, pp. 323–37.

18 See June Drenning Holmquist, *They Chose Minnesota: A Survey of the State's Ethnic Groups* (St. Paul: Minnesota Historical Society, 1981, 1988).

19 George B. Engberg, "The Rise of Organized Labor in Minnesota," in *Selections from Minnesota History: A Fiftieth Anniversary Anthology*, ed. Rhoda R. Gilman and June Drenning Holmquist (St. Paul: Minnesota Historical Society, 1965); Millard L. Gieske, *Minnesota Farmer-Laborism: The Third Party Alternative* (Minneapolis: University of Minnesota Press, 1979).

20 See, for example, Richard M. Valelly, *Radicalism and the States: The Minnesota Farm-Labor Party and the American Political Economy* (Chicago: University of Chicago Press, 1989).

21 See Borchert, *Minnesota's Changing Geography*; John B. Borchert and Neil C. Gustafson, *Atlas of Minnesota Resources and Settlement*, 3d ed. (Minneapolis: Center for Urban and Regional Affairs, University of Minnesota, and Minnesota State Planning Agency, 1980); John Borchert, *The Urbanization of the Upper Midwest, 1930–1960*, Urban Paper no. 2 (Minneapolis: Upper Midwest Economic Study, 1963); and John Borchert, *Upper Midwest Economic Study: A Research Prospectus*, Urban Paper no. 1 (Minneapolis: Upper Midwest Economic Study, 1960).

22 The anecdote was related to one of the authors, then employed by the Pillsbury Corporation, by a member of Pillsbury's economic development staff, which had then made the recommendation to move.

23 See John Fisher, "The Minnesota Experiment: How to Make a Big City Fit to Live In," *Harper's Magazine*, April 1969, pp. 12, 17–18, 20, 24, 26, 28, 30, 32.

24 *Star Tribune*, 10 February 1998, p. A18.

CHAPTER 2

1 Laura K. Auerbach, *Worthy to Be Remembered: A Political History of the Minnesota Democratic-Farmer-Labor Party, 1944–1984* (Minneapolis: Democratic-Farmer-Labor Party of Minnesota, 1984); Gieske, *Minnesota Farmer-Laborism*; John Earl Haynes, *Dubious Alliance: The Making of Minnesota's Democratic Farmer Labor Party* (Minneapolis: University of Minnesota Press, 1984).

2 See C. Theodore Mitau, *Politics in Minnesota*, rev. ed. (Minneapolis: University of Minnesota Press, 1970), and William L. Hathaway, *Minnesota Politics and Parties Today* (St. Paul: Carter and Lacey, 1978).

3 See Auerbach, *Worthy to Be Remembered*; Gieske, *Minnesota Farmer-Laborism*; Haynes, *Dubious Alliance*; Robert L. Morlan, *Political Prairie Fire: The Non-Partisan League, 1915–1922* (Minneapolis: University of Minnesota Press, 1955); Carl H. Chrislock, *The Progressive Era in Minnesota, 1899–1918* (St. Paul: Minnesota Historical Society, 1971); and Carl H. Chrislock, "The Politics of Protest in Minnesota, 1890–1901: From Populism to Progressivism" (Ph.D. dissertation, University of Minnesota, 1954).

4 William Watts Folwell, *A History of Minnesota*, vol. 4 (St. Paul: Minnesota Historical Society, 1930).

CHAPTER 3

1 Daniel J. Elazar and Stephen Schechter, eds., *State Constitutional Design in Federal Systems*, Publius: The Journal of Federalism 12 (winter 1982); Daniel J. Elazar, *The American Constitutional Tradition* (Lincoln: University of Nebraska Press, 1988).

2 See Peter Onuf, *Statehood and Union: A History of the Northwest Ordinance* (Bloomington: Indiana University Press, 1987).

3 "The Federalist #1," from Jacob E. Cooke, *The Federalist: The Definitive Edition of the Historic Essays by Alexander Hamilton, James Madison, and John Jay* (Middletown CT: Wesleyan University Press, 1961), pp. 3–7.

4 See the series entitled "Reference Guide to the State Constitutions of the United States," ed. G. Alan Tarr (Westport CT: Greenwood Press). See also G. Alan Tarr, ed., *Constitutional Politics in the States: Contemporary Controversies and Historical Patterns* (Westport CT: Greenwood Press, 1996).

5 Minnesota Constitutional Convention, *The Debates and Proceedings of the Minnesota Constitutional Convention, Including the Organic Act of the Territory* (St. Paul: E. S. Goodrich, 1857).

CHAPTER 4

1 John F. Bibby and Thomas M. Holbrook, "Parties and Elections," in *Politics in the American States*, 7th ed., ed. Virginia Gray, Russell Hanson, and Herbert Jacob (Washington DC: CQ Press, 1999), table 3.4.

2 Patricia Lopez Baden, "State's Unofficial Voter-Turnout Level Put at 60.4%," *Star Tribune*, 10 November 1998, p. A10.

3 Baden, "State's Unofficial Voter-Turnout Level."

4 Kim Quaile Hill and Jan E. Leighley, "The Policy Consequences of Class Bias in State Electorates," *American Journal of Political Science* 36 (May 1992): 351–65.

5 Dane Smith, "The 'L' Word," *Star Tribune*, 18 November 1994, p. 22A.

6 "Divided We Stand: A Minnesota Poll Report on Shared Values, Social Tolerance, and Community Attachment," *Star Tribune*, 1995. These data are reported on p. 1 of the appendix to the background report prepared to accompany poll results reported in the *Star Tribune* on 2 April 1995. The poll was a statewide survey of 1,103 adults conducted by telephone 16–23 February 1995. The sampling error is plus or minus 3 percent at the 95 percent confidence level.

7 "Divided We Stand." All data in this paragraph come from this source.

8 Virginia Gray and Peter Eisinger, *American States and Cities*, 2d ed. (New York: Longmans, 1997), pp. 68–69. Research indicates that state regulations do not determine the number of registered groups; see David Lowery and Virginia Gray, "How Some Rules Just Don't Matter: The Regulation of Lobbyists," *Public Choice* 91 (1997): 139–47.

9 Unpublished research by Virginia Gray and David Lowery, 1999.

10 Virginia Gray and David Lowery, "The World of Contract Lobbying," paper presented at the Annual Meeting of the Midwest Political Science Association, Chicago, April 1995, p. 8.

11 Gray and Lowery, "World of Contract Lobbying," pp. 9–10.

12 Virginia Gray and David Lowery, "The Demography of Interest Organization Communities: Institutions, Associations, and Membership Groups," *American Politics Quarterly* 23 (January 1995): 3–32. All information in this section is from this source.

13 Clive Thomas and Ronald Hrebenar, "Interest Groups in the States," in *Politics in the American States*, 7th ed., ed. Virginia Gray, Russell Hanson, and Herbert Jacob (Washington DC: CQ Press, 1999), table 4.6.

14 Dane Smith, "The Lobbyists," *Star Tribune*, 5 May 1995, p. 20A.

15 Jack B. Coffman and Thomas J. Collins, "Bankrolling the Legislature," *St. Paul Pioneer Press*, special reprint section, April 1992, p. 5.

16 Conrad deFiebre, "Public Sector Is Their Special Interest," *Star Tribune*, 11 March 1998, p. B4.

17 Gray and Lowery, "World of Contract Lobbying," p. 11.

18 Virginia Gray, unpublished survey of Minnesota interest groups, 1984.

19 Smith, "Lobbyists," p. 20A.

20 Virginia Gray, "The Origin and Impact of Lobbying Laws in the American States," paper presented at the Annual Meeting of the Law and Society Association, Glasgow, Scotland, July 1996.

21 Virginia Gray, unpublished survey of Minnesota legislators, fall 1997.

CHAPTER 5

1 An interesting history of this merger can be found in Haynes, *Dubious Alliance*.

2 Bob von Sternberg, "Perot's Support Surrounded Twin Cities, Independent Scored Well among Men, the Young," *Star Tribune*, 7 November 1992.

3 Wayne Washington, "Reform Party's Election Performance Doesn't Disappoint Barkley, Two Percentage-Point Improvement over 1994 Makes Candidate Proud," *Star Tribune*, 7 November 1996.

4 Malcolm E. Jewell and Sarah M. Morehouse, "Preprimary Endorsements: An Asset or Liability for State Political Parties?" paper presented at the 1995 Annual Meeting of the American Political Science Association, Chicago, 30 August–3 September 1995, p. 2.

5 George H. Mayer, *The Political Career of Floyd B. Olson* (St. Paul: Minnesota Historical Society Press, Borealis Books, 1987), p. 38.

6 *Minneapolis Tribune*, 10 September 1958, p. 22A.

7 Sarah M. Morehouse, "Money versus Party Effort: Nominating for Governor," *American Journal of Political Science* 34 (August 1990): 706–24; also see Sarah McCally Morehouse, *The Governor and Party Leader, Campaigning and Governing* (Ann Arbor: University of Michigan Press, 1998), p. 199.

8 Morehouse, "Money versus Party Effort," p. 717.

9 Joseph A. Kunkel III, "Party Endorsement and Incumbency in Minnesota Legislative Nominations," *Legislative Studies Quarterly* 13 (May 1988): 219.

10 For an excellent summary of the broader issue, especially at the state level, see Alan Rosenthal, *The Decline of Representative Democracy* (Washington DC: CQ Press, 1998).

11 For the last reform proposals to this system, see Joan Anderson Growe, *Report of the Growe Commission on Electoral Reform* (St. Paul: Office of the Secretary of State, January 1995).

12 Jewell and Morehouse, "Preprimary Endorsements," p. 19.

13 410 U.S. 113.

14 Republican Party of Minnesota, *1970–1971 Republican Platform*, adopted 18–20 June 1970, St. Paul, p. 12.

15 Democratic-Farmer-Labor Party of Minnesota, *Democratic-Farmer-Labor Party Minnesota Platform,* 1974, St. Paul, pp. 31–33.

16 Independent-Republican Party of Minnesota, *Minnesota 1992 Independent-Republican State Platform*, p. 7.

17 Minnesota Democratic-Farmer-Labor Party, *Ongoing Platform, 1994*, p. 16.

18 *Star Tribune*, 9 June 1996, p. A9.

19 Steven E. Schier, "No Fluke: Political Trends Fueled Ventura's Victory," *Star Tribune*, 17 November 1998, p. A15.

20 Jack B. Coffman, "Who's the Campaign Cash Cow? Say 'Moo,'" *St. Paul Pioneer Press*, 18 August 1997, p. 1A.

21 Jack B. Coffman, "Campaign Subsidy Still Dropping: Candidates in General Election Will Need More Private Donations," *St. Paul Pioneer Press*, 2 July 1998, <http://www.pioneerplanet.com> [September 1998].

22 Conrad deFiebre, "Protest Candidacy Brings State's Fourth Major Party," *Star Tribune*, 10 November 1998, Metro section.

23 George Fagg, Eighth Circuit Court of Appeals, as quoted in Paul Gustafson, "Appellate Court's Rules Could Aid Third Parties in State Elections," *St. Paul Pioneer Press*, 6 January 1996, p. 2B.

CHAPTER 6

1 Citizens Conference on State Legislatures, *The Sometimes Governments* (Kansas City MO: Citizens Conference on State Legislatures, 1973).

2 Alan Rosenthal, *The Third House* (Washington DC: CQ Press, 1993), p. 10.

3 "Statestats: A Second Look at the Cost of Legislatures," *State Legislatures* (November 1994): 5.

4 Royce Hanson, *Tribune of the People* (Minneapolis: University of Minnesota Press, 1989), p. xi.

5 Citizens League, *Reform the Election Process, Restore the Public Trust* (Minneapolis: Citizens League, 1992), pp. 51–52.

6 Citizens League, *Reform the Election Process*, appendix 6.

7 Malcolm E. Jewell and Marcia Lynn Whicker, *Legislative Leadership in the American States* (Ann Arbor: University of Michigan Press, 1994).

8 Hanson, *Tribune of the People*, p. 60.

9 Rod Searle, *Minnesota Standoff: The Politics of Deadlock* (Waseca MN: Alton Press, 1990).

10 Wayne L. Francis, *The Legislative Committee Game* (Columbus: Ohio State University Press, 1989), p. 44.

11 Sarah Janecek, *Politics in Minnesota: The Directory* (St. Paul: Minnesota Political Press, 1995).

12 Cynthia Opheim, "Reinventing Images: State Legislative Efforts to Reach the Public," *State and Local Government Review* 28 (spring 1996): 136–46.

13 Donald Ostrom, "The Minnesota Legislature," in *Perspectives on Minnesota Government and Politics*, 4th ed., ed. Steve Hoffman, Donald Ostrom, Homer Williamson, and Kay Wolsborn (Edina MN: Burgess Publishing, 1998), p. 77.

14 Virginia Gray, unpublished survey of Minnesota legislative staff, 1997.

15 Hanson, *Tribune of the People*, p. 126.

16 Janecek, *Politics in Minnesota*.

17 Hanson, *Tribune of the People*, p. 144.

18 "State to Appeal Ruling on Wage Law, School Construction," *St. Paul Pioneer Press*, 11 July 1998, p. 2B.

19 Hanson, *Tribune of the People*, p. 238.

20 Jewell and Whicker, *Legislative Leadership*, p. 204.

21 Mahtesian, "Sick Legislature Syndrome."

CHAPTER 7

1 Interview, 20 November 1996, Minneapolis.

2 Secretary of State, *Minnesota Legislative Manual, 1995–1996* (St. Paul: State of Minnesota, 1995), p. 164.

3 *State of Minnesota ex rel Robert W. Mattson, Treasurer of the State of Minnesota v. Peter J. Kiedrowski, commissioner of Finance of the State of Minnesota*, 7 August 1986.

4 Thad Beyle, "Governors: The Middlemen and Women in Our Political System," chap. 6 in *Politics in the American States: A Comparative Analysis*, 6th ed., ed. Virginia Gray and Herbert Jacob (Washington DC: CQ Press, 1996), pp. 228–37.

5 An 1887 article in the then fashionable academic publication *Contemporary Review* criticized Minnesota for violating the principles of laissez-faire because the legislature had enacted so many regulations of business. The author, Albert Shaw, noted with great displeasure the number of people involved in regulating railroads, insurance companies, physicians, dentists, and sources of pollution. Shaw was particularly perturbed about the inspection of the logging industry: "Not a log is floated down stream from the woods to the saw-mill for which it is destined without official cognizance." See Albert Shaw, "The American State and the American Man," *Contemporary Review* 51 (January–June 1887): 695–711.

6 Richard C. Elling, "Administering State Programs: Performance and Politics," in *Politics in the American States*, 7th ed., ed. Virginia Gray, Russell Hanson, and Herbert Jacob (Washington DC: CQ Press, 1999), table 8.1.

7 Elling, "Administering State Programs," table 8.1.

8 Elling, "Administering State Programs," table 8.2.

9 Minnesota Planning, *A Cut Above: Minnesota's National Rankings* (St. Paul: State of Minnesota, 1994), p. 3.

10 Patricia Lopez Baden, "Minnesota Gets AAA Bond Rating," *Star Tribune*, 25 July 1997, Metro Section.

11 Russell W. Fridley, *Evaluation of Minnesota Governors* (St. Paul: Minnesota Historical Society, 1966).

12 Daniel J. Elazar, *The Office of Governor in Illinois, 1818–1933: A Case Study of Gubernatorial Roles and Styles* (Philadelphia: Center for the Study of Federalism, Temple University, 1976), pp. 134–36.

13 Gene Newhall and Richard Williams, "Gov. Freeman, Andersen Cross Words in Debate," *St. Paul Pioneer Press*, 10 October 1960.

14 Gene Newhall, *St. Paul Pioneer Press*, 24 March 1963.

15 A full accounting of this amazing election can be had in Robert F. Stinnett and Charles H. Backstrom, *Recount* (Washington DC: National Document Publishers, 1964).

16 Lewis Patterson, "Rolvaag Cites Record, Eyes Next Term," *St. Paul Dispatch*, 25 March 1965.

17 Interview, 4 December 1996, St. Paul.

18 Governor Bob Graham, "A Magical Vision and Other Ingredients of Leadership," in *Governors on Governing*, National Governors Association, ed. Robert D. Behn (Lanham MD: University Press of America, 1991), pp. 57–64.

19 *A Look at the Record: The First Three Years of the LeVander Administration*, prepared and distributed by the Minnesota Republican State Central Committee, George Thiss, chairman, p. 17. Thanks to Jean LeVander King for allowing us use of her copy of this document.

20 *Look at the Record*, pp. 19, 21.

21 Interview, 20 January 1997, Minneapolis.

22 Thanks to Robert Renner of the Messerli & Kramer law firm for providing the documents during an interview 20 December 1996 in St. Paul.

23 Interview, 9 December 1996, St. Louis Park.

24 The comment was made to one of the coauthors during a 1986 interview. Others have indicated Perpich said it in their presence also.

25 Minnesota Poll, "Perpich Exceeds Public's Expectations," *Minneapolis Tribune*, 10 April 1977.

26 Minnesota Poll, "50% Dislike Perpich's Work, but 57% Favor Him over Al Quie," *Minneapolis Tribune*, 28 May 1978.

27 "Mall of America—Five Years Old," from PRNewswire, at <http://www.startribune.com> [September 1998], 8 August 1997.

28 Robert Whereatt and Dane Smith, "Carlson Rating Is Lowest for Governor since '44" [the year the Minnesota Poll began], *Star Tribune*, 30 January 1992.

29 "State Budget Forecast: Don't Spend Windfall on Election-Year Spree," *St. Paul Pioneer Press*, 1 December 1995, editorial.

30 Jean Hopfensperger, "Poverty, Social Issues Show Rift among Candidates," *Star Tribune*, 13 October 1998; Tom Meersman and Anne O'Connor, "Ventura Spends Holiday Talking to Vets, Students," *Star Tribune*, 12 November 1998.

CHAPTER 8

1 Roland C. Amundson, *A Search for Place: The History of the Minnesota Judicial Center* (St. Paul: Minnesota Court of Appeals, 1995), p. 22.

2 The Board of Law Examiners, the Board of Continuing Legal Education, the Board of Legal Certification, and the Lawyers Professional Responsibility Board.

3 Henry R. Glick, "Innovation in State Judicial Administration: Effects on Court Management and Organization," *American Politics Quarterly* 9 (January 1981): 49–69.

4 David B. Rottman, *State Court Organization, 1993* (Washington DC: U.S. Department of Justice, Bureau of Justice Statistics, 1995).

5 Robert L. Spangenberg and Marea L. Beeman, "Indigent Defense Systems in the United States," *Law and Contemporary Problems* 58 (winter 1995): 31–49.

6 Interview with Kevin Kajer, fiscal director, State Board of Public Defense, 28 October 1996, Minneapolis.

7 From a report for the American Bar Association Bar Information Program by the Spangenberg Group, 1001 Watertown Street, West Newton MA.

8 Interview with A. M. ("Sandy") Keith, 19 August 1995, St. Paul.

9 Brian J. Ostrom and Neal B. Kauder, *Examining the Work of State Courts, 1996: A National Perspective from the Court Statistics Project* (Williamsburg VA: National Center for State Courts, 1997), pp. 21, 28.

10 Kathleen Blatz, "State of the Judiciary," speech delivered at the Minnesota State Bar Association annual convention in Duluth, 25 June 1998. Text available at <http://www.courts.state.mn.us/stofjudic.html> [September 1998].

11 Virginia Rybin, "Swift Justice Is the Best Deterrent, State Supreme Court Chief Says," *St. Paul Pioneer Press Dispatch*, 20 August 1991, Metro final edition, p. 2B.

12 *1995 Annual Report, Minnesota State Court System*, issued by State Court Administrator Sue K. Dosal, 6 June 1996.

13 Peter S. Popovich, "Beginning a Judicial Tradition: Formative Years of the Min-

nesota Court of Appeals, 1983–1987," in cooperation with the State Court Administrator's Office, St. Paul, November 1987, pp. 41–42.

14 Virginia Rybin, "Retirement Summons Chief Justice," *Duluth News Tribune*, 29 January 1989, p. 1B.

15 Harry P. Stumpf, *American Judicial Politics* (San Diego CA: Harcourt Brace Jovanovich, 1988), p. 174.

16 Joan Anderson Growe, *The Minnesota Legislative Manual, 1997–1998* (St. Paul: Election Division, Secretary of State, June 1997), pp. 228–52.

17 Canon 5, Minnesota Code of Judicial Conduct, <http://www.state.mn.us/ebranch/judstnds> [September 1998].

18 Peter Harris, "Ecology and Culture in the Communication of Precedent among State Supreme Courts, 1870–1970," *Law and Society Review* 19, 3 (1985): 443–86.

19 Gregory A. Caldeira, "The Transmission of Legal Precedent: A Study of State Supreme Courts," *American Political Science Review* 79, 1 (1985): 178–93.

20 Lawrence M. Friedman, Robert A. Kagan, Bliss Cartwright, and Stanton Wheeler, "State Supreme Courts: A Century of Style and Citation," *Stanford Law Review* 33 (May 1981): 773–818.

21 Henry R. Glick, "Court Politics and the Judicial Process," chap. 7 in *Politics in the American States*, 7th ed., ed. Virginia Gray, Russell Hanson, and Herbert Jacob (Washington DC: CQ Press, 1999).

22 John Kincaid, "The New Judicial Federalism," *Journal of State Government* 61 (September–October 1988): 163.

23 *State v. Russell*, 477 N.W. 2d 886.

24 *Mitchell v. Steffan*, 504 N.W. 2d 198.

25 Jean Hopfensperger, "Supreme Court Bans Two-Tier Welfare Laws," *Star Tribune*, 18 May 1999, p. 1A.

26 *Gray v. Commissioner of Public Safety*, 519 N.W. 2d 187.

27 Phillip Kronebusch, "Minnesota Courts: Basic Structures, Processes, and Policies," in *Perspectives on Minnesota Government and Politics*, 4th ed., ed. Steve Hoffman, Donald Ostrom, Homer Williamson, and Kay Wolsborn (Edina MN: Burgess Publishing, 1998), chap. 4.

28 *Women of the State of Minnesota as Represented by Jane Doe v. Maria Gomez in Her Official Capacity as Commissioner of Human Services*, 542 N.W. 2d 17.

29 David Phelps, "It's All Over, Bar the Legacy," *Star Tribune*, 29 June 1998, p. 8A.

30 The per capita settlements before Minnesota's were $750.65 in Florida, $788.31 in Texas, and $1,230.32 in Mississippi; Minnesota's was $1,301.75. Settlement numbers from David Phelps and Melissa Levy, "$7 Billion Deal; Minnesota, In-

dustry Settle Suit before Jury Starts Deliberations," *Star Tribune*, 9 May 1998, p. 1A. State population statistics from Kathleen O'Leary Morgan, Scott Morgan, and Mark A. Uhlig, eds., *State Rankings, 1998* (Lawrence KS: Morgan Quinto, 1998), p. vi.

31 Darrell K. Gilliard and Allen J. Beck, "Prisoners in 1997," *Bureau of Justice Statistics Bulletin* (August 1998): 3; on the Web at <http://www.ojp.usdoj.gov/bjs/pub/> [September 1998].

32 Ostrom and Kauder, *Examining the Work of State Courts*, p. 46.

33 Ostrom and Kauder, *Examining the Work of State Courts*, p. 63.

34 Dirk Johnson, "Nice City's Nasty Distinction: Murder Soars in Minneapolis," *New York Times*, 30 June 1996, p. 1A.

35 Criminal Justice Center, Minnesota Planning Agency, <http://www.mnplan.state.mn.us/cgi-bin/crimjust> [September 1998].

36 Johnson, "Nasty Distinction," p. 18.

37 Bob von Sternberg, "Deadly Business: Drugs, Gangs, and Cash Made 1995 Minneapolis' Most Homicidal Year," *Star Tribune*, 17 December 1995, p. 1A.

38 Associated Press, "Urban America Follows N.Y.'s Lead as Homicide Rates Dip Dramatically; Boston, New York at 30-Year Lows; Local Trend Dimmer," *St. Paul Pioneer Press*, 1 January 1997, p. 7A.

39 Federal Bureau of Investigation, *Uniform Crime Reports*, 1997 Preliminary Annual Release, 17 May 1998, p. 4.

40 Federal Bureau of Investigation, *Uniform Crime Reports*.

41 Johnson, "Nasty Distinction," p. 18.

42 "Drug Court, Hennepin County Experiment Pays Off," *Star Tribune*, 19 May 1998, p. 12A.

43 <http://www.drugcourt.org/docs/fact_sht.htm> [September 1998].

44 "Drug Court, Hennepin County Experiment Pays Off."

CHAPTER 9

1 Annie E. Casey Foundation, *Kids Count Data Book, 1997* (Baltimore: Annie E. Casey Foundation), p. 80.

2 Daniel J. Elazar, *The American Partnership* (Chicago: University of Chicago Press, 1962), p. 291.

3 As distinct from direct federal expenditures and transfers to individuals, which tended to flow more heavily to the larger states.

4 Kathleen O'Leary Morgan, Scott Morgan, and Nel Quinto, eds., *State Rankings, 1997* (Lawrence KS: Morgan Quinto, 1997), p. 261.

5 Morgan et al., *State Rankings, 1997*, p. 11.

6 Monica E. Friar, Herman B. Leonard, and J. H. Walder, *The Federal Budget and the States for Fiscal Year 1995* (Boston: Taubman Center for State and Local Government, Kennedy School of Government, Harvard University, 1996).

7 Morgan et al., *State Rankings, 1997*, pp. 263, 265.

8 Morgan et al., *State Rankings, 1997*, p. 85.

9 Morgan et al., *State Rankings, 1997*, pp. 81, 405.

10 *Cherokee Nation v. Georgia*, 30 U.S. 1 (1831); also *Worcester v. Georgia*, 31 U.S. 515 (1832) established that state laws do not apply in Indian country.

11 *California v. Cabazon Band of Mission Indians*, 480 U.S. 202 (1987).

12 D. J. Tice, "Getting Dealt Back In," *St. Paul Pioneer Press*, 6 August 1998, at <http://www.pioneerplanet.com/archive/millelacs/docs/thursday2.htm> [September 1998].

13 *International Gambling and Wagering Business*, August 1997, p. 43.

14 Dennis Lien, "The Last Word: Mille Lacs Treaty Stands," *St. Paul Pioneer Press*, 25 March 1999, p. 1A.

15 Thomas J. Collins and Les Suzakamo, "Dreams in Exile: The Hmong in St. Paul," *St. Paul Pioneer Press*, 16 November 1989, p. 1B.

16 Joseph A. Amato, *To Call It Home: The New Immigrants of Southwestern Minnesota* (Marshall MN: Crossing Press, 1996), pp. 13–24 and 28.

17 Reed Karaim, "Minnesota Is Loser in Guard Case," *St. Paul Pioneer Press*, 12 June 1990, p. 1A; Norman Beckman, "Limiting State Involvement in Foreign Policy: The Governors and the National Guard in *Perpich v. Defense*," *Publius: The Journal of Federalism* 21 (summer 1991): 109–23.

CHAPTER 10

1 American Council on Intergovernmental Relations, *Significant Features of Fiscal Federalism*, vol. 2 (Washington DC: American Council on Intergovernmental Relations, 1998), pp. 211, 215.

2 Minnesota Planning, *Minnesota Milestones: 1996 Progress Report*, July 1996, at <http://www.mnplan.state.mn.us> [September 1998], p. 42.

3 U.S. Bureau of the Census, *Statistical Abstract of the United States, 1998* (Washington DC: U.S. Bureau of the Census, 1998), p. 460.

4 Robert Tannenwald and Jonathan Cowan, "Fiscal Capacity, Fiscal Need, and Fiscal Comfort among U.S. States: New Evidence," *Publius: The Journal of Federalism* 27 (summer 1997): 115.

5 Tannenwald and Cowan, "Fiscal Capacity," p. 124.

6 Kendra A. Hovey and Harold A. Hovey, *CQ's State Fact Finder: Rankings across America, 1998* (Washington DC: CQ Press, 1998), p. 157.

7 Minnesota Council of Economic Advisers, *1994 Economic Report to the Governor* (St. Paul: State of Minnesota, 1994).

8 Thomas F. Luce Jr., "Minnesota: Innovation in an Era of Constraint," in *The Fiscal Crisis of the States: Lessons for the Future*, ed. Steven D. Gold (Washington DC: Georgetown University Press, 1995), p. 328.

9 American Council on Intergovernmental Relations, *Fiscal Federalism*, 2:116.

10 Jack L. Walker, "The Diffusion of Innovations among the American States," *American Political Science Review* 63 (September 1969): 880–99.

11 David Osborne and Ted Gaebler, *Reinventing Government: How the Entrepreneurial Spirit Is Transforming the Public Sector* (New York: Penguin Books, 1992), p. 272.

12 Michael Barzelay, *Breaking through Bureaucracy: A New Vision for Managing in Government* (Berkeley: University of California Press, 1992), p. 39.

13 Minnesota Department of Administration, *Minnesota's STEP Program: A Guide for Managing Change* (St. Paul: State of Minnesota, 1987), p. 6; Michael Barzelay and Robert A. Leone, "Creating an Innovative Managerial Culture: The Minnesota 'STEP' Strategy," *Journal of State Government* 60 (July–August 1987): 170.

14 Osborne and Gaebler, *Reinventing Government*, pp. 91–92.

15 Michael Barzelay and Babak J. Armajani, "Managing State Government Operations: Changing Visions of Staff Agencies," *Journal of Policy Analysis and Management* 9, 3 (1990): 317.

16 Sara M. Evans and Barbara J. Nelson, *Wage Justice: Comparable Worth and the Paradox of Technocratic Reform* (Chicago: University of Chicago Press, 1989), p. 9. All data in this section come from this source. For a critical view of the Minnesota experience, see Steven E. Rhoads, *Incomparable Worth: Pay Equity Meets the Market* (New York: Cambridge University Press, 1993).

17 "Minnesota: A State That Works," *Time*, 13 August 1973, p. 35.

18 Paula J. King, "Policy Entrepreneurs: Catalysts in the Policy Innovation Process" (Ph.D. dissertation, University of Minnesota, 1989), pp. 256–57.

19 Tim L. Mazzoni, "The Changing Politics of State Education Policy Making: A Twenty-Year Minnesota Perspective," *Educational Evaluation and Policy Analysis* 15 (winter 1993): 365.

20 John E. Chubb and Terry M. Moe, *Politics, Markets, and America's Schools* (Washington DC: Brookings Institution Press, 1990).

21 Peter W. Cookson Jr., *School Choice: The Struggle for the Soul of American Education* (New Haven: Yale University Press, 1994), p. 43.

22 Roman Augustoviz, "Imbalance of Power," *Star Tribune*, 4 February 1996, p. 10C.

23 Interview with David M. Green, committee administrator, Family and Early Childhood Education Finance Division, House Education Committee, 30 July 1997.

24 Howard M. Leichter, "Minnesota: The Trip from Acrimony to Accommodation," in *Five States that Could Not Wait: Lessons for Health Reform from Florida, Hawaii, Minnesota, Oregon, and Vermont*, ed. Daniel M. Fox and John K. Iglehart (Cambridge MA: Blackwell, 1994), p. 95. Also see his revised chapter, "Health Care Reform in Minnesota: A Journey, Not a Destination," in Leichter, *Health Policy Reform in America: Innovations from the States*, 2d ed. (Armonk NY: M. E. Sharpe, 1997), pp. 217–36.

25 Robin Toner, "Health Care in Minnesota: Model for U.S. or Novelty?" *New York Times*, 9 October 1993, p. 9.

26 Leichter, "Minnesota," p. 111. The information in the rest of the section comes from the same source.

27 Martin R. Saiz and Susan E. Clarke, "Economic Development and Infrastructure Policy," in *Politics in the American States*, 7th ed., ed. Virginia Gray, Russell Hanson, and Herbert Jacob (Washington DC: CQ Press, 1999), tables 14-2 and 14-3.

28 Robert Kudrle and Cynthia Kite, "Evaluating International Business Development: Lessons for Minnesota," *CURA Reporter* 17 (May 1987): 1.

29 Margaret Dewar, "Development Analysis Confronts Politics: Industrial Policy on Minnesota's Iron Range," *Journal of the American Planning Association* 52 (summer 1986): 291. All information in this section comes from the same source.

30 Pat Doyle, "Rural Development Agency's Lottery Funds at Stake," *Star Tribune*, 25 February 1990, p. B7.

31 Robert Guskind, "Friendly Skies," *National Journal*, 21 December 1991, p. 3063.

32 David Phelps, "State Rescue of Northwest Still Controversial," *Star Tribune*, 19 May 1996, p. A14.

33 Citizens League, *Help Wanted: More Opportunities than People* (Minneapolis: Citizens League, 1998).

CHAPTER II

1 Bureau of the Census, "1992 Census of Governments, Number 2, Popularly Elected Officials," table 3, <http://www.census.gov/govs/www/govstruc. html> [September 1998].

2 Judith H. Dutcher, Minnesota State Auditor, *Revenues, Expenditures, and Debt of Minnesota Cities over 2,500 in Population, December 31, 1996*, 23 April 1998, inside front cover.

3 Morgan et al., *State Rankings, 1998*, p. 139.

4 Morgan et al., *State Rankings, 1998*, p. 144.

5 Morgan et al., *State Rankings, 1998*, pp. 123, 133.

6 <http://children.state.mn.us> [September 1998].

7 Association of Minnesota Counties, *Congratulations: Now You're a County Commissioner!* (St. Paul: Association of Minnesota Counties, n.d.), p. 5.

8 Minnesota State Demographer's Office, *Faces of the Future: Minnesota County Population Projections, 1995–2025*, <http://www.mnplan.state.mn.us/> [September 1998].

9 Association of Minnesota Counties, *1997 Salary Survey* (St. Paul: Association of Minnesota Counties, n.d.).

10 Association of Minnesota Counties, *County Government Structure* (St. Paul: Association of Minnesota Counties, n.d.).

11 Dutcher, *Cities over 2,500, 1996*, pp. 77, 79, 80, 85, 92.

12 Compiled from Judith H. Dutcher, Minnesota State Auditor, *Revenues, Expenditures, and Debt of Minnesota Cities under 2,500 in Population, December 31, 1995*, 30 June 1997, and Judith H. Dutcher, Minnesota State Auditor, *Revenues, Expenditures, and Debt of Minnesota Cities over 2,500 in Population, December 31, 1995*, 30 June 1997.

13 Dutcher, *Cities over 2,500, 1996*, p. 7; Judith H. Dutcher, Minnesota State Auditor, *Revenues, Expenditures, and Debt of Cities under 2,500 in Population, December 31, 1996*, 23 April 1998, p. 6.

14 Government Information Division, Office of the State Auditor, *An Analysis of Minnesota Municipal Liquor Store Operations in 1996*, 17 June 1998, p. 1.

15 Dutcher, *Cities under 2,500, 1996*, p. 3.

16 Dutcher, *Cities over 2,500, 1996*, p. 4.

17 Dutcher, *Cities over 2,500, 1996*, p. 6.

18 *Focus MCDA*, at <http://www.mtn.org/mcda> [September 1998], under "Guiding Principles."

19 Alexis de Tocqueville, *Democracy in America*, ed. J. P. Mayer (New York: Harper and Row, 1969), p. 62.

20 Minn. Stat. 414.01, subd. 1 (2).

21 John Fischer, "The Easy Chair," *Harper's Magazine*, April 1969.

22 Arthur Naftalin and John Brandl, *The Twin Cities Regional Strategy* (Minneapolis: Metropolitan Council of the Twin Cities, publication no. 08–80–058, November 1980), p. 24.

23 John Harrigan, "Minneapolis–St. Paul: Structuring Metropolitan Government," in *Regional Politics: America in a Post City Age*, ed. H. V. Savitch and Ronald K. Vogel (Thousand Oaks CA: Sage, 1996), p. 215.

24 Harrigan, "Minneapolis–St. Paul," p. 218.

25 Myron Orfield, *Metro Politics: A Regional Agenda for Community and Stability* (Washington DC: Brookings Institution Press, 1997), p. 17.

26 Harrigan, "Minneapolis–St. Paul," p. 219.

27 Morgan et al., *State Rankings, 1998*, p. 281.

28 Citizens League and the Minnesota Taxpayers Association, *Minnesota Homestead Property Tax Review, 1997* (St. Paul: Citizens League, September 1997), p. 2.

29 Morgan et al., *State Rankings, 1998*, p. 402.

30 *Minnesota's Private Colleges, 1997*, a brochure distributed by the Minnesota Private College Council, Fund and Research Foundation.

CHAPTER 12

1 Gunther, *Inside U.S.A.*, p. 296; "Minnesota: A State That Works"; "Minnesota: The Land of Good Examples."

2 John Fenton, *Midwest Politics* (New York: Holt, Rinehart, and Winston, 1966).

3 Rodney E. Hero and Caroline J. Tolbert, "A Racial/Ethnic Diversity Interpretation of Politics and Policy in the States of the U.S.," *American Journal of Political Science* (August 1996): 851–71; see also the update by Hero, "Social Diversity and Political Processes in the States of the U.S.," paper presented at the Annual Meeting of the American Political Science Association, Washington DC, August 1997.

4 Minnesota Department of Trade and Economic Development Home Page, at <http://www.dted.state.mn.us/mnecon/glance/perf.html> [September 1998], 30 May 1997.

5 Minnesota Department of Economic Security Home Page, at <http://www.des.state.mn.us//mi/laus/us—mn.htm> [September 1998]. Data are seasonally adjusted.

6 Morgan et al., *State Rankings, 1998*, p. iv.

7 Ted Kolderie, personal communication, 2 September 1997.

8 Minnesota Planning State Demographic Center, "Faces of the Future," May 1998, p. 4, at <http://www.mnplan.state.mn.us/> [September 1998].

9 Kimberly Hayes Taylor, "The Hmong: A New Wave," *Star Tribune*, 25 October 1998, p. A1.

10 Calculated from data in Minnesota Planning State Demographic Center, "Faces of the Future," p. 4.

11 Dirk Johnson, "Ethnic Change Tests Mettle of Minneapolis Liberalism," *New York Times*, 18 October 1997, p. A8.

12 Chris Tomlinson, "Somalis, Fleeing Clan Wars, Start Over in Minnesota," *St. Paul Pioneer Press*, 17 November 1997, p. 3C; Kristin Tillotson, "Somalis Adapt to Life in a Strange Land," *Star Tribune*, 22 March 1998, p. A12.

13 Maureen M. Smith, "The Language Challenge," *Star Tribune*, 24 May 1997, pp. A1, A17.

14 Tomlinson, "Somalis."

15 "Minnesota: A State That Works," p. 31.

16 Minnesota Planning, "State of Diversity," November 1993, p. 6.

17 Myron Orfield, *Metropolitics: A Regional Agenda for Community and Stability* (Washington DC: Brookings Institution Press, 1997), p. 3. His conclusions were confirmed in a later study by Sanders Korenman, Leslie Dwight, and John E. Sjaastad, "The Rise of African American Poverty in the Twin Cities, 1980 to 1990," *CURA Reporter* 27 (September 1997): 1–12.

18 Johnson, "Ethnic Change Tests Mettle," p. A8.

19 Mahtesian, "Sick Legislature Syndrome."

20 *Politics in Minnesota* 15 (29 May 1997): 3.

Index